BATTLEFIELD
YORKSHIRE

BATTLEFIELD YORKSHIRE

From the Romans to the English
Civil War

David Cooke

Pen & Sword
MILITARY

First published in Great Britain in 2006 by
Pen & Sword Military
an imprint of
Pen & Sword Books Ltd
47 Church Street
Barnsley
South Yorkshire
S70 2AS

ISBN 1 84415 424 6

A CIP catalogue record for this book is available from the British Library.

Typeset in Palatino by
Phoenix Typesetting, Auldgirth, Dumfriesshire

Printed and bound in England by
Biddles Ltd, King's Lynn

Pen & Sword Books Ltd incorporates the Imprints of Pen & Sword Aviation, Pen & Sword Maritime, Pen & Sword Military, Wharncliffe Books, Pen & Sword Select, Pen & Sword Military Classics and Leo Cooper.

For a complete list of Pen & Sword titles please contact
PEN & SWORD BOOKS LIMITED
47 Church Street, Barnsley, South Yorkshire, S70 2AS, England
E-mail: enquiries@pen-and-sword.co.uk
Website: www.pen-and-sword.co.uk

CONTENTS

LIST OF MAPS

INTRODUCTION

In AD 71 the Romans established a garrison fortress for the IXth Legion on the banks of a river, now called the Ouse, in the heart of Brigantian territory. The Brigantes had been a client state of Rome but after a short-lived revolt against their queen, Cartimandua, led by her ex-husband, Venutius, the Romans had stepped in and assumed control of the area. The fortress was built on the north bank of the Ouse, while a civilian settlement grew on the south bank. Over the centuries the name, and function, of the site changed, from Eboracum, to Jorvik, to York, and the fortress became a city and gave its name to the surrounding area – Yorkshire.

York was born from a military campaign and since then has had a rich military

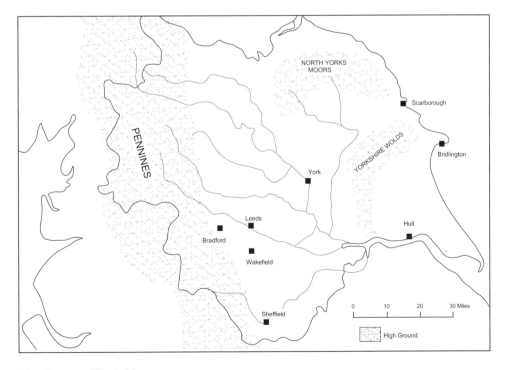

The County of Yorkshire

history. The county can claim the largest battle on English soil, although there is still disagreement as to whether it is Towton or Marston Moor. Towton was the bloodiest battle, with 28,000 casualties reported by the chroniclers of the time, although this is almost certainly a vastly inflated figure. Marston Moor was the largest battle of the English Civil Wars, and had the highest casualty figures, with over 4,000 dead being buried by the local population in the days following the battle – a much more reliable figure than that for Towton.

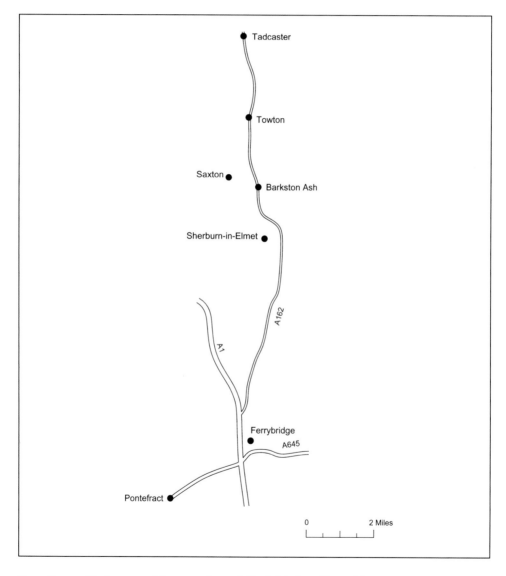

Pontefract to Tadcaster – A journey through Yorkshire's military history

The county has been the site of civil wars, foreign invasions and dynastical struggles. It has also seen many of the foremost fighting men of their periods taking part in life-or-death struggles. Penda, king of Mercia, Harald Hardrada, king of Norway, Warwick the Kingmaker, Black Tom Fairfax, Oliver Cromwell and Prince Rupert of the Rhine, to name but a few, all took part in battles within the county, and two of them lost their lives.

The topography of the county had a major effect on where battles were fought. You only have to look at a relief map of Yorkshire to see that both the east and west sides of the county are constrained by high ground, which was very unsuitable for armies to operate. To the west are the Pennines, and in the north of the county the Yorkshire Dales, while to the east are the Wolds and North Yorkshire Moors. Along the north-south belt of low ground ran the Great North Road, now replaced by the A1, and it was along this road that armies moved into the county from the north and south. Another method of entry was along the River Ouse and this was used on a number of occasions by sea-borne raiders and invaders, such as the Vikings.

Many of the battles fought within the county fall within this belt of low-lying ground, although there are exceptions. Let me give you an example, by taking a short car ride from Pontefract to Tadcaster along the A162, which closely follows the course of the old Great North Road. Pontefract has a rich military history. In 1460 the Lancastrian army left Pontefract to attack Richard, Duke of York, at his castle at Sandal near Wakefield. This led to the Battle of Wakefield in which the Yorkist army was routed and the Duke of York and his son were killed. Pontefract Castle was besieged several times during the Civil Wars and a mounted action was fought within sight of the castle in 1645 when a force of Royalist cavalry successfully resupplied the beleaguered garrison.

Now move on a few miles to Ferrybridge. This was the scene of two small actions during the Wars of the Roses and the English Civil Wars. After a few more miles we come to Sherburn-in-Elmet. Once again this was the site of two actions, both during the First Civil War. The first was a cavalry raid led by Sir Thomas Fairfax. The second was a battle of two halves. A large body of Royalist cavalry defeated the garrison during the morning then was surprised and routed by a pursuing body of Parliamentary horse in the afternoon.

The next place of interest along the road is Barkston Ash. Following the action at Ferrybridge in 1461, Lord Clifford led his men back towards the main Lancastrian army camped at Towton, hotly pursued by the Yorkist army. He turned to face his pursuers at a place called Dintingdale where his force was overwhelmed and Clifford killed. There is disagreement as to where Dintingdale actually was, as the name is no longer in use. One possible site is Barkston Ash. A second possible site is a short distance along the road where a minor road to Saxton leaves the A162.

Continuing along the main road you will notice a ridge line on the left-hand side, running at right angles to the road, with a lone tree close to its eastern end. This is the ridge along which the Yorkist army deployed at the Battle of Towton, and the Duke

Looking south from the Towton battlefield towards Ferrybridge. The A162 runs to the left of the lone tree on the ridge and Ferrybridge power station can be seen on the horizon at the right-hand side of the illustration. Between these two points numerous military actions have taken place.

of Norfolk marched his force along the same road as you are driving on, to reinforce King Edward and win the day. Between the ridge and the next village, Towton, is the battlefield. As you pass the junction on the left as you enter the village, which leads onto the battlefield, you pass a gateway, which is the entrance to Towton Hall. This was the site of an archaeological dig of a battle grave pit.

Further on through the village, on the left-hand side, is the Rockingham Arms. Just beyond it is a small lane which drops down the hill to the Cock Beck. This is where the modern road and the Great North Road part company for a short distance. The old road followed the course of this track down to the river, which it crossed on a narrow bridge, before it followed the valley towards Tadcaster. A bridge still exists today, and remnants of an older bridge's stone footings can be seen at the side of it. A few years ago I was taking part in a walk around the battlefield. The guide was recounting the story of how the river could be crossed at this point on a bridge of bodies in the aftermath of the Battle of Towton, when it suddenly struck me how many fighting men, and their leaders, must have tramped down the hill and crossed the various bridges that have existed on the site, as they marched towards York. King Harold Godwinsson crossed the bridge as he led his army on its march to Stamford Bridge in September 1066, and recrossed it as he returned south to face Duke William of Normandy at Hastings. The Lancastrian army would have crossed the bridge before the Battle of Towton (1461), and the Yorkist army, including King Edward IV and Warwick the Kingmaker, would have crossed after their victory, as they marched to York. Sir Thomas Fairfax also used this route to attack Tadcaster in the build up to his worst defeat, at Seacroft Moor in 1643. Thousands of men who passed this way died in the subsequent actions and never returned home. It is a moving thought.

Continuing our journey we finally reach Tadcaster, famed for its breweries. It is from Tadcaster that King Harold commenced his approach march to Stamford Bridge where one of the greatest warrior kings of the period, King Harald Sigurdsson of Norway, later known as Hardrada, met his end. Tadcaster was also the site of the first battle between Lord Ferdinando Fairfax and the Earl of Newcastle, in December 1642, as the two commanders vied for control of the county.

Looking slightly further afield from Tadcaster, we come to York, the site of a number of actions and sieges throughout the period covered by this book. It is also the centre of a ring of battles. To the west is Marston Moor. Along the southern arc of the circle are Towton, Gate Fulford and Stamford Bridge, to the south-west, south and south-east respectively, and to the north lie Byland and Myton. Further north are the battlefields of Boroughbridge and Northallerton, both battles from the medieval period.

As you can see by now, you don't have to venture far to reach a site of one, or more, military actions, be it a battle, an assault on a defended town, or a siege. During the Civil Wars many towns and villages were the site of a military action, be it a minor skirmish between two bodies of foraging cavalry, or a full-blown assault involving thousands of men. Walk through the shopping centre of many towns, Leeds, Wakefield and Selby for example, and you are walking through a battlefield.

The purpose of this book is not just to recount a list of battles but how the battles were fought and how the men taking part were equipped and organised. The book is split into five sections covering the Roman period, the Dark Ages, the Medieval period, the Wars of the Roses and the English Civil Wars. It will quickly become obvious that some periods are covered in more depth than others. Let me assure you that this is not due to a lack of interest in a particular period but a lack of evidence! The earlier the period, the fewer the contemporary accounts and the less detail they contain. In some instances, even though we have details of an action we cannot be sure of its exact location. Winwidfield is a good example. It took place somewhere to the east of Leeds but various sites have been put forward including Garforth and Whin Moor, close to Seacroft. Without finding a grave pit or battlefield debris it is impossible to pin down exactly where the battle took place. The location of the Battle of Heathfield, or Hatfield, the battle that preceded Winwidfield, is known from artefacts found on the battlefield which were originally stored in the local church, but have since been moved to the Royal Armouries at Leeds. Brunanburgh, another Dark Ages battle, may not have even been fought in Yorkshire, as several other sites claim it including a site in Lancashire and one on the Wirral. Once again, unless the appropriate battlefield artefacts are discovered on one of the sites, the location of the battle may never be known with any certainty.

The final section of the book is a series of battlefield walks. Obviously, it is very difficult to give a tour of a battlefield when the actual location is uncertain and so the walks will cover only battles where the site, and some detail of events are known.

CHAPTER ONE

THE EAGLES OF ROME

Background

In AD 43 a large Roman army landed at Richborough in Kent. It comprised four legions – *II Augusta*, *IX Hispana*, *XIV Gemina* and *XX Valeria* – and a large force of auxiliary cavalry and infantry. Bloody battles were fought at the crossings of the Medway and Thames as the Roman army pushed north. British resistance crystallised around a Catuvellaunian leader called Caratacus. The Catuvellauni controlled the area of the Thames Valley and with their main allies, the Trinovantes, formed the main opposition to the Roman invasion.

The Romans' initial target was the Trinovantes' capital at Camoludunum (Colchester), and the army was joined by the Emperor Claudius prior to the attack on the town. Roman accounts tell us that Claudius brought with him a small number of elephants and camels which seems to be surprising until it is realised that Claudius was well aware of the effect these creatures had on horses that were not used to them. It was also known that one of the most effective weapons used by the British was the light, two-horsed chariot, and Claudius may well have brought the elephants and camels across the Channel to counter them.

After the fall of Camoludunum Claudius returned to Rome and Aulus Plautius, the commander of the Roman army, was left to continue with the conquest. Plautius divided his force, sending the *II Augusta*, commanded by Vespasian, who will appear again later in the story, into the south-west to subdue the Durotriges and Dumnonii. The main army continued in pursuit of Caratacus, who was by this time building a reputation for himself as a resolute opponent of Rome, and is mentioned in histories as far afield as Greece.

Over a period of time Caratacus withdrew into the land of the Silures, in southern Wales, fighting the Romans all the way. The Silurians had little previous contact with the Romans and put up a savage resistance, eventually retreating into central Wales, where the Ordovices ruled. Caratacus seems to have had the ability to pull together the normally feuding tribes to face a more dangerous opponent, and managed to oppose the Romans for eight years, something few other tribal leaders managed to do. Eventually, in 51, the Britons were defeated in a savage battle at a hill fort in central Wales, although the exact location is not known – a major problem with accounts from the Roman period. Once again Caratacus avoided the Romans, although his wife and several other family members were captured. Caratacus and a small band of followers fled north into the land of the Brigantes.

The Brigantes ruled a large area in the north of Britain, covering most of Yorkshire and Lancashire, and almost as far as the present Scottish border. They had stood aloof from the fighting in the south but could see which way the wind was blowing. That said, the Romans had already had some involvement with the Brigantes. In 47 Ostorius Scapula, who had replaced Plautius as governor, was on campaign in the north of Wales when a leadership struggle broke out among the Brigantes. Scapula could not allow his northern flank to be destabilised, and withdrew his troops from Wales and moved in support of one of the rival parties. It is even possible that one of the rival leaders had asked the Romans for support. This was possibly Cartimandua, who seems to have come out of the struggle with a greatly enhanced status – she is referred to in Roman accounts as a queen, a title, along with king, usually reserved for the rulers of client states. In 51, when Caratacus arrived in Brigantian territory, Cartimandua used the opportunity to enhance her status even further by having him arrested and handed over to the Romans. Surprisingly, after putting up such a staunch resistance, Caratacus was pardoned and spent the rest of his life living peacefully in Rome.

Cartimandua ruled until 68 or 69. During this period the relationship between the queen and her husband, Venutius, worsened to the extent that Venutius divorced her. After this, Cartimandua seems to have taken up with one of her ex-husband's companions, Vellocatus, who is referred to as Venutius's *armigerum* (armour bearer). This scandal outraged many of the Brigantes and sowed the seeds of opposition to Cartimandua's rule.

In 68 the Emperor Nero died and the Roman Empire dissolved into a civil war. In one year, four emperors were acknowledged, some simultaneously! Large numbers of troops were withdrawn from Britain to support one or other of the rivals. The departure of one legion, the *XIV Gemina*, and detachments of the other three, plus an unspecified number of auxiliaries, denuded the province's garrison by up to a third. Venutius, who had a reputation as an able military leader, seems to have used the departure of this large part of the garrison as an opportunity to settle his differences with Cartimandua. A large proportion of the Brigantes supported him and the Roman governor, Marcus Vettius Bolanus, had to send a task force to rescue Cartimandua. A mixed auxiliary cohort, comprising both cavalry and infantry, fought its way into Brigantian territory, rescued the queen, then withdrew, clashing with Venutius's forces on several occasions. Bolanus did not have the troops available to subdue the now hostile tribe and Venutius ruled over the Brigantes unchallenged, although not as a client but as an enemy of Rome. What happened to Cartimandua is not recorded and she disappears from the historical record after her rescue.

After a bloody civil war, Vespasian emerged as the victor and sole claimant to the Roman throne in 69. Bolanus had supported one of his rivals, Vitellius, and was replaced as governor in 71 by Quintus Petillius Cerealis who was related to Vespasian.

Cerealis was both a seasoned soldier and had experience of fighting the Britons. During the Boudican rising he had commanded the *IX Hispana*, which had been badly mauled by Boudica's Icenii and Trinovantes tribesmen, as it marched south from Lindum (Lincoln) to suppress the rising. The legion was so cut up that it withdrew into its garrison fortress and took no further part in the fighting. However, his recent military experience had been more successful. On the Rhine frontier a Batavian auxiliary leader, Civilis, had raised German troops in support of Vespasian. Falsely accused of treason, Civilis declared himself independent and a force commanded by Cerealis was despatched to put down the revolt, finally defeating the Germans at the Battle of Vetera.

As a new legion, *II Adiutrix Pia Fidelis*, arrived in Britain at the same time as Cerealis, it is possible that it was part of his Rhine army that he had brought with him to replace the *XIV Gemina*, and bring back up to four the total number of legions in the province. The governor now had the strength to finally settle the Brigantian problem. Leaving the new legion at Lindum he moved north with the *IX Hispana* and supporting auxiliaries, towards the Trent and into Brigantian lands. Although the Romans had twice sent troops to support factions within the Brigantes, this was the first time they had attempted to conquer the area, and so the Romans came to Yorkshire.

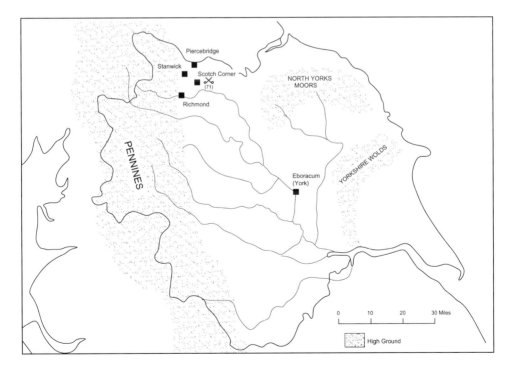

The conquest of the Brigantes

Organisation, equipment and tactics

The Romans

The first century Roman army was one of the most efficient military machines in the history of warfare. It was highly trained and well equipped, and was usually more than a match for the tribal opponents it regularly fought as the Roman Empire expanded.

The core of any Roman army was the legion. A prerequisite for a legionary at this time was Roman citizenship, non-citizens forming the auxiliary units that supported the legions. The basic building block of the legion was the century, commanded by a centurion. Surprisingly, a century did not comprise 100 men, but eighty. Six centuries formed a cohort, and each legion had ten cohorts. The exception to this rule was the first cohort of each legion which was formed of five double strength centuries, thus making it almost twice the strength of the other nine cohorts. A

cohort was commanded by its senior centurion, and the commander of the 1st Cohort was the senior centurion in the legion, a man of great importance. The commander of a legion was called a legate; this post was usually a step on the ladder to more important political posts, even the ultimate post – emperor. Vespasian is a good example of this. As a legate he commanded the *II Augusta* during the invasion of Britain and ended his career as emperor. Each legate was supported by a number of staff officers called tribunes, who often commanded detachments from the legion, or small task forces on specific missions. Once again the post was a step in an individual's political career.

The Roman legionary of this period is what most people think of as a Roman soldier. He was well armoured with a segmented breastplate and shoulder guards, called *lorica segmentata*, which had replaced the earlier mail shirt (*lorica hamata*). On his head he wore a metal

Roman legionaries on the march with standards to the front of the column (Tim Lynch).

helmet with extended cheek and neck guards, and he carried a large rectangular shield called a *scutum*.

The legionary was equipped with a short, stabbing sword, the *gladius*, which he wore suspended from a baldric on his right hip. At first this may seem surprising as it is natural to wear a sword on the left (if you are right-handed) and draw the sword across the body, but this is what the Romans were trying to avoid – drawing a sword in this manner leaves the right arm raised and the body vulnerable to a thrust. To draw his sword the legionary would push the hilt down and back, then slide the sword out towards the rear. The short length of the Roman sword allowed him to do this. Drawing a sword in this fashion brought the legionary into the ideal position to stab forwards and yet kept his body fully protected.

He also carried a number of heavy throwing spears called *pilum*. These had a hardened point on a long, soft metal shaft with a heavy weight, usually an iron ball, at its bottom end where it joined the wooden shaft. Thrown at short range, the weight of the spear allowed it to punch through armour and shields and the soft metal shaft then bent, preventing the enemy using the spear in return. Even if the spear did not kill or injure its target, it could become a major encumbrance, hanging from his shield. Several volleys before contact could be devastating against an undisciplined foe such as British tribesmen.

The legions were supported by auxiliary cohorts, either infantry or cavalry, although some cohorts were mixed – the one used to rescue Cartimandua, for example. Auxiliaries were usually non-citizens and were raised among conquered people or from outside the borders of the Empire. An auxiliary unit was not usually stationed close to home, to prevent it becoming embroiled in local risings. Many auxiliary units stationed in Britain were of German or Balkan origin.

Auxiliary infantry were organised in a similar fashion to legionaries, with the century as the base unit. Depending on the type, a cohort could be formed from a varying number of centuries – a *Cohors Quingenaria* had six, while a *Cohors Milliaria* had ten. They were trained in a similar fashion to the legionaries but could also operate in more open order and in difficult terrain.

For protection the auxiliary infantryman was equipped with a thigh-length, short-sleeved mail shirt, a helmet similar to the legionary and a large oval shield. His weapons were a number of light javelins and a longer sword called a *spatha*. The *spatha* was a dual-purpose weapon and could be used for either cutting or thrusting. The javelin was a longer-range weapon that could be used just before contact, in a similar manner to the *pilum* or as a missile weapon when skirmishing. Some auxiliary units were formed from archers who were equipped in a similar fashion to standard auxiliary infantrymen but replaced the javelin and shield with a bow.

Earlier Roman armies had always been handicapped by a lack of integral cavalry, their mounted contingents being recruited, in the main, from tribal allies, who were not always reliable. For example, during his conquest of Gaul, Julius Caesar used both Gallic and German allied cavalry, troops that had on other occasions fought against him. By the first century measures had been put in place to remedy this situation and many, if not all, of the mounted units serving in Britain were regular auxiliary troops, recruited and trained in a similar fashion to their infantry compatriots and stationed far from their homes.

The basic block of an auxiliary cavalry unit was the *turmae* which was made up of thirty rank and file. A varying number of *turmae* formed an *alae*, the cavalry equivalent of an infantry cohort. An *Ala Quingenaria* had sixteen turmae, while an *Ala Milliaria* had twenty-four. Auxiliary cavalrymen were equipped in a similar fashion to auxiliary infantrymen with a mail shirt, helmet and oval shield for protection, and a *spatha* and javelins for offence. In the case of the mounted troops, the *spatha* was invariably used for slashing rather than stabbing.

As has already been mentioned, the Romans also had a small number of mixed cohorts called *Cohors Equitata* which had either six centuries of infantry and four *turmae* of cavalry, or ten centuries and eight turmae, depending on whether it was a *Quingenaria* or *Milliaria* unit.

The Britons

The Britons who opposed the Roman invaders were a typical tribal force with little formal training or organisation. They were a 'heroic' culture, with a man's fighting prowess often determining his station in life. The tribes were ruled over by a warrior caste, which formed the nobility, while the remainder were farmers or tradesmen. The nobility led their supporters when they went to war. Although we refer to the inhabitants of our island as Britons, it should not be assumed that they had a national identity as we do today – the notion of a united 'England' was centuries away. Each tribe thought of itself as a distinct entity – one of the downfalls of many of Rome's tribal opponents. Prior to the Roman invasion there was continual internecine warfare between the various tribes – sometimes tribes would ally against an opponent but at other times fight with one another. When the Romans landed many tribes opposed them while others actively provided support. Some tribes remained neutral until the invaders were at their doors, by which time it was too late. Had the Britons come together as a single opposing force the Romans would have had a much tougher time than they did but it took an exceptional leader to get beyond the inter-tribal bickering and gather a force from a number of different tribes. Caratacus was such a leader, as was Boudica. Unfortunately, their forces were never strong enough to defeat the Romans. Venutius was known as an able military leader, and he may have been able to forge an alliance with other tribes had he been given sufficient time.

A typical British force was composed of four elements – chariots, cavalry, infantry and skirmishers. The ratio of mounted troops would have varied from tribe to tribe depending on the terrain in which they lived. Hill tribes would probably have smaller mounted contingents than ones that lived on lower ground. Many of the nobles would have ridden to battle and skirmished with the enemy from light, very manoeuvrable chariots, pulled by two ponies. These could be highly effective but should not be thought of as charging into a solid enemy line. The chariots would gallop towards the enemy line, turn through ninety degrees, and gallop along the enemy line throwing javelins as they went, before turning away to repeat the process. The cavalry contingent was mounted on the small British ponies and equipped with javelins, and swords. The main body of a British army was made up of the infantry warbands – supporters of the chariot-borne nobles who dismounted to join them in the main charge. Once again, they would have been equipped with javelins and swords and protected by large elongated hexagonal or oval shields. The final element was the skirmishers. These were adolescents, too young to fight in the main charge but more than capable of skirmishing with the enemy with slings and bows. Armour would have been in short supply and only the nobles would have worn a mail shirt although a larger proportion of the army would have had a helmet. Some of the more elaborate helmets had horns and wings adorning them and it was the Britons who wore this style of helmet, not the Vikings as often portrayed by Hollywood. Most of the army would have been wearing their everyday clothes or stripped to the waist.

A typical battle

Having looked at the two armies, it is now time to look at how they would have interacted with one another on the battlefield. The Romans were often outnumbered by their opposition and so would look for good ground: rising ground with protection such as woods to the flanks and rear. The legions would form the centre while the auxiliaries would protect their flanks or form a screen to protect the heavy infantry from enemy skirmishers. On the low ground the British warriors would straggle onto the battlefield and form into clumps behind their leaders, often referred to as warbands. The leaders would still be in their chariots while skirmishers would move forward to engage the enemy and try to draw them into moving forward from their advantageous position. The Britons would be shouting taunts and challenges at the enemy, blowing their horns and waving their standards. The Roman army stood in silent, serried ranks.

After an initial exchange of missile fire between the opposing skirmishers, the British chariots would have advanced, galloping towards the Roman line, before swinging away and casting javelins. The occasional Roman soldier would fall and be carried back to the medical services in the rear while Roman counter-fire would cause casualties among the chariots. This would go on for some time before the chariots withdrew and the nobles dismounted and joined their infantrymen. The softening up was over and now it was time for the main assault.

The British warbands would move forward, breaking into a jog and then a run, as they approached the Roman lines, each man vying to be the first into contact. The Romans continued to stand in silence. As the Britons approached to within twenty or thirty yards a trumpet would sound in the Roman lines, the legionaries' right arms would go back and the first volley of *pila* would arc towards the enemy. Thousands of heavy spears would crash into the British ranks, skewering men, puncturing shields and causing mayhem. Men would trip over the fallen in front of them and others would have to cast aside shields pierced by a *pilum* and made unmanageable. Before the Britons had time to recover a second and third volley of *pila* would continue the work. Another trumpet would sound and the legionaries would draw their swords, raise their shields and prepare to attack.

The Roman advance was not a headlong charge like their tribal opponents but a steady grinding movement, a wall of shields with the deadly short swords stabbing between them. The Britons' long swords could only be used in a swinging motion and their edges quickly became notched as they beat against the metal rims of the Roman shields. Pressure built as the men at the rear continued to advance and quickly their compatriots at the front became so crushed that they were unable to raise their sword arms and were completely at the mercy of the Roman swords. A Briton fought in the front ranks until he fell wounded or dead. If a Roman was wounded he would be pulled out of the line and given medical attention: at regular intervals the front rank was replaced by a supporting rank passing through it, thus ensuring a constant supply of fresh, or partly rested, men at the front.

On the flanks the Roman auxiliary cavalry and infantry would drive off the British cavalry and apply pressure to the flanks of their infantry mass. The British cavalry stood little chance against their opponents who were both armoured and mounted on larger, heavier horses. As the auxiliaries closed in on the British flanks, and the solid

Roman legionaries advancing – a sight to put fear into any British tribesman! (Tim Lynch)

wall of legionaries continued their remorseless advance, the British army would begin to disintegrate, a trickle at first, but then a torrent. This is the time that the real slaughter began. On at least one occasion a British army had brought a mass of baggage wagons and dependants to the field. These formed an amphitheatre to watch their men destroy the hated invaders but this viewing point quickly became a barrier to their army; as it was routed and pinned against the baggage wagons they were slaughtered.

The Britons quickly learnt that they could not face the Romans in the open field and changed their tactics. Ambushing detachments and raiding supply columns would never defeat the Romans but would impede their advance. Rather than stand in the open the Britons resorted to defending their hill forts but the Romans proved themselves as adept at attacking these fortifications as they were at fighting in the open. Using their attached artillery, bolt-shooting ballista and bowmen to clear the palisades, the Romans would launch an assault with their legionaries, often in *testudo* (tortoise) formation. This was a formation intended for just such situations. The legionaries formed a column, with an unbroken wall of shields protecting the front, flanks and top of the formation. The hail of slingshot and javelins may have halted the Romans but subsequent assaults would follow and once the defences were breached, the slaughter would begin.

The conquest of the Brigantes

Unfortunately very little information has come down to us about the campaign of AD 71. Cerealis's first move was to establish a firm base of operations and he chose a spot on the River Ouse that could be reached by sea-going vessels, thus providing him with a secure line of supply. This probably started as a simple marching camp – at the close of each day's march a Roman army in, or close to, enemy territory would build a marching camp to protect it from a surprise attack. This camp developed into a legionary fortress, complete with stone walls. Its name was Eboracum (York).

The only near contemporary account we have of the campaign is from Tacitus:

> *When Britain with the rest of the world was recovered by Vespasian, Petillius Cerealis at once struck terror into their hearts by invading the commonwealth of the Brigantes, which is said to be the most numerous tribe of the whole province: many battles were fought, sometimes bloody battles, and by permanent conquest or by forays he annexed a large portion of the Brigantes.*

It is probable that the final battle of this series was fought close to Scotch Corner and followed a similar course to that described above. As this lies on the Romans' line of march to the Brigantian capital at Stanwick, about seven miles north of Richmond, and only four miles north of Scotch Corner, it is likely that this was a last-ditch attempt by Venutius to halt the Romans before they reached his capital. The attempt was unsuccessful. Between 1951 and 1952 Sir Mortimer Wheeler excavated a large fortified Iron Age settlement at Stanwick. Its fortifications are among the largest in the

Part of the Roman defences of York. The lower half of the tower is of Roman construction while the upper half was added during the medieval period.

country. Due to the settlement's size it is generally accepted as the Brigantine, and thus Venutius' capital. It was a common Roman strategy to push towards an enemy's capital and bring them to battle. This has already been mentioned in the background section of this chapter, when the Roman invasion force attacked towards Camoludunum, the Trinovantian capital. By the end of the campaign, most of the Brigantian territory in what is now Yorkshire had been conquered and Venutius had withdrawn across the Pennines into his remaining territory in Lancashire and Cumbria. To ensure the newly conquered territory remained secure, Cerealis stationed the *XI Hispana* at Eboracum and built an auxiliary border fort at Piercebridge. It is probable that the Roman fort at Ilkley was built during this period to block another route across the Pennines.

Cerealis was replaced by Sextus Julius Frontinus as Governor whose first priority was to bring the Silures tribe in the south of Wales to heel. Venutius was left alone for seven years but in 79 and 80 the Roman commander Agricola completed the conquest of the Brigantes and pushed the border as far as the Firth of Tay. Yorkshire was now firmly under Roman control.

Beneath York Minster lie the remains of the Roman garrison headquarters, some of which can still be seen today. The remains include the main entrance through which Constantine passed on his way to claim an empire.

This statue of the Emperor Constantine stands outside York Minster.

York considers Constantine to be its own emperor, as is shown on this advertising sign for an exhibition at the Yorkshire Museum.

One other notable event from the Roman period is celebrated by a statue outside York Minster. In the year 306 the Emperor Constantius visited York. On 25 June he died and his soldiers acclaimed his son, Constantine, as the new emperor. In the under-croft of York Minster are the remains of the Roman headquarters building, including what survives of its main entrance. It is through this door that Constantine began his march to claim his throne. His main rival was Maxentius and the two clashed at the Milvian Bridge, close to Rome. On the eve of the Battle Constantine is said to have had a vision of a cross superimposed on the sun and heard the words *In hoc signo vinces* – 'In this sign conquer'. On the following day Constantine defeated Maxentius and successfully claimed the throne. He went on to legalise Christianity within the empire and become the first Christian emperor. A statue of Constantine now stands outside York Minster.

CHAPTER TWO

SHIELD WALL

Background

In AD 410 Honorius, emperor of the Western Roman Empire, wrote to the citizens of Britain stating that they would have to defend themselves against the depredations of the Germanic tribes. The Roman army had been withdrawn from Britain to defend mainland Europe from the advancing Frankish and Gothic tribesmen. By the early part of the fifth century a westward migration of the Germanic tribes was in full flow, driven on by the advance of the Huns, under their king, Attila. Both eastern and

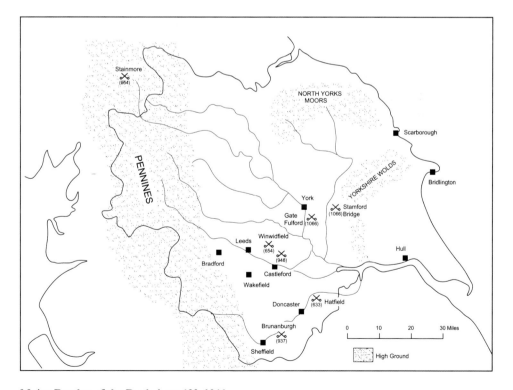

Major Battles of the Dark Ages 633–1066

western empires were under severe pressure as the 'barbarians' – Franks, Visigoths, Ostrogoths and Vandals – pushed into the civilised lands of Gaul and the Balkans. To make matters worse the Roman army had declined since its heyday in the first and second centuries and barbarian tribes were allowed into the empire to act as mercenaries to reinforce the reduced numbers of Roman soldiers. This was not a successful policy and saw the fall of much of the western empire.

Britain had its own problems. A number of Germanic tribes from northern Germany and Denmark – Angles, Saxons and Jutes to name three of the main ones – had begun to raid across the North Sea and the Romans had built a number of Saxon Shore forts to defend the south and East Anglian coasts from their depredations. Once the Roman army had departed for the continent the manning of these defences was left to local levies. Over the next 150 years the British, often called Romano-British, fought a rearguard action against the Germanic incursions and were slowly forced back into the fringes of the island: Cornwall, Wales, Western Scotland and the Highlands. During the same period a number of Anglo-Saxon kingdoms came into being. Northumbria is the one we are most interested in, as this covered most of Yorkshire and beyond, well into the north-east and the borders of Scotland. Its southern neighbour was Mercia which held sway over most of the Midlands, while Wessex controlled the south and south-west and East Anglia covered the same area as its namesake today. These kingdoms fought numerous wars between themselves and the surviving British kingdoms, but it was an external force that brought an end to their independent existence – the Vikings.

Between 780 and 1066 a series of wars were fought against the Vikings, warriors of mainly Norwegian or Danish origin. Initially the Vikings appeared as raiders, landing, looting then returning to their ships. Later these raiders wintered in Britain and began to settle the areas they controlled, assimilating the local population as they went. At times the Vikings controlled much of what would shortly become England and only determined counter-attacks by King Alfred regained the southern half of the country. Alfred's descendants set about uniting the kingdoms, and under Athelstan and Edgar England finally became one nation.

During the late tenth and early eleventh centuries the Danes returned and under their king, Svein Forkbeard, and his son, Cnut, conquered the whole of England. The Anglo-Saxon line of kings returned with the saintly Edward the Confessor who died without a successor in 1066. The English ruling council, the Witan, elected Harold Godwinsson as king, but this was disputed by two foreign rulers – King Harald Sigurdsson of Norway and Duke William of Normandy. This led to two invasions, one in the north and one in the south. The Norwegians invaded Yorkshire and were initially successful, beating the local forces at Gate Fulford close to York. King Harold rushed north and defeated the invaders at Stamford Bridge, before returning south to face the Normans at Hastings, where he met defeat and death. The Norman Conquest ushered in a new period of English history.

The Dark Ages can be split into three sub-periods – the rise of the Anglo-Saxons, the Vikings and 1066, and each of these will be looked at in turn, paying particular attention to events in Yorkshire, although events beyond the borders of the county will be covered to set the scene. As with the previous chapter on the Roman conquest of the Brigantes, there is a dearth of contemporary accounts, particularly during the early part of the period. Not only do we not have any detail of the fighting but in a number of cases cannot even be sure where the battles were fought. As the period progressed more written evidence becomes available, and by 1066 we have enough detail to construct events with a reasonable amount of accuracy.

The rise of the Anglo-Saxons

With the departure of the Romans, Romano-British society began to fragment into numerous independent kingdoms. Most of Yorkshire came under the control of Ebrauc, a corruption of the Roman name for York, Eboracum. The south and west of the county was part of the kingdom of Rheged, and to the north Bryneich held most of what is now Northumberland and County Durham and encroached into the north of Yorkshire. The names of some of the British kingdoms can be traced back to their pre-Roman tribal roots. The three kingdoms controlling much of the south and south-west of Britain were Atrebatia, Durotrigia and Dumnonia, named after the Atrebates, Durotriges and Dumnonii respectively.

In the middle of the fifth century the Angles and Saxons were groups of barbarian raiders to the British and, other than in southern and eastern coastal areas, had little impact on the day-to-day life of the average Briton. This was to change in 449. The *Anglo-Saxon Chronicles* tell of the first inroads by the Germanic tribesmen:

> *449. In this year Marcian and Valentinian obtained the kingdom and ruled for seven years. In their days Vortigern* [a British king] *invited the Angles hither, and they then came hither to Britain in three ships at a place Heopwinesfleot* [Ebbesfleet in Kent]. *King Vortigern gave them land to the south-east of this land on condition that they fought against the Picts. They then fought against the Picts and had victory wherever they came. They then sent to Angel; ordered them to send more aid and to be told of the worthlessness of the Britons and of the excellence of the land. They then at once sent hither a larger force to help the others.*

Vortigern had opened the floodgates, much as the Romans had done on the continent when they allowed the Germanic tribes to enter the empire to fight as mercenaries. The German reinforcements came from three distinct tribes – the Jutes, the Old Saxons and the Angles. The Jutes settled in Kent and the Isle of Wight, the Saxons along the southern coast and the Angles in East Anglia. Several of our county and regional names stem from these German invaders. Wessex, Sussex and Essex derive from the West, South and East Saxons respectively, while Norfolk and Suffolk come from two groups of Angles, the North folk and the South folk.

Initially the new arrivals were used as mercenaries to fight against the Picts but as their numbers built they began to build small homelands in Kent and Norfolk. In 455 they revolted against Vortigern's control:

> *455. In this year Hengest and Horsa fought against king Vortigern at a place which is called Aegelesprep* [Aylesford in Kent], *and his brother Horsa was slain. And after that Hengest succeeded to the kingdom and Aesc, his son.*

In the following year Hengest and his son drove the Britons out of Kent. The *Anglo-Saxon Chronicles* go on to list a series of invasions by different groups of Anglo-Saxons, mainly along the south coast.

In the north life continued, little troubled by the events in the south, but this does not seem to have been a wholly peaceful period. By 475 the balance of power had shifted among the northern British kingdoms, with new ones appearing and older ones changing in size and the territories they controlled. In Yorkshire the kingdoms of Elmet and Deira had come into being. Elmet is still celebrated in a number of place names which point to the antiquity of some of these towns. Two examples are Sherburn-in-Elmet and Barwick-in-Elmet. One dark cloud lay on the horizon. Close to the Wash an Anglian kingdom had arisen, Mercia, which would play a major part in Yorkshire's military history over the next 300 years.

Over the next seventy-five years the trend continued with more waves of German immigrants expanding their control over large tracts of land, while the British kingdoms continued to shrink. There is still much debate among archaeologists and historians as to how the Anglo-Saxon expansion took place. For many years it was thought that the Anglo-Saxons drove the Britons from their lands but more recent evidence points towards only the ruling classes being driven out, while the remainder of the populace continued with little disruption, simply changing their allegiance to their new leaders.

In 547 an event that was to have a major effect on Yorkshire took place with the founding of the Northumbrian kingdom. The *Anglo-Saxon Chronicles* tell us that:

> *547. In this year Ida, from whom originally sprang the royal race of the Northumbrians, succeeded to the kingdom and reigned twelve years. He built Bamburgh, which was first enclosed by a stockade and thereafter by a rampart.*

This was the beginning of a massive expansion by the Northumbrians. From a small enclave on the coast of modern Northumberland the kingdom expanded to control all the north of England, from the Scottish borders to Lancashire and Lincolnshire. The only exception to this was Cumbria which was controlled by the British kingdom of North Rheged. For most of its length the southern boundary of the kingdom bordered Mercia which had also expanded considerably, while to its west it was bordered by the British kingdom of Gwynedd which controlled most of northern Wales.

During this period of expansion Northumbria fought a number of wars against other British and Anglo-Saxon kingdoms. In 603 Aethelfrith, King of Northumbria, had a victorious campaign against the Scots of Dalriada, a kingdom on the west coast of Scotland. This was followed in 605 by another successful campaign against the Welsh, most probably Gwynedd, who Aethelfrith defeated at Chester. Unfortunately, none of Aethelfrith's campaigns are recorded as having taken place in Yorkshire, which was by this time the heartland of the kingdom and surrounded by a sizeable buffer zone. Aethelfrith continued to rule until 617 which points to his having been a very successful military commander. In 617 he met his match when his army was defeated, and Aethelfrith slain, by the East Anglians under their king, Raedwald, who has been put forward as the individual buried in the Sutton Hoo ship burial in Suffolk, which contained the finest collection of Anglo-Saxon artefacts ever found in the country. It is well worth a visit to the British Museum in London just to see them. With Aethelfrith's death, Edwin gained the throne of Northumbria.

Open warfare was not the only form of political machinations taking place at the time, and the *Anglo-Saxon Chronicles* report an attempted assassination on the king of Northumbria:

> *626. In this year Eomer came from Cwichelm, king of Wessex: he meant to stab king Edwin, but he stabbed Lilla, his thane, and Forthere, and wounded the king. That same night a daughter was born to Edwin, who was called Eanfled. Then the king promised Paulinus [Bishop of York] to give his daughter to God, if he by prayers would obtain from God that he might overthrow his enemy who had sent the assassin there.*

Paulinus' prayers seem to have been answered and Edwin led his army into Wessex and 'slew five kings there and killed a great number of the people'. Edwin was true to his word and his daughter was baptised at Easter in the wooden church of St Peter in York, which stood where York Minster is now. Edwin subsequently had a stone church built on the same site. In 627 Edwin and many of his supporters were also baptised in York.

Another event took place in 626 which would have major repercussions in Yorkshire – Penda came to the throne of Mercia. Initially, there seems to have been a delicate peace between the two kingdoms. Penda and many of his people were still pagans while the Northumbrians were, in the main, Christian. Penda gave permission for Paulinus to preach in Lindsey, now part of Lincolnshire, and his success is recorded in the *Anglo-Saxon Chronicles*:

> *627. In this year king Edwin was baptized by Paulinus; and this same Paulinus also preached Christianity in Lindsey, where the first to convert was a certain powerful man called Blecca with all his chief men.*

At some time between 626 and 633, although it is not certain exactly when, Edwin fought a successful campaign against Cadwallon, King of Gwynedd, capturing Anglesey and driving Cadwallon into exile. By this time Edwin was accepted as Bretwalda, over-king, by all of England except Kent. Northumbria's growing power, and Paulinus' success at converting some of his subjects to Christianity, led Penda into an alliance with Cadwallon, when the latter returned to reclaim his kingdom in 633. In the autumn of that year the two kings led their combined armies into Northumbria and engaged Edwin in battle at Hatfield, near Doncaster.

Organisation and tactics of the Anglo-Saxons

Before we move on to look at the events of 633, and its aftermath, it is worth digressing to look at how an Anglo-Saxon army was organised and equipped, and how they fought. Much of what follows is relevant to the whole period covered by this chapter. Few major changes took place in the equipment and tactics of an English army until the Normans introduced the mounted knight in 1066 – an Anglo-Saxon warrior from 633 would have felt at home standing in the shield wall at Stamford Bridge 400 years later.

It is often taught in schools that the feudal system was introduced by the Normans after the conquest. This is far from the truth for Anglo-Saxon England had a deeply engrained feudal system from the time of the arrival of the German tribesmen. It was based on a warrior's allegiance to his lord, be it a king or a chieftain. In return for this allegiance a warrior would be granted land and given gifts. At this period the land grant was not a permanent one and lasted only as long as a warrior supported his lord, or until he died, when the land would return to the lord. Later in the period land was granted on a permanent basis to the church or to individuals and this land would remain within the family, and would return to the lord only if a land owner failed in his duty.

Sixth century Anglo-Saxon kingdoms were very similar in their make up, being formed of a number of tribal groups, many of which had retained the names they had used back in their homelands in northern Germany and Denmark. At the top of the tree was the king, who owned all the land within the kingdom. He then gave gifts of land to his thanes, who could be kings in their own right, as the leader of one of the kingdom's sub-tribes. These in turn gifted estates to their followers, and so on. Each individual who was granted land owed his allegiance to his immediate superior, and ultimately to the king. This payment was usually carried out in the form of military service, although on occasion other forms of payment were accepted in lieu of military service, for example, providing supplies to the king's court. The penalties for not carrying out military duty could be severe ranging from large fines to the con-fiscation of lands or even being put to death.

When a king called his thanes to provide military support they, in turn, would call on their supporters. It was usually only freemen who owed this allegiance and the lower classes of serfs and slaves were left alone to farm the land or carry out their trades. A seventh century army should not be thought of as tens of thousands, or even thousands, of men strong for most would have been in the hundreds. To illustrate this, slightly later in the period, during the Viking invasions, a Viking force was called the Great Army. This immediately assumes a massive force but in actual fact is thought to have been only 2–3,000 men strong and some historians have put the figure as low as 400. If this was considered an exceptionally large army then the average Anglo-Saxon force would have been much smaller.

Although many of the Anglo-Saxon warriors rode to battle, they usually fought on foot. The bulk of the army would have been spearmen, armed with a spear which could be used as a thrusting weapon or thrown. Swords were rare at this period and only the select few would have carried them. Carrying a sword was a sign of prestige and many had been passed down through the family from generation to generation – some even had names and legends attached to them. Most warriors would have carried a long knife as a back-up to their spear and some form of missile weapon, usually one or more javelins. Armour would also have been a rarity. Once again it was only the upper eche-lons who could afford a mail shirt but some of the lower rank warriors would have been equipped with leather armour for their torsos. The bulk of the army would have worn their everyday clothes. An average Anglo-Saxon warrior's main protection was his shield, with its prominent central metal boss which could also be used as an offensive weapon by smashing it into an opponent's face.

Having briefly looked at how an Anglo-Saxon army was formed and equipped it is now time to look at how it fought. As has already been mentioned, most of what follows is relevant to the whole period covered by this chapter, and for all the armies that fought in England. Few early accounts give any detail into how the armies actually fought but we are fortunate to have an epic poem, the *Song of Maldon*, which does give some insights into a battle at this time.

The standard battle formation throughout the period was the shield wall, also known as the 'bord-weal' or 'scyld-burh' by the English. The better-equipped warriors would have formed the front ranks, with the less well-equipped filling in behind. The whole line would be five or six men deep but this could vary due to the circumstances an army found itself in. For example, an army that was heavily out-numbered would extend its line, at the expense of its depth, to try to prevent its shield wall from being outflanked. It could also draw back, or refuse, its flanks. An army could be forced into a deeper formation by terrain and this occurred at one of the battles discussed later in the chapter.

Once the opposing shield walls formed, how did they engage one another? It almost certainly bore little resemblance to Hollywood's version of a Dark Ages, or medieval, battlefield. As the shield walls closed on one another there would have been no mad, headlong charge, as was shown in the film *Braveheart*, for example. The idea of a shield wall was to keep a solid front to the enemy; such a charge would have resulted in the disintegration of the shield wall before contact had been made, which would have given a major advantage to an opponent. At the Battle of Sherston in 1016, Florence of Worcester describes a slow, steady advance to maintain the shield wall's formation.

The troops in the line knew what was about to happen. As the two lines closed, a mass of missile fire would be exchanged. William of Poitiers described the reception that the English shield wall gave to the advancing Norman infantry at Hastings:

> *So the Norman infantry advanced closer, provoking the English, and causing wounds and death with their missiles. The latter resisted bravely, each according to their means. They threw javelins and all sorts of darts, the most lethal of axes and stones fixed to pieces of wood. Under this deadly hail you might have thought that our men would be crushed.*

With this 'deadly hail' of missiles about to begin it is hardly surprising that an army tried to maintain a close, tight formation, with shields overlapping.

As has already been mentioned, the best description of a shield wall fight comes from the *Song of Maldon*. The Battle of Maldon took place in 991. The local troops, commanded by Earl Brihtnoth, confronted a Viking army near Maldon in Essex. Brihtnoth was killed early in the fighting and some of his men fled the field but the remainder continued to fight for some time. What the poem does not describe is a continuous, close-quarter fight between the shield walls. Brihtnoth's retainers, who form the heroes of the poem, seem to be fighting in fits and starts. One of them would exhort his comrades to greater efforts and then exchange missile fire with one of the Vikings. Another would shout out his lineage and then engage an advancing Viking warrior. Yet another would tell his comrades how he intends to die at his lord's side then advance into the Viking line, to be cut down after killing several opponents.

How would a fight between two shield walls have progressed? First, the shield walls would have formed with shields overlapping and bristling with spear points. Before the advance to contact, individuals may have advanced from one or the other army and issued challenges to single combat. This was just a warm-up act, although the loss of a famous champion could adversely affect an army's morale. Once this was over the armies would have closed on one another, with shields overlapping. Then a hail of missiles would have been exchanged, with some casualties caused on both sides, but if the formations had remained tight they would have been relatively few. It must have been a very daunting prospect to charge into a solid wall of shields, bristling with spears but, at some point, contact had to be made. Whether the two solid lines crashed into one another is open to debate, and the *Song of Maldon* mentions no such collision. What seems more likely is a gradual wearing down process. Small groups, or individuals, would try to force an opening in the enemy shield wall and if they were successful others close to them would try to reinforce their success, while their opponents would try to eject them and re-form the line.

So, the two shield walls would not be in constant contact with each other but would be separated by a few yards. Missiles and insults would be exchanged across this space. In a battle such as Stamford Bridge (1066) where each line could have a frontage of 1,000 men covering a distance of half a mile, dozens of groups would be attempting to break into the enemy lines at any given point in time and as these attempts were resolved, others would begin. The lines must have surged back and forth constantly. Eventually, a successful break-in to the enemy formation would occur and the enemy's morale would begin to crack. This was the point when the losing commander had to commit his reserve but if no such reserve was available the shield wall would be broken and the rout would begin. By far the highest numbers of casualties were caused when an army turned and fled and a pursuit would often go on until nightfall.

The battles of Hatfield and Winwidfield

Having briefly digressed to discuss how an Anglo-Saxon army was equipped and how it fought, it is now time to return to the autumn of 633. The combined forces of Penda's Mercia and Cadwallon's Gwynedd clashed with Edwin's Northumbrians close to Hatfield, near Doncaster. The battle is known by a number of different names – Hatfield, Hatfield Chase and Heathfield. The *Anglo-Saxon Chronicles* state:

> *633. In this year King Edwin was slain by Cadwallon and Penda at Hatfield Chase on 14 October; and he had ruled seven years. His son Osfrith was also slain with him. Then afterwards went Cadwallon and Penda and laid waste to the whole of Northumbria. When Paulinus saw this, then he took Aethelburth, Edwin's widow, and went by ship to Kent.*

Bede in his *Ecclesiastical History of the English People* gives the date of the battle as 12 October. Unfortunately, this is all the information we have about the battle. It would have been a 'shield wall' battle as described above, with the Mercians and Welsh forming separate shield walls facing the smaller Northumbrian formation. It is likely that King Edwin had to deploy his men in a shallower formation to cover the same frontage as his opponents, and this would have been a contributory factor in his defeat.

With the defeat of the Northumbrian army the two allies were free to ravage through the kingdom, burning and killing as they went. Initially, Northumbria split into two separate kingdoms, Bernicia in the north and Deira in the south, but by 634 the kingdom had been recombined by Oswald. After raiding into Northumbria Penda returned to Mercia but Cadwallon continued to attack the Northumbrians until he was defeated at the Battle of Heavenfield, in present day Northumberland. With Oswald's defeat of Cadwallon Northumbria began to grow in power. Once again it was Penda of Mercia who brought this to a halt when he defeated the Northumbrians at the Battle of Maserfeld, near Telford in Shropshire, on 5 August 641. Oswald was killed at the battle and was succeeded to the throne by Oswy, who would reign for twenty-eight years, a very long reign for a seventh century Anglo-Saxon king.

There followed a fragile peace between the two kingdoms for the next thirteen years. In 654 this peace broke down and Penda invaded Northumbria with a large army. Oswy gathered his forces and met and defeated him at the battle of Winwidfield. Once again the *Anglo-Saxon Chronicles* give few details of the battle:

> *654. In this year Oswy slew Penda at Winwidfield and thirty princes with him, and some of them were kings; one of them was Aethelhere, brother of Anna, king of East Anglia.*

A much more entertaining account of the battle was written by Edmund Bogg in 1893:

In the year 655 [based on Bede who dates many events one year later than the Anglo-Saxon Chronicles], *he* [Penda] *gathered around his banners a mighty army, consisting of thirty legions of tried soldiers, commanded by generals who had led them to victory on many battlefields. Once again he felt a desire to shatter the growing power of Northumbria and utterly destroy the Christian faith, which the pagan priests represented to him as tending to overthrow the sacred altars, in the groves where he loved to worship along with his kingdom. Marching in a north-easterly direction towards the old Kingdom of Elmet, crossing the River Aire at Leeds, and taking up his position on Winwoed field* [one of many variations of the spelling of the battle's name], *now Whinmoor, awaited the coming of his foes. In vain Oswin* [Oswy] *tried by every means in his power to conciliate the Mercian king by the offer of gold and silver ornaments and other costly gifts.*

Oswin at length growing impatient, cried, 'If the pagans will not accept our gifts let us offer them to one who will' vowing at the same time that if successful he would dedicate his daughter to God and endow twelve monasteries in his realm. The Northumbrian army was only small compared with the hosts of the Mercians, but, putting their trust in God they boldly marched into battle. The dreadful fight took place on 15 November 655. In vain the Mercians tried to penetrate the ranks of Oswin's army.

The power of heathendom was lost for ever when he, who for fifty years had been the cause of so much misery and bloodshed, lay with his generals and thousands of his army, a ghastly and confused heap of slain, their blood changing the waters of the little rivulet to crimson. The wreck of the Mercian army fled southward, and in their frantic rush from the field of battle many fell into the river Cock and were trampled underfoot until their bodies formed a bridge for their flying comrades, who in turn were swept away and drowned when attempting to cross the swollen waters of the River Aire.

This is a very entertaining account and typical of the Victorian period. But how much fact is there in it? Bogg has the battle taking place on Whinmoor which lies just to the east of Seacroft – the A64 crosses it as the road leaves Leeds for York. Two other sites have been put forward: Barwick-in-Elmet and Garforth. All three sites, Whinmoor, Barwick and Garforth, are close to one another, and close to the road from Leeds to York. The western end of Whinmoor saw another battle, Seacroft Moor, in 1643, when Sir Thomas Fairfax led his men in a fighting retreat from Tadcaster to Leeds (see Chapter 5). If Bogg's statement that the Mercians crossed the Aire at Leeds is correct, and as the Northumbrian army probably approached from York, their capital and an obvious place for the army to muster, Whinmoor is a likely candidate. Unfortunately, that is about as useful as saying a battle was near Barnsley as far as pinning down the battlefield is concerned. It is worth considering though, if you are driving along the A64 from Leeds to York that you are passing through one battlefield – Seacroft Moor – and probably within sight of another – Winwidfield.

Where does Bogg get his 'thirty legions' from? It is a strong possibility that he has read a little too much into the *Anglo-Saxon Chronicles* mention of thirty 'princes' being slain at the battle. It has already been mentioned that all Anglo-Saxon kingdoms were made up of a number of sub-groups which retained the tribal names of their founders. Each of the 'princes' would have been a sub-group leader, or part of a ruling family. Penda also had a number of allied contingents with him and the *Anglo-Saxon Chronicles* mention Aethelhere, the brother of the East Anglian king, being among the thirty slain princes. East Anglia was still an independent kingdom but was under Penda's sway. Penda also had at least one British ally, Cadfael of Gwynedd. The *Historia Brittonum* reports Cadfael as 'rising up in the night, escaped together with his army' and this earned him the nickname Cadomedd – battle shirker!

It is almost certain that Penda, with his British and East Anglian allies, outnumbered Oswy's Northumbrians, but Oswy's men were victorious and it is here that we come to another problem in Bogg's account. Bogg talks about the routing Mercian army reaching the River Cock and a bridge of bodies forming across the river. The River Cock is well to the east of the battlefield and runs along the western edge of the Towton battlefield, to the south of Tadcaster. For the Mercians to reach the River Cock, assuming they had come from Leeds, they would have had to pass through the Northumbrian lines. It is much more likely that many of them were drowned in the Aire, as Bogg goes on to say, as this would have taken them back along their line of advance from Leeds, an obvious route for fleeing troops to take. Accounts of the Battle of Towton (1461) talk of a bridge of bodies across the River Cock, or Cock Beck as it is known locally, and it is possible that Bogg confused the two incidents. It seems highly unlikely that any Mercians routed in this direction.

What do we know with any certainty? Simply that the Mercians were defeated and Penda and many of his leaders were killed. We can make a number of reasonably safe assumptions though. The battle was fought on Whinmoor, close to the A64 and Barwick-in-Elmet, with the Mercians advancing from Leeds and the Northumbrians coming from York. The Northumbrian army was outnumbered but won a hard fought victory, with many Mercian troops being cut down in the pursuit towards Leeds and many more drowning as they tried to cross the River Aire to safety. Among the slain were Penda and thirty of his tribal leaders.

After Winwidfield the power of Mercia was much reduced. Things continued much as before, with raids and open warfare between the two kingdoms. In 716 the *Anglo-Saxon Chronicles* record the death in battle of another Northumbrian king, Osred, who was killed in a battle somewhere south of the Northumbrian/Mercian border. In 741 the same source records York burning down but there is no mention of a military cause for this and it could simply have been a fire sweeping through the mainly wooden buildings of the town. Over the next 100 years a succession of kings followed and many of them did not die peacefully in their beds. The *Anglo-Saxon Chronicles* records kings being murdered, expelled and abdicating, but does not record any military actions. It should not be assumed that this period was peaceful because of the lack of recorded military campaigns and fighting would have been a regular occurrence, both with external and internal enemies. In 793 an event took place which would have a major effect on the Anglo-Saxon kingdoms and on the island as a whole – the arrival of the Vikings.

The fury of the Northmen

In AD 793 the *Anglo-Saxon Chronicles* reported a portentous event:

> *793. In this year terrible portents appeared over Northumbria, and miserably fright-ened the inhabitants: these were exceptional flashes of lightning, and fiery dragons were seen flying in the air. A great famine followed these signs; and a little after that in the same year on 8 January* [8 June in other sources] *the harrying of the heathen miserably destroyed God's church in Lindisfarne by rapine and slaughter.*

Another report of the attack on Lindisfarne came from Alcuin, a monk from York who spent many years at the court of King Charlemagne and often corresponded with the king of Northumbria:

Viking raiders – a sight to put fear into any Saxon villager (John Wilson).

Never before has such a terror appeared in Britain as we have now suffered from a pagan race, nor was it thought that such an inroad from the sea could be made. Behold the church of St Cuthbert, spattered with the blood of the priests of God, despoiled of all its ornaments; a place more venerable than all in Britain is given as prey to pagan peoples.

Not only was Lindisfarne venerable but it was also vulnerable, lying on an island off the Northumbrian coast connected by a causeway but completely cut off during high tides. These reports are the first mention of Viking raids although an earlier visit by a party of Norwegians is recorded in the *Anglo-Saxon Chronicles*:

787. In this year Beorhtric [king of Wessex] *took to wife Eadburh, daughter of Offa* [king of Mercia]. *And in his days came three ships of Norwegians from Horthaland: and then the reeve rode thither and tried to compel them to go to the royal manor, for he did not know what they were: and then they slew him. These were the first ships of Danes to come to England.*

This entry is a little contradictory, first mentioning that the ships were Norwegian and then that they were Danish. If they did indeed come from Horthaland, the area around Hardanger Fjord, they were definitely Norwegians.

Initially, the Vikings were little more than a seasonal nuisance as internal power struggles for the Northumbrian throne continued. In 789 Aelfwald, the Northumbrian king, was slain in battle somewhere in the north-east. He was succeeded by his nephew, Osred, who ruled for only a short time before he was driven into exile and Aethelred, not to be confused with the two kings of Wessex of the same name who will be mentioned later, assumed the throne. In 792 Osred returned to reclaim his throne but was seized and killed on 14 September.

The Viking raiders do not seem to have had everything their own way as the *Anglo-Saxon Chronicles* report:

794. And Northumbria was ravaged by the heathen, and Ecgfrith's monastery at Donemup [Jarrow] *looted; and there one of their leaders was slain, and some of their ships besides were shattered by storms: and many of them were drowned there, and some came ashore alive and were at once slain at the river mouth.*

The Northumbrians obviously gave short shrift to any of the Viking raiders they captured!

Things continued in Northumbria in much the same vein until 829. In 802 Egbert succeeded to the throne of Wessex and commenced a series of campaigns which would lead him to be acknowledged as Bretwalda in 829. Bretwalda, meaning overlord or chief king, was a title given to the ruler of Britain. Only seven other kings had attained the title since the Germanic tribes had arrived in Britain. Egbert had conquered all of England south of the Humber and in 829 he crossed the river with his army and marched to Dore, now on the outskirts of Sheffield. Here he was met by a deputation

The Vikings assault a village stockade (John Wilson).

from the king of Northumbria offering him 'submission and peace'. Having agreed to this Egbert marched his army south having attained supremacy over the whole of England. He continued to campaign until his death in 839 after a reign of thirty-seven years, a very long reign for a king of this period.

After Egbert's death his kingdom was divided in two and a succession of weaker kings of Wessex allowed the other Anglo-Saxon kingdoms to emerge as fully in-dependent states once again. In 855 a short entry in the *Anglo-Saxon Chronicles* records another important event in English history: '855. In this year the heathen for the first time wintered in Sheppey'. Up to this point the Vikings had been seasonal raiders but the party wintering on Sheppey showed a marked change in their tactics.

In 865 a large force of Vikings, which has become known as the Great Army, arrived in East Anglia forcing the local populace to submit to them and provide them with horses. In a similar fashion to the English, the Vikings invariably fought on foot, but used horses to provide mobility while on campaign. In 866 the Great Army turned north and crossed the Humber into Yorkshire, as the *Anglo-Saxon Chronicles* state:

866. In this year the host went from East Anglia over the mouth of the Humber to York in Northumbria; and there was great dissension of the people among themselves; and they had repudiated their king Osberht and accepted Aella, a king not of royal birth; and it was late in the year when they set about making war against the host [Great Army], nevertheless they gathered great levies and went to attack the host at York and stormed the city [21 March 867], and some of them got inside; and immense slaughter was made of the Northumbrians there, some inside, some outside, and both kings were slain, and the remnant made peace with the host.

It would seem from this entry that the Great Army had taken York and, after many disagreements, the Northumbrians raised an army and attacked the city. Although some of the Northumbrians managed to penetrate its defences the Vikings defeated them and installed a puppet ruler after both Northumbrian kings were killed in the battle. The capture of York gave the Vikings a good base of operations.

Over the winter of 867-8 the Great Army moved to Nottingham where it fortified its quarters. The king of Mercia called on Wessex for support to drive the pagans from his land and the king of Wessex, Aethelred, and his brother, Alfred, responded to the call. Unfortunately, the Vikings had prepared their defences well and the Saxons were frustrated in their attempts to defeat their enemy. After a short stand-off the king of Mercia made peace with the Vikings and Aethelred and Alfred returned south to Wessex.

In 869 the Great Army returned to York and then marched back into East Anglia. This time the Anglian king, Edmund, did not welcome them and raised his levies to fight. The Anglians were defeated and Edmund was captured and brutally put to death. Next the Great Army turned its attention to Wessex. In 870 the Vikings captured Reading and fought a series of battles against Aethelred's Wessex levies, with honours going to both sides. The campaigning continued into 871 when, after Easter, Aethelred died after a five-year reign and his younger brother, Alfred, ascended the throne. Alfred had yet to prove himself as a king and the nickname 'the Great' was many years in the future.

Alfred carried out a successful defensive campaign and then came to an agreement with the Great Army's leaders, upon which the Vikings withdrew into Mercia. Border skirmishes and raids continued but it was during this period that a section of the Great Army split from the main force and moved north into Northumbria. Halfdan led his men north to the River Tyne where he carried out a successful campaign against the Scots before returning to York and settling the area. Once again this was a new departure for the Vikings – now they were settling the land rather than conquering it and demanding tribute. This was the start of Viking Yorkshire and York would become Jorvik.

In 875 the remainder of the Great Army recommenced its assault on Wessex in earnest. Once again Alfred stopped the invasion and the Vikings returned to Mercia. In January 878 the Vikings launched a surprise assault on Twelfth Night as the Christian men of Wessex celebrated the end of the Christmas festivities. Gathering their forces in secret at Chippenham the Vikings advanced rapidly into Wessex catching Alfred completely off his guard. The year would see the king reach his lowest point and also achieve his greatest victory. By Easter Alfred had been driven back to Athelney in the Somerset Levels and ruled only a few square yards of his kingdom. From his hiding place among the marshes Alfred was able to co-ordinate the gathering of his forces and in May 878, in an amazing turn around of fortune, he defeated the Vikings at the Battle of Edington in Wiltshire, following which the Viking leader Guthrum converted to Christianity and withdrew into East Anglia. Part of the agreement was the division of England into two parts. The southern part comprised Wessex and the western half of Mercia which would be ruled by Alfred, while eastern Mercia, East Anglia and Northumbria would come under the Viking sway, and so the Danelaw came into being.

In the aftermath of the 878 campaign Alfred completely reorganised Wessex's defences, building a number of burghs, or fortified towns, such as Wareham, to act as focus points for the defence of his kingdom during the expected return of the Viking attacks. Although raid and counter-raid took place an unsteady peace reigned until Alfred launched a successful attack on London in 886. In 892 the Vikings opened a major assault on Wessex but Alfred's preparations paid dividends and the attack was unsuccessful with the Vikings been driven back into the Danelaw.

During this period the seeds of an English identity had begun to germinate and many of Alfred's subjects no longer considered themselves as merely men of Wessex or Kent, but as Englishmen. This was not the case in the north which was still firmly under Viking control. York, or Jorvik, had developed into the centre of power of the Danelaw and had become a major trading centre, probably more important than London at the time. Excavations in Coppergate have shown what a thriving commercial centre York was at this time.

In 899 Alfred, after a long and successful reign, died and his son Edward was crowned king. This was not to his cousin Aethelwold's liking and he raised a force, including Danish troops from York, to take the throne from Edward. Aethelwold was unsuccessful and was defeated by Edward who then commenced a long reign. In 924 Edward died and was succeeded by Athelstan, his illegitimate son, who continued his father's campaigns, both military and diplomatic, to unite England, including Northumbria, into one nation.

While the Great Army had been vying against Wessex in England, other Vikings had been carrying out similar campaigns in Ireland, with varying degrees of success. In 911 one of these 'Dublin' Vikings, Ragnald, turned his attention on England and captured York. He ruled for only a short time before been driven out but returned in 919. On his death his brother Sihtric, who had been ruling in Dublin, moved to York and began his reign. In 927 Guthfrith, another Dublin Viking advanced to claim York after Sihtric's death. He was soundly defeated by the Northumbrian troops, returning to Ireland to find Dublin had been taken over by another Viking leader.

While Guthfrith was campaigning in the north, Athelstan began his conquest of England in earnest. First he turned on Cornwall and Wales which he had conquered by April 928. Then he marched into Northumbria which submitted with little, if any, resistance. In 934 he carried out a successful campaign against the Scots before returning to the south of England. Between 934 and 937 an alliance was founded between the Scots and several disparate groups of Vikings from both Ireland and Scandinavia. The Scots king, Constantine, seems to have been the instigator of the alliance, which planned to conquer the north before turning on Athelstan in the south, and the various contingents gathered together in Yorkshire. Athelstan reacted decisively and gathered his army to march north. This march led to the Battle of Brunanburgh.

The campaign and Battle of Brunanburgh

One of the important questions to ask about Brunanburgh is where exactly was the battle fought. There are dozens of sites which claim the battle, so, unlike the previous battles mentioned in this chapter, we cannot even be sure in which county the battle took place. Sites in Lancashire, Yorkshire, the Wirral and Scotland, to name but a few, all claim the battlefield. Alfred H Burne puts forward a convincing argument for a site in South Yorkshire in his book *More Battlefields of England* published in 1952, and this has been supported by a number of other historians, including Michael Wood in *In search of the Dark Ages* (1987), although always with the caveat that we cannot be sure.

So, what evidence is there that the battle had been fought on the banks of the River Don between Rotherham and Sheffield? Let us look at the strategic situation. In 937 Scotland occupied the eastern half of the present country with the western side occupied by the British kingdom of Strathclyde. Constantine would have gathered his own army in south-eastern Scotland which was also a convenient point for the Scandinavian Viking contingents to join his growing force. The Dublin Vikings, under their leader Anlaf (Olaf), were a different matter. After gathering his forces where did Anlaf land to join the allied army? Burne and several other historians put forward the idea that they sailed up the River Ribble in Lancashire before landing and crossing the Pennines along the pass now occupied by the A65, via Skipton and Ilkley, to meet with Constantine at, or close to Tadcaster. This is perfectly plausible but not necessarily correct. Later in this chapter we will look at the events of 1066 when a Norwegian army invaded Yorkshire. When its leader, Harald Sigurdsson, gathered his army in the Orkney Isles, contingents from the area of the Irish Sea, Dublin and the Isle of Man sailed to Orkney to join his army before the whole forced moved south. It is possible that Anlaf and his men did the same and the whole army gathered in Scotland before sailing south.

The allied fleet was immense. Medieval chroniclers give us some clues as to the size of the fleet and its destination. Simeon of Durham states that Constantine and Anlaf had 615 ships – Harald Sigurdsson had only half this number in 1066 – while Florence of Worcester states that the fleet sailed up the River Humber. Where the army disembarked is open to conjecture. Burne wrote that they landed close to Tadcaster. Although this is far from certain, it makes strategic sense. Tadcaster was at a junction of several Roman roads which were still in use at the time. One was the road over the Pennines through Ilkley and Skipton which Burne suggested was the route taken by Anlaf and his men as they marched from Lancashire to join with Constantine. Another road led south through Castleford to Derby and ran close to the River Don between Sheffield and Rotherham. Tadcaster also lies close to the Northumbrian seat of power at York.

Athelstan had placed two earls in charge of Northumbria, Alfgeir and Gudrek, and these two gathered a force to oppose the allied army, now commanded by Anlaf. Egil's Saga, tells of a battle between the two armies which resulted in a bad defeat for the Northumbrians, with Gudrek killed and Alfgeir fleeing south to warn the king. Athelstan gathered his army and marched north to meet the invaders. Having beaten the Northumbrian forces Anlaf led his men south. Both armies were approaching along the same road and clashed at Brunanburgh sometime in September 937 – the exact date is not known.

Between the present-day villages of Brinsworth and Catcliffe runs an east-west ridge, now heavily built on. At the time of the battle it was open heath land, with its eastern flank protected by the River Rother while its western end was covered by a wooded valley. Gentle slopes lay to the north and south. It was along this ridge-line that Athelstan deployed his army to face his opponents as they approached from the north.

We know very little about the actual battle, but a poem in the *Anglo-Saxon Chronicles* gives us some clues:

> *In this year king Athelstan, lord of warriors,*
> *Ring-giver of men, with his brother prince Edmund,*
> *Won undying glory with the edges of swords,*
> *In warfare around Brunanburgh.*
> *With their hammered blades, the sons of Edward*
> *Clove the shield wall and hacked the linden bucklers,*
> *To defend their land, their treasures and their homes,*
> *In frequent battle against each enemy.*
> *The foemen were laid low: the Scots*
> *And the host from the ships fell doomed. The field*
> *Grew dark with the blood of men after the sun,*
> *That glorious luminary, God's bright candle,*
> *Rose high in the morning above the horizon,*
> *Until the noble being of the Lord Eternal*
> *Sank to its rest. There lay many a warrior*
> *Of the men of the North, torn by spears,*
> *Shot o'er his shield; likewise many a Scot*
> *Sated with battle, lay lifeless.*
> *All through the day the West Saxons in troops*
> *Pressed on in pursuit of the hostile peoples,*
> *Fiercely, with swords sharpened on grindstone,*
> *They cut down the fugitives as they fled.*
> *Nor did the Mercians refuse hard fighting*
> *To any of Anlaf's warriors, who invaded*
> *Our land across the tossing waters,*

In the ship's bosom, to meet their doom
In the fight. Five young kings,
Stretched lifeless by the swords,
Lay on the field, likewise seven
Of Anlaf's jarls, and a countless host
Of seamen and Scots. There the prince
Of Norsemen, compelled by necessity,
Was forced to flee to the prow of his ship
With a handful of men. In haste the ship
Was launched, and the king fled hence,
Over the watery grey, to save his life.
There, likewise, the aged Constantine,
The grey-haired warrior, set off in flight,
North to his native land. No cause
Had he to exult in that clash of swords,
Bereaved of his kinsmen, robbed of his friends
On the field of battle, by violence deprived
Of them in the struggle. On the place of slaughter
He left his son, mangled by wounds,
Received in the fight. No need to exult
In that clash of blades had the grey-haired warrior,
That practised scoundrel, and no more had Anlaf
Need to gloat, amid the remnants of their host,
That they excelled in martial deeds
Where standards clashed, and spear met spear
And man fought man, upon a field
Where swords were crossed, when they in battle
Fought Edward's sons upon the fateful field.
The sorry Norsemen who escaped the spears
Set out upon the sea of Ding, making for Dublin
O'er deep waters, in ships with nailed sides,
Ashamed and shameless back to Ireland.
Likewise the English king and the prince,
Brothers triumphant in war, together
Returned to their home, the land of Wessex.
To enjoy the carnage, they left behind
The horn-beaked raven with dusky plumage,
And the hungry hawk of battle, the dun-coated
Eagle, who with white-tipped tail shared
The feast with the wolf, grey beast of the forest.
Never before in this island, as the books
Of ancient historians tell us, was an army

> *Put to greater slaughter by the sword*
> *Since the time when Angles and Saxons landed,*
> *Invading Britain from across the wide seas*
> *From the east, when warriors eager for fame,*
> *Proud forgers of war, the Welsh overcame,*
> *And won for themselves a kingdom.*

All very inspiring – but very biased! Another version of the *Anglo-Saxon Chronicles* simply mentions that 'In this year king Athelstan led levies to Brunanburgh', while a third version does not mention the battle at all.

It is difficult to gauge how large the two armies were, although some historians have given ridiculous numbers – in one instance 100,000 for Anlaf's force and in another over 200,000 for the combined total of both armies. Burne gives a figure of about 18,000 for the combined Scots/Viking army and this is a reasonable estimate – Harald Sigurdsson with a fleet of 300 ships had an army of about 10,000, so Anlaf's 615 ships could yield a force of twice that size. Taking into account their losses in the initial battle against the Northumbrians, a figure of 18,000 seems about right. Athelstan's English army must have been of a comparable size, although *Egil's Saga* says it was much smaller than the invaders force.

The battle would have been a classic shield wall fight that went on for much of the day, and the pursuit, once the Scots and Viking shield wall broke, would have continued as long as the weary English troops could keep it up. Anlaf and the remnants of his Dublin forces returned to their ships and headed back to Ireland while Constantine returned to Scotland. The invaders suffered massive casualties including five kings and seven earls. Among the casualties was Constantine's son. Alfred Burne sums up the importance of the battle:

> *The short-lived confederation was broken, never again to be revived. If the Southern capital had been captured North Britain would probably have become the 'predominant power' in this island, and Edinburgh or Perth would now be the capital of the United Kingdom.*

Erik Bloodaxe

In the aftermath of Brunanburgh peace returned to Yorkshire, but only for a short time. In 940 Athelstan passed away after a reign of fourteen years, and was succeeded by his eighteen-year-old brother Edmund, a veteran of the battle. The Northumbrians, who always seemed to consider themselves as an independent nation and submitted to the English kings only when they had no other option, took the opportunity of having a young, inexperienced king on the throne to once again assert their independence. In 941 the Northumbrians offered the throne to Anlaf, who returned to Yorkshire from his base at Dublin.

Initially, Anlaf and the Northumbrians made inroads into Mercia but the young king quickly regained the lost ground and drove the Northumbrians back into their own territory. In 943 Anlaf once again moved south and stormed Tamworth, the old royal capital of Mercia. The *Anglo-Saxon Chronicles* record that there was great slaughter on both sides and that the Northumbrians 'carried great booty away with them'. Once again Edmund responded to the threat and besieged Anlaf in Leicester. Anlaf managed to escape at night but realised that the English were too powerful and came to an agreement with Edmund who stood as sponsor at Anlaf's subsequent baptism. Edmund also stood as sponsor for Raegnald, Anlaf's co-ruler. The peace was short-lived and in 944 Edmund drove the two kings out of Northumbria and brought the whole kingdom under his control. In the following year Edmund invaded and ravaged Strathclyde before handing it over to Malcolm, Constantine's successor as king of Scots.

Edmund reigned for only six years before he was stabbed to death in 946. He was followed by his younger brother Eadred, who, in short order brought Northumbria and the Scots to heel. Troublesome as ever, the Northumbrians required Eadred to bring his army north again in 947 to Tanshelf, which is part of modern day Pontefract and one of the town's railway stations is called Pontefract Tanshelf. Wulfstan, Archbishop of York, and all the Northumbrian nobles pledged their allegiance to the king but in a very short time 'they were false both to their pledges and oaths'. The Northumbrians had invited a Norwegian warrior to rule their kingdom.

Erik Haraldsson, known to history as Erik Bloodaxe, held the throne of Northumbria for two short periods during the 940s and 950s. His father was Harald Finehair who had subdued and then ruled the whole of Norway. When Harald died open warfare broke out between his numerous sons. Erik defeated and killed two of his brothers but his violent nature seems to have turned many of his most powerful subjects against him. These supported his half-brother, Hakon, who returned from Athelstan's court where he had been brought up, to challenge Erik for the throne. With his support dwindling Erik abandoned the country and sailed west. Initially, this seems to have simply been a raiding expedition with Erik and his men plundering down the eastern coast of Scotland. When he arrived in Northumbria, Wulfstan and the North-umbrian nobles, the same men who had only months earlier given their allegiance to Eadred, offered him the throne.

Needless to say, Eadred was not very impressed with the situation and gathered his army and marched into Northumbria in 948. The *Anglo-Saxon Chronicles* record the subsequent events:

> *948. In this year king Eadred harried all Northumbria, because they had taken Eric for their king: on the raid the famous minster at Ripon, which St Wilfred built, was destroyed by fire. Then when the king was on his way home, the host from out of York overtook the king's rearguard at Castleford, and there was great slaughter.*

The Northumbrians bided their time well and waited until only the English rearguard remained north of the Aire, and the main English army was some distance to the south, before they attacked and badly defeated them. Driven back against the River Aire with only the crossing, where the Roman road crossed the river, as an escape route the English were slaughtered. The few survivors who managed to escape across the river reported the defeat to Eadred who, according to the *Anglo-Saxon Chronicles* was 'so enraged that he would have invaded that land a second time and completely devastated it'. The Northumbrian counsellors realised what a serious position they had put themselves in and abandoned Erik before making peace with Eadred and paying reparations to him.

Once again Erik was adrift living the life of a freebooter. Little is known about what he did over the next four years, although there is some garbled evidence to suggest he may have taken part in the slave trade with Moorish Spain as well as the normal raiding expected of a landless Viking at the time. During this period Anlaf Guthfrithsson had returned yet again to York from Dublin to rule Northumbria. He ruled from 949 to 952, which means he must have co-operated with the English king to have been allowed to rule for so long. In 952, in yet another change of ruler, the Northumbrians drove Anlaf out and accepted Erik as their king once again.

Little is known of Erik's second reign, and even less of his death. During the two-year period between 952 and 954, Erik seems to have built a reputation as a warrior king but his violent nature made him few friends and the number of his enemies continued to grow. His end came, fittingly, in battle at Stainmoor near Brough on the present-day A66. Michael Wood provides two quotes which are the sum total of the contemporary, and near contemporary, accounts of Erik's end. From the *Fagrskinna*:

> *Eric had so great an army that five kings followed him because he was a valiant man and a battle-winner. He trusted in himself and his strength so much that he went far up country, and everywhere he went with warfare. Then came against him King Olaf, a tributary king of King Edmund. They fought and Eric was routed by the army of the land; and he fell there with all his force.*

The King Olaf mentioned may be Anlaf Guthfrithsson – Olaf and Anlaf are two versions of the same name. As has already been mentioned, Anlaf must have come to some agreement with the English king, Eadred not Edmund, during his reign and may have been a tributary king. It is not beyond the realms of possibility that he had gathered an army to claim back his kingdom, Northumbria. The *Saga of Hakon the Good* also provides a few details of Erik's last battle:

> *A dreadful battle ensued in which many English fell. But for every one who fell three came in his place out of the country behind, and when the evening came on the loss of men turned against the Norsemen and many were killed.*

With Erik's death Northumbria ceased to be an independent or tributary kingdom and became an English earldom ruled for King Eadred by an appointed earl. Yorkshire would remain relatively peaceful for over 100 years but events further south would lead to the next major military campaign in the county in 1066.

Aethelred the Unready and Cnut

The next major event of note took place in 980 with the renewal of Viking raids on England. In 991 Olaf Tryggvason, who would briefly rule Norway, raided Essex, where he defeated the local levies of Earl Brihtnoth at the Battle of Maldon. Several English kings had followed Eadred until in 978 Aethelred came to the throne. He has come down to us as Aethelred the Unready, although his nickname does not mean he was not ready to rule but comes from the Saxon word 'unraed' which meant ill advised, and this definitely seems to be the case throughout his reign. His first act of folly was to pay Olaf Tryggvason 10,000 lbs of silver to leave England. This first payment of Danegeld opened the floodgates and year after year larger forces of Vikings landed in England.

In 994 Olaf Tryggvason returned to England with Svein Forkbeard, King of Denmark. The pair raided Northumbria and then along the south coast before they were paid off once again, this time with 16,000 lbs of silver. The alliance between Norway and Denmark would not last. For many years Norway had been a vassal state of Denmark and open warfare broke out between the two kings as Svein tried to bring Norway to heel. The campaign culminated in the Battle of Svold where Olaf was killed. Although Svein spent the next ten years consolidating his rule in Denmark and Norway, other bands of Vikings continued to raid.

In 1002 the English paid 24,000 lbs of silver to buy off the raiders and Aethelred decided that enough was enough. On 13 November, believing that the Danish settlers in England were aiding the raiders he issued an order that all Danish men within England should be executed. This order seems to have been carried out to differing degrees from area to area and in some areas the massacre went beyond Danish men to their wives and families. It is thought that Svein Forkbeard's sister was among those killed and this may have prompted his return to England in 1003. Another event that took place in 1002 was Aethelred's marriage to Emma, the daughter of the Duke of Normandy.

The raids continued and the Danegeld grew from 30,000 lbs of silver in 1007, 36,000 in 1008, to 48,000 in 1012. In 1013 Svein came to conquer England, landing at Gainsborough. Northumbria quickly submitted to Svein and declared him their king. His successful campaign continued and by the end of the year most of England was under his control. Early in 1014 Aethelred fled the kingdom and took shelter with his father-in-law in Normandy. Svein was crowned king but ruled for only five weeks before he died and his son, Cnut, assumed the throne. Later in the year Aethelred returned to try to reclaim his kingdom, making a payment of 21,000 lbs of silver to Cnut who continued to rule in the north.

Aethelred died in 1015 and London elected Edmund as king. In a series of battles with Cnut, Edmund defeated his adversary on several occasions, and earned himself the nickname 'Ironside'. Cnut was resilient and continued the fight, finally defeating Edmund at Ashingdon on 18 October 1015. The two warriors decided to divide the country between them, with Edmund ruling Wessex and Cnut ruling the rest of the kingdom. By November 1016 Edmund had died, leaving Cnut to rule the whole of England, and to marry Aethelred's widow, Emma.

Cnut had a long and successful reign. After his death in 1035 the succession to the throne became very confused. Harthacnut was Cnut's heir, but remained in Denmark to assert his right to rule, while his half-brother, Harold Harefoot, attempted to gain the English throne, eventually being crowned in 1037. During this period two of Aethelred's sons made a brief foray from Normandy to try to gain support for the eldest, Edward's, claim to the throne. The brothers were arrested by Godwin, a Saxon who had supported Cnut and now transferred his allegiance to Harold Harefoot. Godwin handed the two Saxon princes to Harold who had the younger brother, Alfred, blinded. Alfred died of his injuries and his older brother would never forgive Godwin for his perceived treachery. Harold ruled for only three years until his death in 1040. Harthacnut, having consolidated his rule in Denmark, then succeeded to the English throne, but would only rule for two years. In 1042 the ruling council of England, the Witan, invited Edward to return from Normandy to become king and he was crowned on 3 April 1043.

The house of Godwin

Although Godwin, Earl of Wessex, was directly implicated in the death of Edward's brother, he was a very powerful man, possibly the most powerful in the kingdom, and he retained his lands and titles, and his place in the king's council, when Edward came to the throne. England's history between 1043 and 1066 is really the story of Earl Godwin and his sons and their interactions with King Edward. Godwin's position was further reinforced when the king married his eldest daughter, Edith, on 23 January 1045. This marriage produced no offspring and some historians have written that it could have been totally platonic, with the relationship being more that of a father and daughter.

The relationship between Godwin and the King seems to have been very turbulent. The first break came in September 1051. Edward, who had spent much of his life at the Norman court, gave preferential treatment to his Norman friends, particularly when he was appointing bishops. Indeed, the Archbishop of Canterbury, Robert, was a Norman and stoked the fires of Edward's resentment towards Godwin. Things came to a head with the arrival in England of another of Edward's Norman friends, Eustace of Boulogne, to pay the King a visit. The *Anglo-Saxon Chronicles* report the trouble caused on Eustace's arrival at Dover:

> *In this same year Eustace landed at Dover; he was married to king Edward's sister. His men behaved foolishly when looking for quarters, and slew a man from the town; and another man from the town slew their companion, with the result that there lay dead seven of his companions; and much evil was done on either side with horse and*

with weapons, until the townsfolk assembled, whereupon they fled away until they came to the king at Gloucester, and he gave them protection.

Edward then ordered Godwin to 'carry war into Kent to Dover' to punish them for the supposed affront to his Norman brother-in-law, a command which Godwin refused to obey. Godwin was already enraged by the King having allowed another Norman to build a castle, a rarity in England at the time, in Herefordshire, on land belonging to Godwin. From the protection of the castle, the French 'inflicted all the injuries and insults they possibly could upon the king's men in that region'. Godwin decided enough was enough. A show of strength would be sufficient to force the King to rid himself of his foreign friends. With this in mind Godwin and his sons, Harold and Svein, raised troops from their earldoms and met at Beverstone before approaching the King at Gloucester. Upon their approach the King sent messengers to Leofric, Earl of Mercia, and Siward, Earl of Northumbria, to raise troops and bring them to his aid. Florence of Worcester writes of the subsequent events:

They [Godwin and his sons] *encamped at a place called Langtree, and sent messengers to the king at Gloucester, threatening war unless he gave up Count Eustace and his companions and also the Normans and the men from Boulogne who held the castle at Dovercliff. For a time the king was alarmed and in great distress, not knowing what to do, but when he found out that the forces of Earls Leofric, Siward and Ralph were coming in, he stoutly replied that he would in no wise deliver up Eustace and the rest.*

The King seems to have had his resolve hardened by Robert, the Norman Archbishop of Canterbury, who raised the old spectre of his brother Alfred's death and Godwin's implication in it. A stand-off had been reached. Common sense prevailed as 'some of them considered it would be great folly if they joined battle, because well-nigh all the noblest in England were present in those two companies, and they were convinced they would be leaving the country open to the invasion of our enemies, and bringing utter ruin upon ourselves'. Hostages were exchanged and a meeting in London was agreed to by both parties, to take place on 24 September.

As the date of the meeting approached, both sides continued to raise troops. The king's forces were quartered in London while Godwin's were at Southwark, with the river separating the two armies. As the forces of the northern Earls continued to grow, Godwin's began to shrink and a decision had to be made. Did he appear before the King with a much-reduced army or should he await a better day? Discretion got the better of valour and Godwin and his sons fled the country. Godwin, Svein, Tostig and Gyrth fled to Flanders while Harold and Leofwine left for Ireland. Edward had won the day. All of Godwin's possessions, and those of his family, were confiscated, and Godwin's daughter, the Queen, was sent to a convent.

During Godwin's exile another event took place which would have serious repercussions on England's history, when Duke William of Normandy paid Edward a visit. The two were related through Edward's mother, Emma, who was William's great-aunt, and knew one another well from Edward's time at the Norman court. William later claimed that Edward had agreed that he would be his heir and, as this was the only time they met before Edward's death, it is highly likely that it was during this visit that the agreement was reached. Edward had no right to come to such an agreement as English kings were still, in theory, elected by the Witan.

Early in 1052 the Godwins began their return to England. Initially, Harold began a raiding campaign along the south coast in preparation for joining his father's fleet from Flanders. Edward gathered a fleet of forty ships at Sandwich but was unable to prevent Godwin's fleet combining with his son's at the Isle of Wight. From there the combined fleets sailed along the coast and into the Thames, arriving at Southwark on 14 September. Godwin had sent a letter from Sandwich to the King telling him that he would march on London. Edward responded by calling for all his loyal supporters to gather at the city but few had appeared before Godwin's arrival at Southwark, many of them biding their time to see how events turned out. This time the boot was on the other foot and the King, with a small force, was opposed by Godwin's much larger army. Edward had no choice but to come to an agreement, as Florence of Worcester reported:

> *Meanwhile, Earl Godwine with his fleet sailed up the Thames against the tide. He reached Southwark on the Feast of the Exaltation of the Holy Cross* [14 September] *(which was a Monday) and there waited until the flood tide came up. During this time he had meetings with the citizens of London both in person and by deputy. These he had previously placated by means of many promises, and he brought nearly all of them over to his side. So when everything was arranged and set in order he weighed anchor immediately the tide came up, and sailed up the river along the southern bank, meeting no opposition at the bridge. The land army also arrived, and putting itself in array along the bank of the river, showed a close and imposing front. Then the fleet made for the northern bank, as though for the purpose of enclosing the numerous fleet and army of the king. But inasmuch as there were very few men of any prowess either with the king or with Godwine who were not Englishmen, nearly all were very reluctant to fight against their kinsmen and fellow-countrymen. This circumstance enabled the wiser sort on both sides to affect a peace between the king and the earl, and both disbanded their troops.*

On the following morning the King called a meeting of the Witan and Godwin and his sons were restored to their titles and possessions, and the Queen was brought back from the convent. Godwin was not to enjoy the fruits of his success for very long. On 12 April 1053 'the hand of death came upon Earl Godwin' as he attended a feast with the king. The *Anglo-Saxon Chronicles* record Godwin's death as follows:

> *In this year the king was at Winchester at Easter, and with him earl Godwine and earl Harold, his son, and Tostig. When on the second day of Easter he sat at table with the king, he suddenly sank down against his footstool, speechless and helpless: he was*

carried into the king's chamber and it was thought it would pass off, but it was not to be; yet he lingered on like this, unable to speak and helpless, until the Thursday, and then gave up his life.

These are the classic symptoms of a cerebral haemorrhage. A much more sinister complexion is placed on Godwin's death in a poem called *La Estoire de Seint Aedward le Rei* written by a Norman some eighty years after the event. The King once again brought up the subject of his brother's death. Godwin, who by now was heartily sick of having this thrown in his face, responded:

> *Now he takes a piece of bread and holds it up,*
> *And says, 'If I can enjoy*
> *This morsel which you see me hold,*
> *Which I will eat in the sight of you all,*
> *Then all at the table will see*
> *That I am not to blame for this death;*
> *So I am either acquitted or found guilty.'*
> *King Edward blesses the morsel,*
> *And says, 'May God grant that the proof be true.'*
> *The earl puts it in his mouth,*
> *The morsel is fixed like a stick*
> *In the opening of the throat*
> *Of the traitorous felon glutton,*
> *So that all the table can see it.*
> *His eyes roll back in his head,*
> *His flesh blackens and becomes pale.*
> *All are astonished in the hall:*
> *He loses breath and speech*
> *From the morsel which sticks fast.*
> *Dead is the bloody felon;*
> *Which gave virtue to the morsel;*
> *At last was the murder proved.*
> *'Now,' cries the King,*
> *'Drag out this stinking dog.'*

Was this a Norman writer's attempt to blacken the family of the last English king by asserting that his father had been a murderer, or was it really a case of divine intervention? Upon his father's death Harold succeeded to the Earldom of Wessex.

With the death of Godwin, Edward's grudge against his family ceased. Harold became the King's right-hand man and by the end of the reign virtually ruled the nation as his 'subregulus' or under-king. By 1064 Harold's brothers, Tostig, Gyrth and Leofwine, had already received their own earldoms from a grateful king, and Tostig was reported to be a great favourite of Edward.

In 1064 Harold undertook a mission to Normandy for the King to confirm William's succession to the throne. Although English sources are silent on this subject, three French sources mention it: William of Poitiers, William of Jumieges and the Bayeux Tapestry. This is hardly surprising as French writers attempted to blacken Harold's name and justify William's invasion. What is more surprising is that the incident is mentioned in an Icelandic saga – Snorri Sturluson's *King Harald's Saga* – which adds veracity to the episode. The crux of the story is that Harold swore an oath to support William's claim to the throne, as William of Poitiers wrote:

> *At a gathering at Bonneville, Harold took an oath of faithfulness to him according to the sacred rite of the Christians. And, as highly respected men of the utmost sincerity have related, who were witnesses to the event, in the last item in the oath he would be the agent of duke William at the court of king Edward for as long as the king lived; that he would try with all his authority and power, to ensure for him the possession of the kingdom of England on Edward's death.*

After Harold's return to England, things continued peacefully until the following year when an event took place which was to have serious repercussions. In October 1065 Northumbria rose against its earl, Tostig. After killing a number of his huscarls and retainers, an army of northerners headed south. At their head was Morcar, son of Earl Aelfgar. Morcar's brother Edwin, who was Earl of Mercia, with the levies of his earldom, met them at Northampton. Tostig was hunting with the King at Britford when news of the revolt reached them. Despite his rage Edward sent Harold to listen to the rebels' demands. Harold met with them at Northampton and was informed that Tostig had 'robbed God first, and then despoiled of life and land all those over whom he could tyrannize'. At the same meeting Tostig was declared an outlaw by the northern thegns and Morcar was declared their earl. With Harold's support for the Northumbrians, Edward acquiesced to their demands and Tostig was exiled on 1 November.

Tostig was to return to England during the following year in support of the final claimant to the throne, King Harald Sigurdsson of Norway. Ever since the time of Cnut, the kings of Denmark and Norway had claimed the throne of England. For some time the two kingdoms had been combined but had separated upon the death of Magnus the Good. Svein Ulfsson, king of Denmark, had also claimed the English throne but had been unable to force his claim as he had been at war for many years with Harald of Norway. With the conclusion of a peace treaty between the two nations, King Harald's mind could turn to other things. He is known to history as Hardrada or Hardradi (ruthless) although the name was not used during his lifetime. He was a phenomenal warrior whose restless mind was always searching for a new outlet. Tostig was to provide him with one.

The death of King Edward and the succession

As the year 1066 began, England's king lay dying in his palace on Thorney Island (now Westminster). On the night of 4/5 January the great men of the nation gathered in the King's room waiting for the end. The *Vita Aedwardi Regis* records the King's last moments:

> *When he was sick unto death and his men stood and wept bitterly, he said, 'Do not weep, but intercede with God for my soul, and give me leave to go to Him.' Then he addressed his last words to the queen who was sitting at his feet, in this wise, 'May God be gracious to this my wife for the zealous solicitude of her service. For she has served me devotedly, and has always stood close by my side like a beloved daughter. And so from the forgiving God may she obtain the reward of eternal happiness.' And stretching forth his hand to his governor, her brother, Harold, he said, 'I commend this woman and all the kingdom to your protection. Serve and honour her with faithful obedience as your lady and sister, which she is, and do not despoil her, as long as she lives, of any due honour got from me. Likewise I also commend those men who have left their native land for love of me, and have up till now served me faithfully. Take from them an oath of fealty, if they should so wish, and protect and retain them, or send them with your safe conduct safely across the sea to their own homes with all that they have acquired in my service. Let the grave for my burial be prepared in the minster [Westminster Abbey] in the place which shall be assigned to you'. Now and then he also comforted the queen to ease her natural grief. 'Fear not', he said, 'I shall not die now, but by God's mercy regain my strength.' Nor did he mislead by these words, for he has not died but has passed from death to life, to live with Christ.*

Queen Edith commissioned the *Vita Aedwardi* upon the King's death and, it should therefore, be an accurate account of his dying moments. Unfortunately, the queen was also the daughter of Earl Godwin and his family are painted whiter than white in it. Some doubt is therefore thrown upon Edward bequeathing the nation to Harold. Does any other contemporary evidence support it? One version of the *Anglo-Saxon Chronicles* states that 'Earl Harold succeeded to the kingdom of England as the king granted it to him and as he was elected thereto'. With two independent contemporary accounts stating that Edward had bequeathed the kingdom to Harold, and no account disputing this fact, it should be beyond doubt. Unfortunately, one event still leaves a nagging doubt and that is the speed of Harold's crowning. Edward was buried in Westminster Abbey on the morning of 6 January and within a few hours Harold was crowned in the same church. If Harold's claim to the throne was well founded what was the rush?

On the other hand, two French accounts tell the same story from the other side. William of Poitiers writes that:

> *Suddenly news came that England had lost its king, Edward, and Harold had been crowned in his place. This foolish Englishman did not await a public election, but on*

the day of mourning when the good king was buried and the whole nation lamented, he broke his oath [to William] *and seized the throne by acclamation, thanks to the support of some iniquitous partisans. He received an unholy consecration at the hands of Stigand* [Archbishop of Canterbury], *who had been deprived of the office of priest by the just zeal of a papal anathema.*

William of Jumieges is in agreement and writes: 'Then Harold immediately seized the kingdom, thus violating the oath which he had sworn to the Duke'. These writers go to the opposite extreme from the *Vita Aedwardi* and try to blacken Harold's name. This is hardly surprising as they were writing after William had gained the throne and were trying to belittle his predecessor. Where does the truth lie?

On the morning of Edward's funeral the same men who had attended him in his final hours met to decide upon his successor. This band of 'iniquitous partisans' was the King's Witan, or personal council, and it was their duty to decide on a successor. No record survives of their discussion and most of them were dead by the end of the year. Harold may well have argued the case for Duke William succeeding to the throne and may have done so because he had given William his oath to support his claim. Once it was clear that the Witan would not allow a foreign king to sit on the throne, the obvious candidate was Harold himself. Having done his best to support William, Harold believed he was absolved from his oath and could accept the Witan's nomination.

This still leaves the question of the haste of Harold's coronation. Although England had been settled for many years, outside forces dictated that a strong king be enthroned as soon as possible. Firstly, the north of England had to be watched closely. Northumbria, although now an earldom, had been an independent nation up to almost the end of the tenth century. The Earl of Northumbria, Morcar, and his brother, Edwin of Mercia, controlled a large proportion of England. If a power struggle broke out, they might decide to declare themselves independent once again. Secondly, Tostig was still in Flanders with his father-in-law. He could be expected to put in an appearance and try to reclaim his earldom. Finally, Duke William could not be expected to sit idly by while his claim to England's throne was ignored. Bearing these external forces in mind, Harold's rapid enthronement begins to make sense.

Harold the King

Duke William must have received the news of Harold's coronation with incredulity which rapidly turned to anger. Messengers passed between the two and Harold's answer inflamed William even more. With this, William decided on a drastic course of action, no less than the seaborne invasion and conquest of England. While William planned his invasion, Harold addressed himself to the problems at hand.

With the sea-going vessels of the time, crossing the channel was no mean feat and was usually confined to the spring and summer months. With this in mind Harold perceived his most pressing problem to be Morcar and Edwin, the northern earls. By 16 April, when he returned to Westminster from York, he had visited both earls and received their agreement as to his right to rule the kingdom. On 24 April an omen of great events appeared as a 'long-haired star' and was seen in the night sky for seven days. (Scientists have calculated that this was Halley's Comet on one of its regular visits to our galaxy.) With his northern flank secured, and the year pressing on, he began to gather his forces on the south coast at Sandwich. The *Anglo-Saxon Chronicles* report that Harold 'gathered together greater naval and land levies than any king in this country had ever gathered before'.

In the late spring Tostig returned to the scene when, with a small force of boats and mercenaries, along with his English supporters, he raided along the south coast. Upon been informed that Harold was at Sandwich with overwhelming land and naval forces, he decided to move north and raided up the east coast. Sailing into the mouth of the Humber he landed and harried Lindsey (North Lincolnshire). Edwin and Morcar gathered their forces and drove him out. From here Tostig sailed to Scotland where King Malcolm provided him with shelter. What was Harold's reaction to Tostig's raiding? Quite simply, he chose to ignore it. His spies had informed him of Duke William's preparations and William posed a much greater threat than Tostig's raiding force did. Harold then moved his forces to the Isle of Wight. This would allow him to use the usual prevailing winds to intercept any attempted crossing of the Channel from Normandy.

By this time Tostig had realised that to regain his earldom he needed assistance. Sailing to Denmark, he tried to recruit King Svein to his cause but was unsuccessful. He then sailed north to Norway and met with King Harald Sigurdsson. After some discussion it was agreed that a combined invasion of the north of England would take place that summer. As the summer passed by, King Harold's eyes were fixed firmly on Normandy. His surprise must have been great when the first threat to his kingdom came not from the south but from the north.

The Norwegian invasion

One of the main problems is calculating the size of King Harald's invasion force. It is generally accepted that his army was 9,000–10,000 strong, but when this is compared with the number of ships in his fleet there is an anomaly. Contemporary accounts give a figure for the Norwegian fleet of between 240 and 500 ships, with 300 as the most frequently mentioned figure – two of the *Anglo-Saxon Chronicles* give this number. During the tenth century the smallest Viking warship was a twenty-bencher and had a crew of 100 men. If Harald's fleet was made up of 300 twenty-benchers this would give a figure for their crews, and hence his army, of 30,000 – an improbably high figure.

How can we resolve this anomaly?

The Norwegian army comprised two elements, the Hird and the Leidang. The Hird was made up of professional household soldiers with each leader having his own contingent of Hirdmen. It is known that Harald had 120 Hirdmen, and other Viking jarls and chieftains would have had their own contingents. These men formed the elite nucleus of a Viking army. The Leidang was a levy of all the men of military age from the kingdom. A full Leidang was usually called only when the safety of the kingdom was at risk, and it was more usual to call a half-Leidang for military operations beyond the home territory. In the tenth century a full Leidang would produce an army of 27,000 men. The events under discussion took place 100 years later so the figure for a full Leidang would have almost certainly grown.

Snorri Sturluson, in *Harald's Saga*, writes:

> *King Harald sailed south with his own men to meet the main army. A great host was gathered there, and it is said that King Harald had over two hundred ships, apart from supply ships and smaller craft.*

Harald's fleet gathered at the Solund Isles before it departed for England and was only 200 ships strong, plus an unspecified number of supply and auxiliary ships. Unfortunately, this still gives a figure of 20,000 men. Although Snorri writes that Harald had 200 longships when his fleet gathered at the Solund Isles it is not clear if he actually sailed with this number. In the mid-tenth century the period of service for the Leidang was only two months. By the twelfth century it had grown to four. Using the higher figure, this still does not give much time to organise and carry out an invasion. It is obvious that Harald intended to winter in England, should his invasion be successful, as he brought his wife and daughters to Orkney with the intention of bringing them to England once he had established a foothold. Is it possible that Harald disbanded the Leidang and sailed with only the Hird?

There is at least one precedent for this. Snorri writes that during the build up to the Battle of Nissa (9 August 1062) Harald 'sent back all the farmers' levy, keeping only 150 ships'. The Hird and the mercenary element of Harald's army manned these 150 ships. At the time of the Nissa campaign Harald was facing only one enemy, King Svein of Denmark. Svein had proved himself to be an opportunist and, although Harald was at peace with Denmark, it is not beyond belief that Svein would have used Harald's absence to begin a new round of hostilities. With this in mind, it is unlikely that Harald would have stripped his country of all its professional warriors. Someone had to provide a nucleus, and the leadership, of the army, should Svein have taken this course of action. If this is accepted, then it is quite possible that Harald sailed with a relatively small, elite, force of only 6,000-7,000 men. This was then reinforced to a total of 9-10,000 by the Orkney contingent, Tostig's men, freebooters and mercenaries, drawn from as far afield as Iceland, the Isle of Man and Ireland.

So King Harald sailed into the Humber with, possibly, 150 assorted warships. There is still a large anomaly with the number of ships reported. Accepting the above explanation, and the figure of 300 ships for Harald's entire fleet, where did the remainder of the ships come from? Snorri Sturluson provides an answer. When the Norwegian fleet gathered at the Solund Isles it contained a large number of supply vessels. An experienced commander, such as Harald was, would have made careful preparations for his invasion. One final point: Duke William crossed the channel with a similar-sized fleet, which contained an army of only 7,000 men. Of course, another explanation is that the chroniclers simply exaggerated the size of the Norwegian fleet. After all, other chroniclers in the same period reported an English army of 400,000 and a Norman army of 60,000 at Hastings!

The English armies that faced Harald's invasion were very similar in composition to those throughout the period, as previously described. One major difference was the addition of the huscarls to an English army. These, in many ways, resembled the Viking Hirdmen, which is hardly surprising as many of them were Scandinavian mercenaries. King Harold had a force of 3,000 Royal Huscarls at his disposal, while many of his earls commanded smaller forces. The huscarls were professional soldiers and had a reputation as fine warriors, as Snorri Sturluson reported:

> *Some people reckoned up all King Harald's great achievements, and said that nothing would be too difficult for him; but there were others who said that England would be very hard to conquer – it was very populous, and the warriors who were known as the king's Housecarls were so valiant that any one of them was worth any two of the best men in King Harald's army.*

The huscarls formed the nucleus of an English army and very often formed the front ranks of the shield wall while the Fyrd filled in behind them.

The first firm date we have during the campaign is 20 September 1066 when the armies of the northern earls, Edwin and Morcar, fought with King Harald's army at Gate Fulford. Contemporary accounts speak of many events taking place 'during the summer' and 'in the autumn'. Harald's first move was to sail his elite force to the Orkneys, although the King stopped off at the Shetland Isles on the way. On Orkney the earls, Paul and Erland, joined him with a contingent of Orkneymen, and large numbers of freebooters arrived from Ireland and the Isle of Man. When Harald's fleet of 300 war and supply ships sailed, his wife and daughters were left on Orkney to await the success of the expedition.

The fleet sailed down the east coast into the mouth of the River Tyne where it was joined by Tostig's fleet of twelve small ships. The combined fleet then continued down the coast and into the Humber. Snorri Sturluson mentions that the fleet landed three times between the Tyne and the Humber. The first landing was at an unspecified place in Cleveland and few details are given. The second landing was at Scarborough and Snorri writes:

> *King Harald then made for Scarborough and fought with the townsmen. He climbed up on to the rock that stands there* [where Scarborough Castle now stands], *and had a huge pyre built on top of it and set alight; when the pyre was ablaze they used long pitchforks to hurl the burning faggots down into the town. One after another the houses caught fire, until the town was completely destroyed. The Norwegians killed a great*

number of people there and seized all the booty they could lay their hands on. The
English then had no choice, if they wanted to stay alive, but submit to King Harald.
In this way he subdued the country wherever he went.

The third landing was on the coast of Holderness before reaching the Humber. These
landings are confirmed by an entry in the *Orkneyinga Saga*. The Norwegian fleet sailed
along the Humber until it reached the mouth of the Ouse and then proceeded towards
York, landing at Riccall. A small English fleet had protected the river but once its
commander saw the size of the enemy fleet he withdrew along the Wharfe to
Tadcaster, leaving the Norwegians to continue their landing and fortify their position.
It was a standard Viking tactic to land at a bend in a river where the headland formed
by the river's course could be easily fortified, providing an easily defensible base of
operations. It is probable that the Norwegians landed on 17 or 18 September. With
their preparations made, on 20 November the Norwegian army marched along the
banks of the Ouse towards York. During this period the northern earls had not been

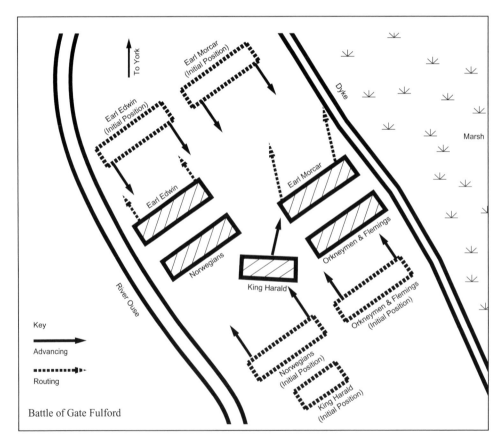

The Battle of Gate Fulford

idle. Edwin and Morcar had raised their Mercian and Northumbrian levies and gathered them at York. With the approach of the Norwegian army the earls led their men from the city and clashed with the Norwegians at Gate Fulford.

The Battle of Gate Fulford

It is difficult to pin down exactly where the battle took place, although it is obvious it was close to the village of Gate Fulford which is mentioned in the Domesday Book and, hence, existed at the time of the battle. Snorri Sturluson gives a short description of Harald's deployment, stating that he 'began to draw up his army, with one flank reaching down to the river and the other stretching inland towards a dyke where there was a deep and wide swamp full of water'. Both the *Anglo-Saxon Chronicles* and Florence of Worcester support the fact that the battle was fought close to the river. As Gate Fulford, and the modern day village of Fulford, lie on the east bank of the Ouse it is a fair assumption that the battle also took place on the east bank, although artefact finds have yet to prove this.

The two armies each contained approximately 9,000–10,000 men, which would give a frontage for the shield walls of at least half a mile. The battle lines stretched from the River Ouse until they reached a dyke, beyond which was a wide area of wet and boggy ground. The terrain rose gently from the flood plain and then descended to the marsh

Gate Fulford. The River Ouse in full flood. Although it is not certain where the battle of Gate Fulford took place the flooded land in this photograph is a likely candidate.

– the A19 now runs along this ridge of higher ground and Gate Fulford would have stood on it above the river's flood plain.

King Harald deployed his men in two divisions. On the left, against the river, were his most reliable men and these would have been his Norwegian troops. Snorri Sturluson reports that the Norwegian line was thickest at this side. In the light of subsequent events, it is clear that this thickening of the line was the result of Harald holding a reserve, under his direct command, behind the left of his line. Snorri confirms this: 'King Harald's standard was near the river, where his forces were thickest'. He also goes on to write, 'but the thinnest and least reliable part of his line was at the dyke'. It is probable that his non-Norwegian contingents, the Orkneymen and Tostig's Flemings, formed the right of Harald's line.

The English also formed in two divisions. On the right against the Ouse were Edwin's Mercian levies, while on the left were the Northumbrians, commanded by their earl, Morcar. The English seem to have had no overall commander and there is no mention of any reserves. As the frontage of the battlefield was constricted by the river and dyke, the depth of the English shield walls may have been deeper than usual. The English army was larger than the Norwegian one and probably numbered slightly over 10,000.

Once the troops were in position the lines advanced. Initially, Morcar, and his Northumbrians, had the better of the day, driving the Norwegian right back and causing heavy casualties on it. This success was to be the English army's undoing. While Morcar pushed the Orkneymen and Flemings back, Harald's Norwegians had halted his brother's Mercians. On both sides the two halves of the army began to separate. If Morcar could have broken Harald's right he could then have attacked the flank of the Norwegian contingent, but this was not to be. It was King Harald who struck the decisive blow. Snorri Sturluson describes this attack:

> *When King Harald saw that the English flank was advancing down the dyke and was now opposite them, he sounded the attack and urged his men forward, with his banner, 'Land-Waster', carried in front. The Norwegian onslaught was so fierce that everything gave way before it, and a great number of the English were killed.*

Harald had chosen his time well. Morcar, engaged frontally by Harald's right, was struck in the flank by the Norwegian King's reserve. Attacked from two sides, the English left disintegrated. With their left in rout, hotly pursued by the Norwegian right, the remainder of the English army was quickly outflanked and broken. The fighting had been hard, with heavy losses on both sides but the English were to suffer many more casualties in the rout. Snorri quotes the words of the poet Stein Herdisarson:

> *Many were lost in the water;*
> *The drowned sank to the bottom.*
> *Warriors lay thickly fallen*

> *Around the young Earl Morcar.*
> *Harald's son, young Olaf,*
> *Pursued the fleeing English*
> *Running before King Harald.*
> *Praise the brave prince Olaf.*

The mention of Earl Morcar's death is in error. Both Edwin and Morcar survived the battle and returned to York. Several accounts speak of large numbers of English been drowned in the pursuit, for example, Snorri writes:

> *The English army quickly broke into flight, some fleeing up the river, and others down the river; but most of them fled into the swamp, where the dead piled up so thickly that the Norwegians could cross the swamp dry-shod.*

This theme of being able to cross a water obstacle dry-shod occurs in a number of accounts of medieval battles, for example, the 'bridge of bodies' at Towton. As Snorri reports a large number of English drowning in the swamp, Florence of Worcester reports similar losses in the Ouse:

> *But after a long contest the English were unable to withstand the attacks of the Norwegians and fled with great loss. More were drowned in the river than slain on the field.*

It is difficult to ascertain at what time the battle commenced and for how long it continued. Most sources speak of a long, hard-fought battle. However long the battle lasted, Harald had time to march to York with part of his army and the *Anglo-Saxon Chronicles* give some details:

> *After the battle king Harald of Norway and earl Tostig entered York with as great a force as seemed to them necessary and received hostages from the borough, besides assistance in the way of provisions, and so retired thence to their ships. They offered to conclude an abiding peace with the citizens provided that they all marched southwards with them to conquer this realm.*

Florence of Worcester is in agreement with this, stating that both sides exchanged 150 hostages each. With the exchange of hostages the Norwegian army returned to Riccall. A further meeting, and exchange of hostages, would take place on the following Monday at Stamford Bridge. King Harald was close to achieving his first objective, securing a foothold in England and a secure base of operations at York. It is hardly surprising that the local populous came to an agreement. Their earl and his brother had been decisively beaten and their army had suffered grievous casualties. There was little hope of succour from King Harold who, to the best of their knowledge, was still awaiting the arrival of the Normans on the south coast, for some time to come. Little did they realise that the King had set off northwards on that very day, gathering an army as he marched.

King Harold's reaction

Harold had spent most of the summer waiting for William to cross the Channel. He had gathered a large fleet and army with which to oppose the Norman invasion and stationed it on the Isle of Wight, an ideal spot from which to intercept the enemy fleet. The prevailing winds along the Channel would drive Harold's fleet towards the enemy, while the same winds prevented the Normans from leaving harbour. By early September provisions for his troops were beginning to run out and still there was no sign of William's fleet. It was getting late in the season for a channel crossing and Harold decided to disband his levies. Harold marched back to London with his household troops, while a large part of the fleet sailed along the south coast to London. The *Anglo-Saxon Chronicles* report the loss of a large number of ships during this voyage but do not give a reason. As there is no mention of fighting it is probable that these ship losses were caused by a storm.

Shortly before 20 September Harold received news of Harald Sigurdsson's landing in Yorkshire. He seems to have had little hesitation in setting off north with only his huscarls. He would call out the levies and gather them as he marched. It is worth considering whether his decision to march was a rash one. With hindsight, it is easy to say that it was not. The suddenness of his arrival in Yorkshire contributed to his victory at Stamford Bridge. On the other hand, he was marching into the unknown and he had little intelligence of what had been happening in the north. The army of his northern earls had been defeated on the same day as he left London. The Norwegian army could have been waiting for him, uplifted by victory and reinforced by Northumbrian levies. If Harold had hesitated just a couple of weeks, this could well have been the case. As it was, the scale of the Norwegian victory seems to have made them overconfident and, as will be seen shortly, ill-prepared for King Harold's arrival from the south.

Harold marched rapidly north, covering almost forty miles per day. By the evening of Sunday, 24 September, he had arrived at Tadcaster and it is likely that he had already heard rumours of the defeat of Edwin and Morcar. When he arrived at Tadcaster these rumours were confirmed. He immediately deployed his huscarls into a battle formation, expecting an attack at any moment. The fact that he had only his household troops with him points to the footsore English army being spread out over many miles of road and straggling into Tadcaster throughout the evening. During the night messengers reached Harold from York informing him of the intended meeting between the townsmen and the Norwegians at Stamford Bridge on the following day. Harold had been presented with an ideal opportunity to surprise Harald Sigurdsson – an opportunity he had no hesitation in taking.

Now we must turn to the Norwegian army and look at what it had been doing since its victory. Discussions seem to have continued with the people of York and Snorri Sturluson reports the arrival of a number of Tostig's friends and kinsmen, a welcome addition to Harald's army after the heavy losses it had suffered at Gate Fulford. On

Sunday, 24 September Harald marched part of his army to Stamford Bridge. Snorri Sturluson writes:

> *On Monday, when King Harald Sigurdsson had breakfasted, he ordered the trumpets to sound the order for disembarkation. He got the army ready and divided his forces, choosing which of them were to go with him and which were to stay behind: from each company two men were to go for every one that was left behind.*

> *Earl Tostig prepared his troops for landing to go with King Harald; the men who were left behind to guard the ships were the king's son, Olaf, Earl Paul and Earl Erland of Orkney, and Eystein Ori, the noblest of all the landed men and dearest to the king, to whom the king had promised his daughter Maria in marriage.*

> *The weather was exceptionally fine, with warm sunshine; so the troops left their armour behind and went ashore with only their shields, helmets, and spears, and girt with swords. A number of them also had bows and arrows. They were all feeling very carefree.*

Several interesting points are raised here. Firstly, Snorri mentions that the Norwegians marched on the Monday, although this is almost certainly not the case. King Harold found the Norwegian army already at Stamford Bridge. He had marched from Tadcaster to York early in the morning and had then continued through the city and on to Stamford Bridge. It is likely that the English army arrived at Stamford Bridge by mid-morning. Although Riccall is slightly nearer to Stamford Bridge than Tadcaster, the Norwegian army would have had to set off early to arrive there before the English army. Snorri's account shows little haste in King Harald's preparations and nothing happened until the King had breakfasted. Then the army was divided and, in due course, departed in a carefree, almost holiday, fashion. If all this had happened on the Monday morning the Norwegian army could not have arrived at Stamford Bridge first. It is generally accepted that the march to Stamford Bridge actually took place on the Sunday. The Norwegian King could not have been expecting any hostile action to take place and most of his men, although armed, did not carry their armour, and Harald took only two thirds of his army with him. Add to this the fact that the Norwegians were 'all feeling very carefree' and a picture emerges of a Sunday afternoon jaunt. After all, the English were coming from York to hand over a large number of hostages and once an agreement had been reached the army would march into the city. Then their king would lead them to the south and they would conquer him a kingdom.

At about mid-morning on the 25 September a dust cloud appeared on the horizon, beyond Gate Helmsley on the opposite ridge, but this would have come as no surprise to the Norwegians as they lounged on the ridge above the bridge. This would be the expected English hostages arriving. As the dust cloud approached, figures could be seen within it, both armed and armoured. It would not have taken the Norwegian king long to realise that this was not a party of hostages but an army approaching and he began to form his men for battle. The approaching army was less than a mile away – would he have time?

The Battle of Stamford Bridge

The Norwegian army was scattered over a large area, with men on both sides of the river, and as Harald began to gather his men and form them into a battle line, he also despatched a number of mounted messengers back to the camp at Riccall to call for reinforcements. It would not have been long before Tostig recognised his older brother's standards – the red dragon of Wessex and Harold's personal standard, the 'Fighting Man'. It is at this point that Harald and Tostig must have realised that this

Stamford Bridge. The children of Stamford Bridge have created their own version of the Bayeaux Tapestry.

was no local army approaching but the King's royal army, complete with 3,000 of the renowned huscarls – this would be a hard fight.

Contemporary, or near contemporary, accounts of the battle give few details of the fighting. The one exception to this is Snorri Sturluson's account in *Harald's Saga*. This account was written over 100 years after the battle and is often considered unreliable. What is interesting is that most historians will accept Snorri's account of Gate Fulford at face value but will not accept his account of Stamford Bridge. There seem to be two reasons for this.

The first is his mention of the use of cavalry by the English at the battle: it is the perceived wisdom that the English never used cavalry on the battlefield. However, the *Anglo-Saxon Chronicles* show that on rare occasions English armies did, in fact, use cavalry, for example, at Hereford in 1055. This will be discussed further in due course.

The second reason for not accepting Snorri's account is that there were no survivors in the Norwegian army, so how did the story of the battle get back to Norway? Once again this can be discounted as a reason for not treating Snorri's account as reasonably reliable. Although the Norwegian army suffered massive casualties there *were* survivors and Snorri Sturluson writes of the escape of Strykar, Harald's Marshal and a senior military figure, from the battlefield.

The hard facts of the battle that are agreed by all, or most, of the contemporary accounts are:

✧ *The battle took place five days after Gate Fulford, i.e. 25 September.*

✧ *The battle took place at Stamford Bridge, a crossing of the River Derwent.*

✧ *It was a hard-fought battle with many casualties on both sides.*

✧ *King Harald Sigurdsson and Tostig were both killed.*

✧ *The Norwegians lost the battle and suffered massive casualties in the pursuit.*

These are the basic facts but there must be more to the battle than that.

One of the first questions that springs to mind is why was the battle fought at Stamford Bridge? The direct, and obvious, route for the hostages to use to reach Harald's army was straight down the Ouse to Riccall, although this would have meant passing over the battlefield which, after five days of warm weather and many corpses unburied, would not have been a very nice prospect. Harald was trying to come to an accommodation with the defeated northerners as he needed their support in his assault on the rest of England and he needed York as a base of operations. Stamford Bridge was a well-known local landmark that would have been known to Tostig and his rebel English supporters.

As a visitor approaches that battlefield today, from the direction of York, he has to cross a narrow stone bridge before turning into the village. The position of this bridge

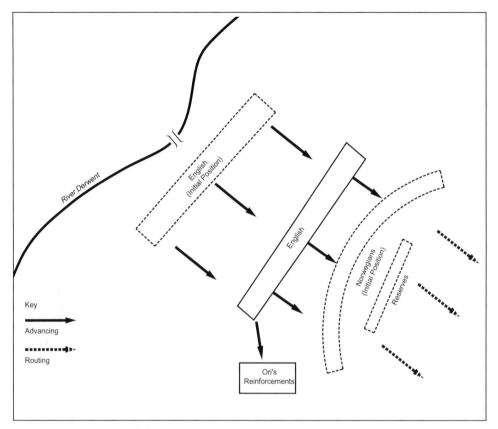

The Battle of Stamford Bridge

has caused some confusion as to the location of the battlefield. On the 1913 edition of the OS 6-inch to the mile map of the area the battlefield is marked directly south of the present eighteenth century bridge even though an area known as the Battle Flat is clearly marked some distance to the east. This is not the position of the bridge that existed in 1066, which actually was situated several hundred yards north-east of the site of the present one. Stamford Bridge is not mentioned in the Domesday Book and did not exist as a village at the time of the battle, although the existence of isolated farms cannot be ruled out. The course of the two Roman roads that met by the bridge can still be traced from modern maps. One ran west to east, through Gate Helmsley straight down to the river and then in a straight line towards the coast. The other ran, roughly, north to south.

The English army descended the gentle slope from Gate Helmsley to the river along the Roman road. Confronting them was a narrow wooden bridge, wide enough for a single cart to cross. Beyond the river the land rises to the 50-foot contour line in just over 100 yards before levelling out into an almost imperceptible slope. It was on the high

Stamford Bridge. Looking along the River Derwent towards the site of the original bridge. Two Roman roads crossed the river at this point. The site of the initial fighting on the west bank is now a caravan site.

ground to the east of the river that King Harald and Tostig formed their main battle line.

The first clash took place on the west bank of the Derwent as the advancing English army overtook the Viking stragglers who were trying to rejoin the main army on the other bank. In some accounts this has been raised to the status of a major clash, lasting some considerable time, with part of the Norwegian army acting as a rear-guard and buying time for Harald to form his shield wall. Although there may have been a clash on the west bank it was insignificant and did not hold up the English for long. It was during this initial fighting that one of the most famous incidents in the battle took place, when a lone Viking warrior held the bridge against all comers.

As the English approached the bridge, the lone warrior, a giant of a man clad in chain mail and brandishing an axe, blocked their path. Laughing in the faces of the English army he cut down anyone who tried to cross the bridge. He withstood a hail of arrows and javelins, holding the bridge for three hours and killing forty men in the process. Then an Englishman rowed a boat under the bridge and killed him with a spear thrust beneath his armour. This is a well-known story from the battle and is mentioned in most accounts, in various forms, with the version above being made up of the most extreme exaggerations. It would be expected that such a tale of Viking heroism would come from one of the sagas, but it actually comes from an English source, the *Anglo-Saxon Chronicles*:

> *The Norwegians fled from the English, but there was one Norwegian who stood firm against the English forces, so that they could not cross the bridge nor clinch victory. An Englishman shot with an arrow but to no avail, and another went under the bridge and stabbed him through under the coat of mail.*

It is interesting to see how the story has grown over the years, with no mention of the warrior being a giant of a man, no axe, and no forty men slain. In fact, there is no mention of a boat and local tradition has it that the Englishman used a tub; indeed, up to late in the nineteenth century, locals baked tub-shaped pies to celebrate the anniversary of the battle. This event is mentioned only in the one account and it is a later addition to that account. The section quoted above is in a different hand from that of the remainder of the entry. One theory is that a monk from a northern religious house visited Abingdon, the source of the chronicle in which it is quoted, read their chronicle then added some details about the battle. Whether this idea is correct or not, the fact that it is mentioned in an English source adds some veracity to the tale. If the story of the gallant Viking defender of the bridge is true then the English army would have cleared the bridge in minutes and then begun to cross the river.

It is interesting to consider why King Harald allowed the English to cross and this is a question that has vexed historians for many years. Several theories have been put forward. One such theory is that King Harald was still in the process of forming his army into its shield wall and was in no position to prevent the English crossing. There is also a precedent for an army being allowed to cross a water obstacle before a battle took place and this is exactly what Brihtnoth had done at the Battle of Maldon.

The real reason that Harald did not attempt to hold the riverbank is probably a combination of tactics and terrain. Firstly, as has already been discussed, the standard fighting formation of both armies at the battle was the shield wall and this was best formed on firm, level ground. If the shield wall could be formed with a slope protecting its front, so much the better, as fighting up the slope would slow the opposition, while the army forming at the top of the slope had the added advantage of impetus in an attack on the enemy. On the 1913 OS map much of the Derwent's banks are shown as 'Liable to Floods'. If this was the case in 1913 it must have been more susceptible to flooding at the time of the battle. The banks of the river would have been boggy and would not have been ideal ground on which to form a shield wall. So King Harald formed his shield wall on firm ground at the top of the slope, while the English army formed theirs close to the banks of the river on the rougher, boggy ground. This also meant that the English would be fighting with their backs to the river, a major disadvantage in the event of a defeat. Harald's army had already defeated a larger force at Gate Fulford and its morale and confidence would have been high. Reinforcements had been sent for and prospects of another victory looked good.

We will now look at the size of the armies at Stamford Bridge but, once again, it is difficult to calculate exact numbers. Working from the estimate of King Harald's initial force of 9,000–10,000, which is generally accepted, his army must have numbered about 5,000 men. He had taken heavy losses at Gate Fulford but had then been reinforced by an unknown number of Tostig's English supporters. At the time of his march to Stamford Bridge he probably had 7,500–8,000 men in his army. Snorri Sturluson states that Harald left one third of his army with the boats, leaving about 5,000 men to march with him. It is almost certain that the English army outnumbered Harald's forces, though it is difficult to know by how much. King Harold Godwinsson left London with 3,000 huscarls from his household, although other figures for the huscarls are as high as 4,000. Gathering troops on his rapid march towards York, he might have assembled an army of some 7,000–8,000.

As the English crossed the bridge, King Harald formed his 5,000 men into a shield wall. Snorri Sturluson writes:

> *King Harald now drew up his army, and formed a long and rather narrow line; the wings bent back until they met, thus forming a wide circle of even depth all the way round, with shields overlapping in front and above.*

Harald formed his men into a longer, shallower, shield wall than was usual, in an effort to prevent the English outflanking his line – a tactic that has been used throughout history. Harald also pulled back the wings of his army, refusing his flanks to the enemy. Although Snorri says the line formed a circle, and this is a possibility, it is open to debate. It is more likely that the line took the form of a flattened semicircle. Harald's archers were deployed directly behind the shield wall to provide supporting fire, while his Hirdmen and Tostig's supporters formed a reserve.

Snorri Sturluson reported an interesting exchange between an English huscarl and Tostig while the two armies were forming their lines:

> *Twenty horsemen from the English king's company of Housecarls came riding up to the Norwegian lines; they were all wearing coats of mail, and so were their horses.*

> *One of the riders said, 'Is Earl Tostig here in this army?'*

> *Tostig replied, 'There is no denying it – you can find him here.'*

> *Another of the riders said, 'Your brother King Harold sends you his greetings, and this message to say you can have peace and the whole of Northumbria as well. Rather than have you refuse to join him, he is prepared to give you one third of his whole kingdom.'*

> *The Earl answered, 'This is very different from all the hostility and humiliation he offered me last winter. If this offer had been made then, many a man who is now dead would still be alive, and England would now be in better state. But if I accept this offer now, what will he offer King Harald Sigurdsson for all his effort?'*

> *The rider said, 'King Harold has already declared how much of England he is prepared to grant him; seven feet of ground, or as much more as he is taller than other men.'*

Earl Tostig said, 'Go now and tell King Harold to make ready for battle. The Norwegians will never be able to say that Earl Tostig abandoned King Harald Sigurdsson to join his enemies when he came west to fight in England. We are united in our aim: either to die with honour, or else conquer England.'

The English riders then returned to their own lines. King Harald asked Tostig who the Englishman was who had spoken and Tostig replied: 'That was King Harold Godwinsson'. King Harald said that if he had been told sooner the English king would not have lived to tell the tale. Although interesting, this exchange was almost certainly added to Snorri's account for dramatic effect.

With the armies in position the Battle of Stamford Bridge now commenced. Snorri writes:

Now the battle began. The English made a cavalry charge on the Norwegians, who met it without flinching. It was no easy matter for the English to ride against the Norwegians because of their arrows, so they rode around them in a circle. There was only skirmishing to begin with, so long as the Norwegians kept their formation. The English cavalry kept charging them and falling back at once when they could make no headway.

Stamford Bridge. All that remains of the Battle Flat, the area of the bloodiest fighting.

The Norwegians observed this, and thought the enemy assaults rather half-hearted; so they launched an attack themselves on the retreating cavalry. But as soon as they had broken their shield wall, the English rode down on them from all sides showering spears and arrows on them.

This is the section of Snorri's account that has caused the most problems to modern historians, his description of English cavalry in action. Unfortunately, it is very difficult to say for definite whether he is right or wrong. There is other evidence to support the use of cavalry in battle, but not much. In the above extract, if the word Norwegian was replaced with English, and English with Norman, it could almost be an account of the battle of Hastings. This has been used as evidence against Snorri's account and there does seem to be some overlap between events in both battles. It is possible that King Harold used some of his mounted huscarls to pin the enemy line while he deployed his army. Snorri describes tactics that would be suitable for such a task. Small bodies of cavalry skirmishing with the enemy, riding close to the enemy line and throwing spears and javelins, but able to attack should the enemy break formation. Once the English line had formed, the mounted troops would dismount and join their comrades. It is interesting, and reinforces this possibility, that Snorri mentions English cavalry only in the first phase of the battle.

So, as the English line formed the Norwegians were held in place by mounted English troops. From King Harald's formation it is clear that he intended to hold his ground and wait for the arrival of reinforcements, rather than attack the English as they formed up. Once the English were ready the real fighting began. The English advanced up the hill at a slow and deliberate pace. The shield walls clashed and both sides began to suffer losses. This first phase may have continued for some time before English numbers began to tell. As the English began to break into the Norwegian formation their shield wall became ragged. Just as he had done at Gate Fulford, King Harald chose the moment to launch his reserve well. Snorri writes:

When King Harald Sigurdsson saw this, he led a charge into the thickest of the fighting. The battle became very fierce, and great numbers were killed on both sides. King Harald Sigurdsson now fell into such a fury of battle that he rushed forward ahead of his troops, fighting two-handed. Neither helmets

Stamford Bridge. Most of the Battle Flat has disappeared under a new housing estate. When the estate was built the builders put up a small information board. This now seems to have disappeared.

nor coats of mail could withstand him, and everyone in his path gave way before him.
It looked as if the English were on the point of being routed.

As the Norwegian reserve attacked, the English line was thrown back in confusion. It looked as though King Harald's decision to fight had been proven correct, but on the point of victory Norway's king was struck down. Cutting his way into the recoiling English ranks, he was struck in the throat by an arrow. Snorri Sturluson quotes the words of two court poets, the main source of the Scandinavian sagas. Thjodolf says:

> *Disaster has befallen us;*
> *I say the army has been duped.*
> *There was no cause for Harald*
> *To bring his forces westward.*
> *Mighty Harald is fallen*
> *And we are all imperilled;*
> *Norway's renowned leader*
> *Has lost his life in England.*

While Arnor, the Earl's Poet, has this to say:

> *It was an evil moment*
> *When Norway's king lay fallen;*
> *Gold-inlaid weapons*
> *Brought death to Norway's leader.*
> *All King Harald's warriors*
> *Preferred to die beside him,*
> *Sharing their brave king's fate,*
> *Rather than beg for mercy.*

This second poem gives a clue to a possible alternative to King Harald being struck down by an arrow: 'Gold-inlaid weapons brought death to Norway's leader'. This hints at King Harald been cut down by a sword or axe. Once again there is a parallel between King Harald's demise and the fall of his opponent at Hastings. There has been much discussion as to how King Harold Godwinsson died – was he struck in the eye by an arrow or cut down by Norman horsemen?

The Bayeux Tapestry shows two figures, close together with the wording: 'Hic Harold rex interfectus est' (Here King Harold has been killed). One is clutching an arrow in the face, while the other is being cut down. It is now generally believed that both figures represent Harold. Initially he was wounded in the face by an arrow and then, while incapacitated, cut down by a party of Norman horsemen, possibly including Duke William. It is possible that King Harald Sigurdsson suffered a similar fate. As he advanced, he was struck in the throat by an arrow and then cut down by one, or more, of the English huscarls. It is impossible to say for certain. Just as King

Harald's attack with his Hirdmen had swung the battle in the Norwegians' favour, his death gave the advantage back to the English.

Both armies needed to reform and a pause in the fighting ensued. The English had been badly shaken by King Harald's counter-attack, while the Norwegian army was disordered by their King's death. Both armies had lost heavy casualties. The Norwegian army re-formed several hundred yards further back, on what is now known as the Battle Flat. Command of the army seems to have devolved on Tostig, who now stood under King Harald's standard, 'Land Waster', surrounded by his own men and the survivors of Harald's Hirdmen, many of whom had fallen with their King. As the two armies re-grouped King Harold Godwinsson offered quarter to his brother and the remaining Norwegians. Snorri Sturluson reports the Norwegian reply:

> *But the Norwegians shouted back with one voice that every one of them would rather die than accept quarter from the English; they roared their war-cry, and the battle started again.*

A second phase of the battle now commenced and once again the shield walls clashed. Numbers began to tell and, although losing heavy casualties, the English began to gain the upper hand. Then another event occurred that swung the advantage back to the Norwegians: with the arrival of Eystein Ori on the battlefield with approximately 2,000 men. These men were heavily armed and armoured. The *Orkneyinga Saga* states that the Earls of Orkney were both with Ori, although this is not confirmed in other sources. The arrival of these reinforcements caused chaos in the English ranks and once again they came close to breaking. Unfortunately, Ori's men had forced-marched from the ships at Riccall on a hot afternoon in mail armour and many of them were on the verge of exhaustion. Although their initial onslaught almost proved decisive, they had no stamina left for a long fight. Snorri reports many of them stripping off their armour and others dying from exhaustion. Once again the English army managed to rally and the final phase of the battle commenced. Most of the leaders of the Norwegian army, and virtually all of Harald's Hirdmen, died on the field. With their leadership gone, and the cream of their army dead, the Norwegians finally broke, fleeing in all directions, closely pursued by the victorious Englishmen. Snorri sums up this rout:

> *It was now late in the afternoon. As was to be expected, not all reacted in the same way; a number of them fled, and others were lucky enough to survive in different ways. It had grown dark before the carnage ended.*

An English account, the *Anglo-Saxon Chronicles*, also speaks of the savage pursuit of the Norwegians:

> *There were slain Harold the Fairhaired and earl Tostig, and the remaining Norwegians were put to flight, while the English fiercely assailed their rear until some of them reached their ships: some were drowned, others burnt to death, and thus*

perished in various ways so that there were few survivors, and the English had possession of the place of slaughter.

These accounts give a picture of a terrible pursuit and any Norwegian overtaken was cut down. Others tried to cross the Derwent or the Ouse and were drowned. Small groups, cornered in a remote farmhouse or barn, were burnt to death. Few of the Norwegians reached their ships but enough survived to pass on the story of the battle, their defeat and the loss of their King.

It is rare that a battle proved as decisive as Stamford Bridge. By nightfall on 25 September 1066 the invading Norwegian army had been smashed. Its remnants were trapped inside its base at Riccall, with the English army close by. The next morning the surviving Norwegian leaders, Prince Olaf and the Earls of Orkney, Paul and Erland, submitted to King Harold. The *Anglo-Saxon Chronicles* record that:

They then went inland to our king, and swore oaths that they would ever maintain peace and friendship with this land; and the king let them sail home with twenty-four ships.

This shows the extent of the Norwegian defeat. Their fleet had been 300 strong when it sailed into the Humber, but when it departed it required only twenty-four ships to take the survivors home. Another source, Florence of Worcester, puts the number of ships even lower, at twenty. The highest possible number of survivors is about 2,400, using a figure of 100 for the crew of a 20-bencher. It is almost certain that the actual number of survivors was considerably lower than this.

King Harold and the English army returned to York with a vast amount of booty. It is said that one ingot of gold, amassed by Harald while he was in Constantinople and Russia, took twelve men to carry it. If this is true, then it is further evidence for Harald's intention to remain in England over the winter – not only did he bring his family but he also brought his treasury. Harald's wife and daughters had remained on Orkney and the Orkneyinga Saga relates a strange tale about the death of one of his daughters:

On the same day that King Harald was killed, indeed at the very same hour, his daughter Maria died quite suddenly, and the people said of them that they had shared one life.

Maria is said to have been Harald's favourite child. Not only had her father been killed at the battle but her husband-to-be, Eystein Ori, had also fallen. Prince Olaf, his mother and sister remained on Orkney for the winter. In the spring of 1067 they set sail for Norway where Olaf was crowned king, ruling for many years alongside his brother Magnus. King Harold Godwinsson was not to be so fortunate.

The English dead were buried on the field while the Norwegians were left where they fell. Their skeletal remains were still clearly visible in 1120. Harold's army, although victorious, had suffered heavy losses. It is difficult to ascertain how many

Englishmen fell in the battle but almost 1,000 of the Royal Huscarls had been killed or wounded – they would be sadly missed over the coming weeks.

As the English celebrated their victory at York a dark cloud was gathering on the horizon. The month of September was almost over, and King Harold must have thought that it was too late in the year for the Duke of Normandy to cross the channel, but he was wrong. On 28 September Duke William landed at Pevensey with an army of approximately 7,000 men and news of this second invasion soon reached Harold. In another rapid march Harold, and his huscarls, retraced their steps to London. It is unlikely that the fyrdmen who had fought at Stamford Bridge accompanied the King. As Harold marched south, William moved his base to Hastings and ravaged the surrounding countryside. Gathering some of his southern levies Harold tried to repeat his surprise attack. By 14 October he was close to the Norman base. Unfortunately for Harold, William received news of his approach and marched his army out to meet him. In a hard fought battle on Senlac Hill the English were defeated and King Harold Godwinsson fell. His body was so badly mutilated that it had to be identified by his lover, Edith Swan-neck. He had ruled for less than ten months. In a rapid campaign William cowed the English and on Christmas Day 1066 he was crowned King of England.

1066 was one of the most momentous years in British history. By the end of the year three kings had sat on the English throne. With the death of King Edward, three rivals had sought the crown. By the end of the year two were dead, both slain in battle. With the coronation of William, England began to look towards the Continent, as opposed to Scandinavia, as she had done for many years. A new chapter in English history had begun.

CHAPTER THREE

SCOTS AND REBELS

The Battle of the Standard (Northallerton)

William of Normandy's coronation did not bring peace to the North. In 1067 he led his army into Northumbria which was subdued in short order. In 1068 William awarded one of his supporters, Robert de Commines, the earldom of Northumbria and then returned into the South. Robert's rule was not to last long, as is reported in the *Anglo-Saxon Chronicles*:

1068. In this year king William gave earl Robert the earldom of Northumberland, but [in 1069] the inhabitants surprised him inside the borough of Durham, and slew

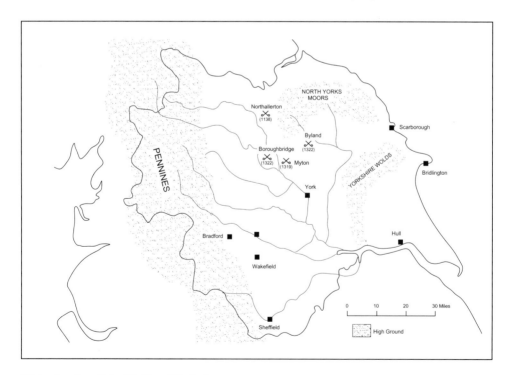

Major battles of the Medieval Period

him and nine hundred of his men. Immediately thereafter came prince Edgar to York with all the Northumbrians, and the citizens came to terms with him. King William came unexpectedly on them from the south with an overwhelming host and routed them, and slew hundreds of those who could not escape. He plundered the borough, and made St Peter's church an object of scorn, and also plundered and humiliated all the others. The prince returned again to Scotland.

Edgar was the only surviving member of the House of Wessex that remained in Britain. He had been sheltering in Scotland but saw the Northumbrian rising as an ideal opportunity to assert his claim to the throne. King William acted swiftly and led a large army into the North. York was sacked and the rebellious northerners put to flight. No evidence of any field actions has come down to us and it is probable that the Northumbrian army dissolved and fled on the approach of the royal army. The northerners had been supported by a large fleet of Danes but William had bribed them to sail away, leaving the Northumbrians unsupported.

The sacking of York was just the beginning and William unleashed his army on the rebellious Northumbrians. William's men laid waste to the area between York and Durham with the sword and the flame. It would take many years for the area to recover from the 'Harrowing of the North' and the Domesday Book entries for the area show ample evidence of the large drop in value of many properties during the period. William's uncompromising reaction to the rising had its desired effect and Yorkshire and the north remained at peace for many years, as the area slowly recovered.

William I was followed by his son, William Rufus, who in turn was followed by his son, Henry I. When Henry died in 1135, without an heir, his nephew Stephen sailed from Normandy and took possession of the throne. Stephen had a rival, his cousin Matilda, who was the daughter of Henry and the dowager German Empress. The English barons were split in their loyalties and a long drawn-out war between the two rival claimants began. Most of the fighting took place in the South and Yorkshire seems to have been little affected by the campaigning. It was the actions of an opportunistic foreign king that led to the next battle on Yorkshire soil.

The Scots king, David, took the opportunity presented by the English king's distraction with the fighting in the South to increase his holdings. He gathered a large army, one of the largest Scottish armies to invade England, and crossed the Tweed into England in the spring of 1138. His army was made up of several disparate parts. Lowland spearmen formed a large part of the army and these men were of mainly Anglo-Saxon descent. Another large contingent came from Galloway, the Galwegians; men of Gaelic descent and only recently brought under the sway of the Scots kings. Contingents also came from the Highlands and the Earl of Orkney sent a force to support King David. One of the most interesting elements of the Scots army was its mounted arm which was made up of French, Norman and disenchanted English knights – for many years to come the Scots nobility would be mainly of Anglo-Norman stock. Many nobles held lands from both the English and Scottish kings and their loyalty seems to have changed as the situation warranted. Robert the Bruce is one of the most famous Scottish kings but on several occasions he fought for King Edward I against the Scots. As will be seen shortly, he was not the first of the Bruce family to have to make a difficult decision as to where his loyalty lay. It is difficult to gauge how large the Scots army was, although it was considered to be a huge army for the time. A figure of 15,000 may be close to the truth, although figures of as low as 12,000 and as high as 25,000 have been given in accounts of the battle.

Once it had crossed the Tweed the Scots army laid waste to the land as it marched down through Northumberland and Durham until it approached the border of Yorkshire. The English king was too distracted in the South to be able to react to the invasion of his territory but he had an able lieutenant in the North, Thurstan, Archbishop of York. Although Thurstan was too old and infirm to lead the army he issued a summons to all loyal men that it was their sacred duty to oppose the Scots invasion. His summons was answered and an army of 10,000-12,000 men was raised. The heart of the English army was its mounted gentry, who were supported by the infantry levies. These levies were usually spearmen but the army which fought at Northallerton contained several thousand archers. These were not the longbowmen of Crècy and Agincourt fame but were equipped with a short bow similar to those used by the Norman archers at Hastings. William of Albemarle commanded and one of his subordinate commanders was Bernard de Balliol, one of whose descendants, John, would be King of Scotland. This is another example of the confused politics of this period of British history.

The English army marched north through Thirsk to Northallerton. On 22 August 1138 the English commanders received news that the Scots were approaching from the direction of Darlington and moved their army to the north side of the town to meet them. The battlefield is very easy to find. The modern A167 leaves Northallerton and heads northwards. The ground begins to rise and the road follows a north-south ridge. About three miles from the town centre is a monument and this roughly marks the English lines. The battlefield is still rural and the only buildings that have impinged on it are a couple of farms, although the farmland is much more enclosed than it was at the time of the battle. On either side of the north-south ridge on which the battle was fought the ground falls away, so it is easy to see the extent of the two battle lines. The English army formed on a low hill, now known as Standard Hill. The ground then drops into a shallow depression before reaching a higher hill about 300 yards to the north. It was on this second hill that the Scots army deployed. The ground was open moorland and was an ideal site for a medieval battle.

Although this was still the period of the mounted charge by heavily armoured knights, the English army fought dismounted. The dismounted knights would have formed the backbone of the army, supported by the levy spearmen. Interspersed along the line were bodies of archers. By far the best source for the battle is that of Aelred, an abbot at Rievaulx Abbey, who wrote soon after the battle and knew participants on both sides. He gives a good description of the English deployment:

Northallerton. Looking from the English lines towards the Scots lines.

> *Being few in number, the southern forces wisely drew up in a single close formation. Taking up position, the leading knights so interspersed the bowmen and spearmen amongst themselves, that protected by their heavy arms they could with the greater security be sharp to launch an attack, or be ready to meet one. The older knights meanwhile, to be the support of the rest, were drawn up about the royal standard, some of them posted above the others even upon the wagon itself.*

The army had been accompanied by a sacred standard to give heart to the troops. A structure resembling a ship's mast had been fixed on a large cart, and a cross had been attached to the top of the mast. From its cross-beam were hung the standards of the four northern saints: John of Beverley, Cuthbert of Durham, Peter of York and Wilfred of Ripon. It is this standard that gives the Battle of Northallerton its alternative name – the Battle of the Standard.

The deployment of the Scots army was not so straightforward. King David's original plan was to form a front line of dismounted knights supported by the bowmen in the army. These would break into the enemy line and would then be supported by the Galwegians and Lowland spearmen. The combined attack would break the English line and victory would be theirs. Unfortunately, the Galwegians were not happy about

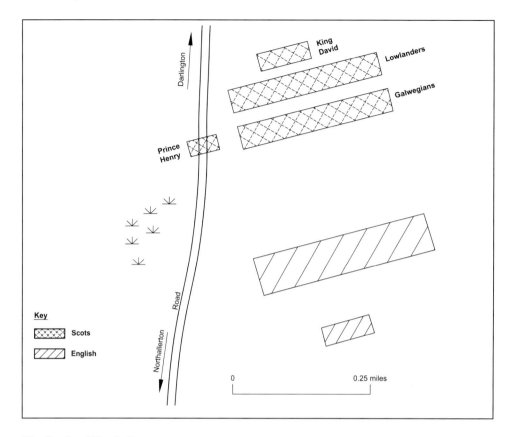

The Battle of Northallerton

playing a supporting role and, after much dispute, a final deployment was decided on. The Galwegians would be given opportunity to prove their boasts and would form the first line. In support were the Lowlanders and on their right flank a contingent of mounted knights under the King's son, Prince Henry, who Aelred gives a shining description of: 'This young man was of so retiring a disposition as to seem the least of them all, while commanding an authority which all revered; and at the same time his gentle manner, his taking ways, and his courtesy, endeared him to everyone.' The third line was made up of the remainder of the knights, who fought dismounted and formed a bodyguard for the king.

Once the two armies had formed the priests moved among the men, blessing, exhorting and leading them in prayer. It was during this period of relative calm that a figure rode from the English lines, Robert de Brus, a direct ancestor of the famous Scottish king of the same name. Although a loyal subject of the English king he also held lands and owed allegiance to the Scots king. He exhorted King David to withdraw his army and reminded him of the support he had been given in the recent past by the English when he successfully seized the throne – many of the English who had supported him stood several hundred yards away ready to oppose him. Aelred gives de Brus a long speech which reduced both him and the Scots king to tears. King David had begun to waver when his nephew, William, who is described as a 'high-spirited man and chief instigator of this war', intervened and charged de Brus with treachery. With the Scots king's resolve hardened, de Brus realised that his efforts would be in vain. He formally withdrew his allegiance to King David and returned to the English lines. Parleying had failed and the matter would be resolved by strength of arms.

With battle inevitable, the two armies began to psyche themselves up, as Aelred describes:

> *Then follows such a sounding of horns, and blaring of trumpets, and the crash of lance striking on lance; the ground is atremble, the air a thunder of sound, and the neighbouring mountains and hills resound to the echo of battle.*

During this interlude Thurstan's deputy, Ralph, Bishop of Orkney, climbed onto a piece of higher ground and 'pronounced' the absolution over the waiting English ranks, to which they replied with a 'mighty shout: Amen, Amen'. This seems to have prompted the Galwegians to begin their charge, as Aelred reports:

> *This was the cue for the Galweymen who with their usual thrice repeated terrible roar so flung themselves on the men of the south that they threw the first line of lancers* [spearmen] *right back from their ground, but repulsed by the armour of the knights they sensed the spirit and strength of the enemy.*

The charge of the lightly armoured Galwegians brought them into contact with the levy spearmen in the English front ranks. Once the English knights, armoured from head to toe, came into contact the enemy, finding their light spears could not penetrate the knights' chainmail armour, were quickly repulsed.

The Galwegians fell back to their start position and rallied. Realising that their light spears were having little effect on the enemy they drew their swords and charged again:

> *However, flying arrows from the south, teeming from their hidden quivers and showering through the air like pouring rain to strike on breast, on face, and even in the enemy's eyes all but brought this movement to a halt. You should have seen the Galweymen, spiny as a hedgehog, pinned on all sides with arrows yet wielding still his sword, and rushing blindly forward in his madness to strike now his enemy, now the empty air with vain blows.*

During this second charge the English archers had much more effect on the lightly armoured Galwegians than they previously had. Why was this? The initial charge may have taken the English by surprise and this allowed the Galwegians to close to contact before the English archery had time to slow them. During the second charge the English archers were waiting and began to pour a heavy fire into the enemy as soon as

Northallerton. Looking from the Scots lines towards the English lines. Much of the fighting took place on the open ground in the centre of the photograph.

they came into range. It may also be that, having been repulsed once, the Galwegians' second charge was not carried out with the speed and fury of their first. Aelred graph-ically describes the effect of the English archery in the quotation above.

While the Galwegians were carrying out their second charge, Prince Henry led his mounted contingent in a sweeping attack on the English left wing, which met with immediate success, as Aelred describes:

> *The extreme flanks, smitten with terror, were already taking to flight when that renowned young prince with his all-conquering line, fell upon the wing against him with the ferocity of a lion; he scattered the opposing sector of the close-knit southern men in all directions like a spider's web, striking down those few who stood their ground, to find himself well beyond the royal standard.*

Henry and his knights had cut their way clean through the English left flank and found themselves well beyond the English lines, close to the present Scotpit Lane. Henry, expecting to be followed by the remainder of the army, attacked the English horse lines and scattered the horses, preventing the escape of the English knights if the Scots were victorious. Aelred also reports that at this stage in the battle some of the English levies had begun to waver – 'the scarce-armed rank and file fled away in terror'. This could have been the turning point of the battle, but a rumour of the Scots king's demise seems to have rallied the English line and brought many of those who had begun to flee back to the fight. As will be seen the rumour was incorrect but it had the desired effect.

We must now return to the main battle which was now rapidly approaching its climax. Once again Aelred gives us details of the closing stages of the action:

And now unable to withstand the rain of arrows any longer, and the swords of the regular soldiery it was the turn of the Galweymen to take flight, having lost already two of their leaders, Ulric and Donald. But the second line, the Laodenses [Lowlanders], was quite unready for this sudden shock and gave way at once. The king at this leapt from his horse and with those barons who were close about him moved forward at the enemy. But now the Scots, too stricken with panic at the flight of the rest who were falling back on all sides, began themselves to leave the king's line until in a short time all had deserted except the few who stood fast by him.

From this description it would appear that, despite the English archery, at least part of the Galwegian line came into hand-to-hand contact but were quickly repulsed. The Lowlanders were struck by the fleeing Galwegians and joined them in their flight. By now the Scottish army was starting to disintegrate and the king began to advance his third line to try to steady the situation. More and more of his troops turned and fled and in a short time the king was left with only his immediate entourage. The English line by now had begun to advance and the king was in grave danger of being over-whelmed with his bodyguard and King David seems to have been ready to accept this fate. Aelred tells us that he was compelled to withdraw from the field by his own knights.

As the king withdrew many of his fleeing men rallied to his banner and formed a rear guard, attempting to protect his fleeing troops from the English pursuers. The king continued to carry out a fighting withdrawal until the remnants of his army reached Carlisle and relative safety. Several times the Scots had turned on their pursuers and driven them off, even capturing a few prisoners in the process.

While the rest of the Scots army had been broken and was in the process of fleeing the field, what had happened to Prince Henry and his knights? By this stage they were well beyond the fighting line, possibly as far as 500 or 600 yards, and Henry could see that no support was forthcoming. He decided that guile was the safest course, as Aelred reports:

We have done what we could, and as far as we are concerned we have carried the field. But now counsel is as much our need as courage. Never is worth more put to the proof than when you refuse to break, though fortune frowns, and if unable to defeat the enemy by force of arms, you yet master him by guile. Remove then, all distinctive signs from our apparel and let us move in amongst the enemy unseen, and join with him in the pursuit, until getting right through we can the sooner rejoin the company of my father which I can still see intact though forced to give ground.

So the prince spoke to his companions and his plan seems to have been successful. The prince was unable to rejoin his father during the retreat from the battle but caught up with him three days later at Carlisle.

The English carried out a merciless pursuit and 'slew numberless Scots and Galwegians'. It is difficult to gauge the casualties suffered by either side in the battle, although it is certain that Scots casualties were much higher than English, as many were cut down in the pursuit. Scots casualties may have been as high as 4,000-5,000, while English casualties may not have exceeded 1,000. Aelred reports that all the English leaders returned safe from the battle and that 'they rendered thanks a thousand times to Almighty God for a victory they had not expected'.

The Battle of the Standard is one of the last entries in the *Anglo-Saxon Chronicles*:

> *1138. In this year David, king of Scotland, invaded this country with immense levies, determined to conquer it. He was met by William, earl of Aumale, to whom the king had entrusted York, and by the other trustworthy men with a few followers: they fought against them, and put the king to flight at the Standard, and slew a great number of his host.*

This sums up succinctly the campaign, and draws a line under the Anglo-Saxon period of history.

The Battle of Myton

For almost 200 years after the Battle of Northallerton, Yorkshire was at peace. Coincidentally, the next spate of battles in the county was started by the Scots and by a direct descent of Robert de Brus who had fought on the English side at Northallerton. It is beyond the scope of this work to go too far into what is now known as the Scottish Wars of Independence but a few facts will help set the scene for the next three battles that took place in the county.

Scotland had remained an independent country after its defeat at Northallerton and seems to have had generally good relations with its southern neighbour. The English kings' warlike tendencies had changed direction and now that England was peaceful their attentions had turned to protecting and enhancing their possessions in France and to taking part in the Crusades. It was the accidental death of the Scots king, Alexander III, in March 1296 that led to a deterioration of relations between the two countries. Alexander, recently married to a new, young, wife, decided to return to her bed after a council meeting, much against the advice of his counsellors. It was a wild stormy night but Alexander and his escort successfully crossed the Firth of Forth. During the subsequent ride towards the royal palace at Kinghorn the king disappeared. He was found the next morning lying at the bottom of a cliff with his neck broken and it was suspected that he had been thrown from his horse.

Although Alexander had outlived his two sons and had not yet produced an heir with his new wife, an heir did exist, his granddaughter Margaret, the Maid of Norway.

The Scottish nobles swore their fealty to the young heiress to the throne and a ship was despatched by the King of England, Edward I, to collect the princess from Norway, illustrating how good the relations between the two countries were. Unfortunately, Margaret died on the Orkney Isles during the journey and Scotland was left without a sovereign. In another example of the close relations between England and Scotland, the Scots nobility turned to Edward I and asked him to make a decision as to who should succeed to the throne. Edward took the task seriously and after much deliberation decided that John Balliol, a descendant of Bernard de Balliol who was one of the English commanders at Northallerton, had the best claim. It was at this point that the relations between the two nations took a definite turn for the worse.

The feudal political situation at the time was very complicated. It has already been mentioned that many nobles held land in both Scotland and England and owed fealty to both kings. Kings could also be in the same situation. Edward owed loyalty to the king of France for some of his continental possessions and the new Scots king, in turn, owed fealty to Edward for his possessions in England. The difference was that while Edward chose to fight for control of his French territories against his overlord, and had the power to do so, Balliol did not and Edward began to treat him as a vassal. It does not take much imagination to realise that this situation was not to the liking of many of the Scots nobles and very quickly they forced their new king into a rebellion against the English king. Edward, soon to be known as 'the Hammer of the Scots', raised an army and invaded Scotland where he defeated the Scots army at Dunbar. Many of the Scots nobility and King John were captured at the battle and imprisoned.

In 1297 another Scots rising took place led by William Wallace and Andrew Moray. The Scots defeated the English forces sent against them at Stirling Bridge before raiding into northern England. Edward, who was campaigning in France, quickly returned to England and led a large army into Scotland. He caught up with the Scots army at Falkirk, where the English archers, many of them equipped with the longbow, peppered the stationary Scots schiltrons – a close ranked formation of spearmen – and then the massed English gentry shattered the Scots army with a mounted charge. For the next eight years Scotland would see no peace. If the English were not fighting them, the two rival Scots factions – the Bruces and the Comyns, supporters of Balliol – would be fighting each other.

In 1305 Edward came to an agreement with the Scots and peace should have descended but the two rival factions still vied with each other for the Scots throne. In 1306 a meeting was arranged between the leaders of the two families at Dumfries Cathedral. During a heated discussion Robert Bruce, often known as Robert the Bruce, stabbed John Comyn and it is difficult to ascertain whether this was a planned attack or carried out in a fit of temper. Bruce was crowned king, but was not to enjoy a peaceful existence for many years. Edward rose from his sick bed and invaded Scotland. Once again the Hammer of the Scots was victorious and it was only his death at Carlisle on 7 July 1306 that saved the new Scots king from total defeat. The new

English king, Edward II, having left garrisons in many Scottish towns and castles, returned to England to consolidate his rule.

King Robert I still had the remaining English garrisons and the Comyn forces to deal with and at one time lost control of virtually the whole of the kingdom. Robert slowly but surely built up his power base and as his support grew defeated the Comyns and began to reclaim his towns and fortresses from the English. By the summer of 1314 the Scots army was blockading the English garrison in Stirling Castle, one of the most powerful and important fortresses in Scotland. This was a challenge that Edward of England could not ignore and, after raising a large army, he invaded Scotland and the two armies met along the Bannockburn on 24 June 1314. At the battle the badly deployed English army was shattered by the advancing Scottish schiltrons and Edward was lucky to escape capture. The English king and his army withdrew south of the border to lick their wounds and King Robert was able to continue clearing the few remaining garrisons.

Edward, with the pride of his father but without his tactical acumen, refused to come to peace with the Scots. King Robert launched a series of raids into the northern counties of England during the period between 1315 and 1318. Many Yorkshire towns suffered the effects of the depredations, including Northallerton, Boroughbridge, Knaresborough and Tadcaster. Edward seems to have done little to prevent these raids and the Scots seem to have roamed the North as they pleased. In the meantime the Scots king continued the reconquest of his kingdom and recaptured the town of Berwick. Although Berwick is now on the English side of the border, at various times in its history it has belonged to both nations. Its capture by the Scots forced a reaction from King Edward.

During the early part of 1319 the English king began to raise a massive army to sort the Scottish problem once and for all. The army is said to have been between 60,000 and 100,000 strong, although this is probably a highly exaggerated figure. By the end of August the English had begun their advance on Berwick. The Scots king had been busy reinforcing Berwick's garrison and poured troops and supplies into the town. This was only one part of the Scots king's plan to repulse the English invasion. While the English were occupied at Berwick he would launch a raiding force into Northumberland, Durham and Yorkshire to cut the English supply lines and threaten the northern boroughs. As the English army set down in front of Berwick – the siege began on 8 September 1319 – the Scots raiders crossed the border, led by their commanders the Earl of Moray and Sir James Douglas, often called the Black Douglas. These two were among Bruce's most experienced commanders and were an inspired choice by the Scots king.

The Scots force crossed the western side of the border close to Carlisle and then followed the Tyne valley across to the east side of the country, where they then began to devastate the counties of Northumberland, Durham and Yorkshire. By 18 September they were encamped to the north-west of York at Myton-on-Swale, close to the town of Boroughbridge. The Archbishop of York got news of the Scottish army's location, possibly through a Scots spy captured in the city and it could have been a deliberate ruse to draw the English onto ground of the Scots commanders' choosing. He attempted to gather what forces he could to oppose them. The northern nobility and knights were all with the king at Berwick, as were many of the local levies. Somehow the Archbishop managed to raise a force from the local townsmen and marched to surprise the Scots at Myton.

Once again, the sizes of the two armies are somewhat problematic. Both are said to have been between 10,000 and 15,000 strong. A recent account of the battle by Graham Bell casts some doubts on this and gives a good argument for the forces being much smaller. Firstly, the Scots were a raiding force, not an invading army – their task was to hit and run and cut the English supply lines. At the Bannockburn the Scots army had only amounted to about 13,000-14,000 men. It seems unlikely that King Robert, having garrisoned Berwick and retained a small force under his own command, would have had 15,000 men to spare. It is unlikely that the Scots army amounted to more than 2,000-3,000 men. As has already been mentioned, the bulk of the Yorkshire troops had marched north with the king, so the Archbishop had few remaining assets from which to build an army of 15,000. The short period of time between the English

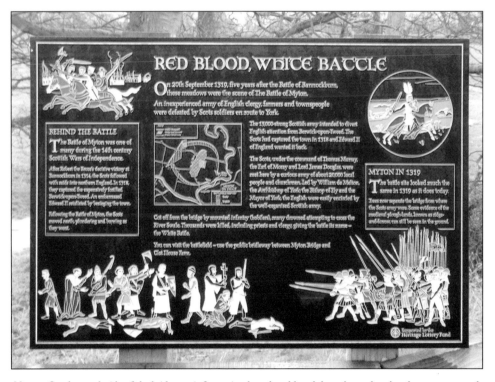

Myton. On the north side of the bridge an information board and bench have been placed and are a very good point to view the battlefield from.

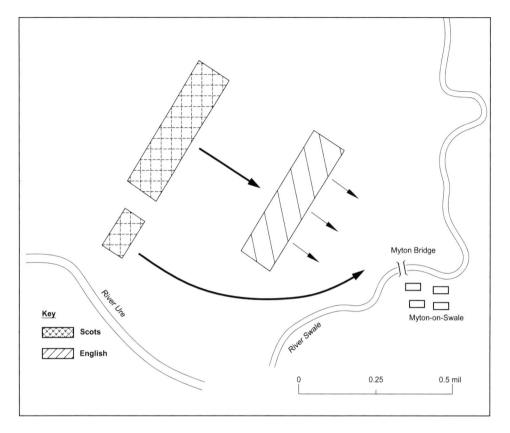

The Battle of Myton

discovering the location of the Scots and the battle also precluded the gathering of such a large force – have no doubt about it, an army of 15,000 men was a very substantial force throughout most of the period covered by this book and could take weeks or months to raise. Bearing this in mind, the English probably had a similar strength to the Scots, although it is known that a body of 300 white-clad monks accompanied the army on its march.

Myton-on-Swale lay on the east bank of the River Swale. Beyond the village a wooden bridge crossed the river onto an area of fairly level ground. The Scots army formed on the high ground which lay to the west and north-west of the crossing. The bulk of the Scots army dismounted and formed into a single schiltron, while a small body remained mounted. The experienced Scots' commanders had a solid plan to defeat the English. First they would allow them to cross the river. Then the schiltron would advance from the high ground to engage the English, while the mounted troops would ride around behind the English army and seize the bridge, thus preventing the English army from retreating. The Scots movements would be covered by a

Myton. Looking north across the bridge at Myton. The English army deployed along the track and the Scots schiltron attacked from the left, while a small body of Scots seized the bridge to prevent the English retreating. The present bridge was built in the nineteenth century and refurbished in 2002.

Myton. Looking from the north end of the bridge towards the north-west. The Scots army deployed on the high ground beyond the line of trees in the middle distance.

Myton. The River Swale is very high in this photograph. Many of the fleeing English troops were drowned along this stretch of the river.

smoke-screen created by setting fire to three large haystacks. As the undisciplined, inexperienced, English force deployed on the ground below the Scots, the plan was put into action.

The first that the English troops, blinded by smoke, knew of the Scots advance was when the compact body of Scots spearmen appeared through the smoke. The bulk of the English troops put up little resistance and fled back towards the bridge. Imagine their shock when they saw that the bridge was held against them by another body of Scottish troops! The English army disintegrated. Most of the English leaders, including the Archbishop of York, managed to escape but many of their men were cut down or drowned in the Swale. Myton was more of a massacre than a battle and was referred to by the Scots as the 'Chapter of Myton' due to the presence of the 300 monks with the English army.

Not only had Moray and Douglas's tactical plan worked like a dream but King Robert's strategic plan also came to fruition. The English northern lords at Berwick, led by the Earl of Lancaster, quickly began to worry about their lands to the south, currently being raided by the Scots. They demanded that the army withdrew from Berwick so that they could protect their possessions. Interestingly, it is thought that the siege of Berwick was broken off on 18 September 1319, the day before the Battle of Myton took place. So the mere presence of the Scottish raiding force may have been enough to force the English army to withdraw. Edward's failure at Berwick would lead to the next battle to be covered – Boroughbridge.

The Battle of Boroughbridge

Although the battle of Boroughbridge took place during the Scots Wars of Independence and the battles before and after it, Myton and Byland, were against invading Scots armies, Boroughbridge was fought between troops loyal to King Edward II and those of the rebellious Thomas, Earl of Lancaster. To get to the root cause of the dispute between Edward and Lancaster we have to go back a number of years to 1311. Edward had homosexual tendencies and promoted his favourites, much to the annoyance of the nobility. Edward had promoted his Gascon lover, Piers Gaveston, to the earldom of Cornwall. Many of the leading nobles took offence at this and in 1311 Thomas, Earl of Lancaster, was a key player in Gaveston's downfall and execution.

During the following years the enmity between the king and the earl grew, but both were distracted by the campaigns against the Scots. Lancaster was one of the first of the northern lords to abandon the siege of Berwick in 1319, to protect his holdings in Yorkshire and Lancashire against the depredations of the Scots and this led to further enmity with the king. Edward by this time had another favourite, Hugh Despenser, a rapacious individual who carried out a campaign of aggrandisement against the English nobility, particularly the marcher lords on the Welsh borders. Once again Lancaster was one of the leaders of the nobility who demanded Despenser's exile at a parliament in 1321. With many of his leading nobles close to rebellion the king acquiesced and Despenser went into exile, where he spent much of his time playing the pirate in the English Channel. He would not be the last exiled English lord to turn to piracy (see next chapter).

In October 1321 Queen Isabelle, wife of Edward II, set off from London on pilgrimage to Canterbury. The Queen had intended to spend the night at Leeds Castle, in Kent, but was refused entry by Lady Badelsmere. Lord Badelsmere had been despatched by the king to treat with the rebellious marcher lords but had joined them. The Queen attempted to storm the castle with her escort, but was repulsed with some loss. Enraged, the king raised a force of Londoners and mercenaries and laid siege to the castle which fell after a short siege. Lady Badelsmere was imprisoned. Her husband had gathered the support of some of the marcher lords and their army marched as far as Kingston-upon-Thames, before withdrawing into the Welsh Marches. This was one of the few times during his reign that Edward showed the energy and military skill of his father, carrying out a successful military campaign along the Severn Valley against the marcher lords.

Throughout this period Lancaster had remained in the North, despite the pleas of

Boroughbridge. A memorial plaque on the south side of the bridge.

THE BATTLE OF
BOROUGHBRIDGE
1322
At the Battle of Boroughbridge,
fought at the then wooden bridge,
King Edward II's army,
commanded by Sir Andrew Harcla,
defeated the rebel forces of the
Earls of Lancaster
and Hereford.

the marcher lords for him to come to their aid. He held several parliaments and is thought to have been in communication with the Scots. Eventually, Lancaster, accompanied by Humphrey de Bohun, Earl of Hereford, and Lord Badelsmere, set off south with a large force of levies. He was too late to aid the marcher lords. By the time Lancaster reached Burton-on-Trent, in early March 1322, the king, with a large force, had closed up to the River Trent. The two armies reached a stand off until the king crossed the river at another crossing, leaving Lancaster with little option but to retreat.

An army in retreat is not a pretty sight and Lancaster's was no exception. By the time he had returned to his castle at Pontefract desertions had substantially reduced his force and it now numbered no more than 1,000 men. The king's army was following steadily behind the rebel force and it was decided that a further retreat would have to be made, to the Earl's castle at Dunstanburgh. The castle was a formidable fortress and within easy reach of Scottish support. Lancaster seems to have been a little reticent to abandon his Yorkshire and Lancashire holdings but was persuaded of the sense of retreating to his Northumberland fortress. The retreat would cross the River Ure at Boroughbridge and then continue north; it was at this town that Lancaster received a surprise on 16 March 1322 – the northern bank of the river was held by troops loyal to the king.

Unbeknown to Lancaster and his allies, the king had ordered Sir Andrew Harcla, Warden of the Western Marches, to gather what forces he could and march south through Yorkshire to prevent Lancaster's possible retreat north. In a rare episode of strategic insight, the king had got it right and Harcla's force was in an ideal position to stop the rebels' northward progress. Harcla deployed his men to block both of the crossings, the bridge and a ford about half a mile to the east. Harcla had about 4,000 men, the bulk of which he deployed at the bridge, with spearmen blocking the crossing while bodies of archers to either flank supported them. The ford was defended with a

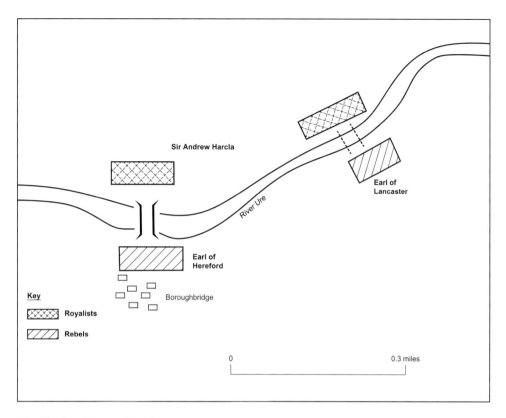

The Battle of Boroughbridge

force of bowmen, supported by spearmen. It is likely that the river was high and the ford may not have been easy to cross; the archers may have added to this by planting defensive stakes to cover the crossing.

Lancaster knew Harcla – indeed it was Lancaster who had knighted him – and tried to negotiate with him but to no effect. Realising he would have to force a crossing, Lancaster then split his forces, almost certainly less than 1,000 men, with the Earl of Hereford and Lord Clifford leading the bulk of the forces in a foot attack on the bridge, while Lancaster led a mounted attack across the ford. Lancaster's attack made little progress and was quickly stopped. At the bridge Hereford's men attempted to cross the narrow bridge. Clifford was wounded by an arrow and Hereford was killed by a spear which had been thrust through a gap in the bridge from underneath by, it is said, a Welsh spearman. This story is similar to that told of the lone Norwegian on the bridge at Stamford Bridge and there may be some confusion between the two. With both their commanders having fallen as casualties, the rebel troops fell back into Boroughbridge.

On the following morning Harcla led his men across the river and attacked the rebel

Boroughbridge. Looking south from Sir Andrew de Harcla's position on the north bank.

troops who, surprisingly, had spent the night in the town. Lancaster, Clifford and Badelsmere were all captured and could have expected little mercy from the king. They were right. Lancaster was taken to Pontefract where he was paraded through the town much to the joy of its citizens – he had not been a popular lord – before he was beheaded. Badelsmere was taken to Canterbury and Clifford to York, where they were tried for treason and hanged. Edward was elated by his successful campaign. He had a victorious army in the North and his rebellious barons had been put down. Now was the time to finish the business with the Scots, who were still raiding into his northern counties.

The Battle of Byland

King Edward gathered his army in preparation for an invasion of Scotland. By early August his strength had grown to about 20,000 men, although numbers between 30,000 and 60,000 are given by some chroniclers. The English army crossed the border and pushed north towards Edinburgh, while a fleet sailed up the east coast of Scotland to assist in keeping the army supplied.

King Robert decided on a 'scorched earth' policy to defeat the English, rather than risking a battle against their superior numbers. This was a sound strategic plan. The territory through which the English army had to pass, both sides of the border, had suffered the depredations of the Scots and was a wasteland. As the Scots army withdrew before their enemy they burnt or removed anything that would be of assistance to them. As the English army marched through East Lothian they found the land around had been laid waste and their foraging expedition brought in few supplies. All one foraging party was able to procure was a lame cow!

By late August the English army had halted east of Edinburgh to await the arrival of the ships. By this time many of the men were suffering from hunger and morale must have been very low. Although losses had begun to mount due to starvation and dysentery, which had broken out among the soldiers, it is likely that the army was still a cohesive body at this time as stragglers and deserters would have been at the mercy of the Scots moss troopers as they attempted to return through the borders to England.

Boroughbridge. Looking north from the rebel positions. At the time of the battle the bridge would have been much narrower and easier to defend. The rebel troops attempted to force a crossing in the teeth of Harcla's archers.

There was still the promise of supplies arriving from the ships which were now approaching the Firth of Forth. Unfortunately, things began to go from bad to worse for Edward. Contrary winds prevented his supply fleet from entering the Firth and the supply situation continued to worsen. The English king had no choice but to withdraw along his invasion route, which was still a waste land with few supplies available, and the English army began its retreat towards the end of August. It was at this stage that Robert the Bruce's plan came to fruition – the English army had been turned back without having to fight it and was in a disorderly retreat back the way it had come. Now was the time for the Scots to strike.

Over the next few weeks the Scots king gathered his forces, including a contingent of highlanders and prepared to move south. Rather than following the English army along the east side of the country, which would have entailed advancing through the ravaged areas, the Scots crossed the border on 30 September and advanced to Carlisle. Several days were spent ravaging the area before the Scots army moved south. King Robert seems to have been fully aware of the English army's movements and its lessening in numbers and morale. After five days raiding in the Carlisle area the king called his army together and set off towards Yorkshire, through the Aire gap. By 13 October the Scots had reached Northallerton.

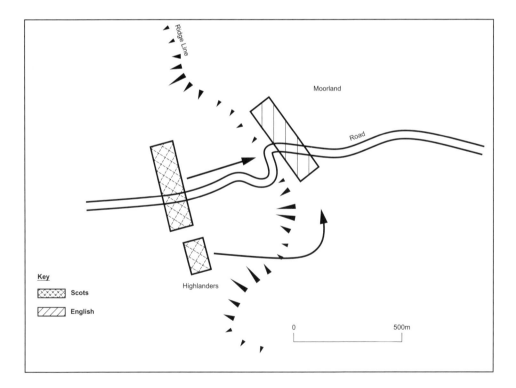

The Battle of Byland

Byland. Looking towards the English position from the Scots' line of advance. The road ascends the ridge in a series of hairpin turns and has a gradient of one in four in places. The ridge is much steeper with cliffs in some places. King Robert sent his highlanders on a flank march to the south of the English position, just off the right of this photograph.

By this time the pitiful remnants of the English army had reached the area to the east of Thirsk close to Rievaulx Abbey, where King Edward and his entourage were quartered. Edward had summoned his lords to gather as many forces to him as they could but the speed of the Scots' advance caught the English before any of these reinforcements could arrive. The Scots king had been presented with an ideal opportunity.

On the morning of the 14 October the Scots advanced towards Rievaulx Abbey, very likely with the intent of capturing the English king. What forces Edward had left, probably no more than 1,000 men, were deployed, under the Earl of Richmond, to prevent the passage of the Scots army. Although there is some confusion as to where the battle took place, it is likely that the English defended the edge of Scawton Moor between the abbeys at Byland and Rievaulx.

The edge of the moor presents a formidable obstacle for an army advancing from the direction of Northallerton as the road ascends the precipitous rise in a series of hairpin turns. The English, who were heavily outnumbered by the 4,000–5,000 Scots present with King Robert, defended the top of the hill and the Scots had no option

Byland. Sutton Bank is one of the possible locations for the battle of Byland. This photograph is looking from the English positions along the A170 towards Thirsk. The Scots advanced along this route to attack the English.

but to attack up the steep slope. Details of the battle are very sketchy but it seems that after the repulse of his first attack, King Robert despatched his highlanders on a flanking movement. As the Scots attacked up the steep slope for a second time, the highlanders struck the English in the flank. The combined Scots attack quickly broke the English line.

With the English in flight, King Robert despatched a body of cavalry to Rievaulx Abbey with the intention of capturing his English counterpart. By the time the Scots horsemen reach Rievaulx King Edward had fled, leaving behind his baggage and the members of a French diplomatic mission. Edward first rode to York and then on to Bridlington and safety. Tradition has it that he was closely pursued by the Scots as far as York and it is easy to imagine the king and his escort galloping up Bootham towards the bar with the Scottish cavalry on their tails! Edward looked for a scapegoat to cover his embarrassment and chose Sir Andrew Harcla, the victor of Boroughbridge. Harcla had been marching to reinforce Edward with a small force but had not arrived in time. He was subsequently tried and executed.

Byland was a something-and-nothing battle, but its repercussions were massive.

Firstly, the English king was finally forced to come to terms with the Scots and a peace treaty lasting thirteen years was agreed, although subsequent events led to a new round of hostilities in 1327. Edward's continued misrule of the nation, and his penchant for advancing favourites, led to another revolt in 1327, when his wife, Isabelle, and her lover, Roger Mortimer, successfully deposed the king and placed Isabelle's infant son, Edward, on the throne. Edward III would go on to be one of England's greatest warrior kings and, unlike his father, had inherited his grand-father's military skills. Edward II, deposed and imprisoned in Berkeley Castle, met a painful death by having a red-hot iron inserted into his anus. His killers did not want to leave a mark on his body!

The first battle in Yorkshire of the Wars of the Roses?

Before moving on to the next chapter, there is one more action in Yorkshire worth mentioning – Bramham Moor. In 1328 England and Scotland signed a peace treaty and conflict along the border ceased. When he reached adulthood, Edward III turned his eyes towards his continental possessions and so began the Hundred Years' War. This was the period when the English longbowmen ruled supreme and the flower of French chivalry felt the sting of their yard shafts. The king and his eldest son, the Black Prince, won great victories at Crècy and Poitiers and England's fortunes on the continent reached a high point.

Edward III was followed by his grandson, Richard II. Richard was not of the same mettle as his grandfather and in 1399 he was deposed by Henry Bolinbroke, Duke of Hereford, often known as Henry of Lancaster. The two cousins had a tempestuous relationship which led to Henry being banished for ten years in 1398. In 1399 Richard seized Henry's vast Lancastrian estates. While the king was campaigning in Ireland Henry invaded England and successfully usurped the throne as King Henry IV, the first of the Lancastrian monarchs. Richard was imprisoned in Pontefract Castle where he subsequently died. It is often said that Richard was starved to death on the orders of King Henry.

Henry's early reign was far from peaceful. Taking advantage of the confusion in England the Welsh, under Owen Glendower, rose and attempted to regain their independence. Henry also had troubles with rebellious lords including the powerful Percy family, one of the most prominent families in the North of England. On 21 July 1403, the royal army met a rebel force commanded by Sir Henry Percy, often known as Hotspur, at Shrewsbury. The rebels were defeated, Hotspur killed and his father, the Earl of Northumberland, fled to Scotland. Early in 1408 Northumberland returned to England with a small Scots army. Once he had gathered a small force of his northern retainers the combined army continued south until it reached Bramham Moor, to the east of Bramham village, where he was intercepted by Sir Thomas Rokeby, a staunch supporter of King Henry and the Sheriff of Yorkshire. Little is known of the ensuing battle other that it started at about two o'clock in the afternoon and Rokeby's army won. Northumberland was probably killed during the rout, although he may have been captured and executed at York.

Some authors have asserted that Shrewsbury was the first battle of the Wars of the Roses, not without some merit – rebels supporting the Plantagenet family against the ruling House of Lancaster. If this is the case then was Bramham Moor the first battle of the Wars of the Roses on Yorkshire soil? I'll let you decide. What I find interesting is that during what is generally accepted as the Wars of the Roses, the Percy Earls of Northumberland were staunch supporters of the Lancastrian king. At the time of Shrewsbury and Bramham Moor they were his staunchest English opponents. What a difference forty years made!

When Henry IV died in 1413 he was succeeded by his son Henry V, of Agincourt fame. During the second Lancastrian Henry's reign, English fortunes in France blossomed. His untimely death left the infant Henry VI on the throne and this led directly to the next round of battles in Yorkshire – the Wars of the Roses.

CHAPTER FOUR

BOW AND BILL

The Wars of the Roses

Many books have been written on the Wars of the Roses but one misconception still exists, that the wars were fought between Yorkshire and Lancashire. This is far from the truth. The wars were a dynastic struggle between the ruling House of Lancaster and the House of York, with nobles supporting one side or the other as the situation suited them. It comes as quite a surprise to many Yorkshire people when it is explained to them that they would probably have supported Lancaster not York. Henry VI was the ruling Lancastrian king and much of his support came from the

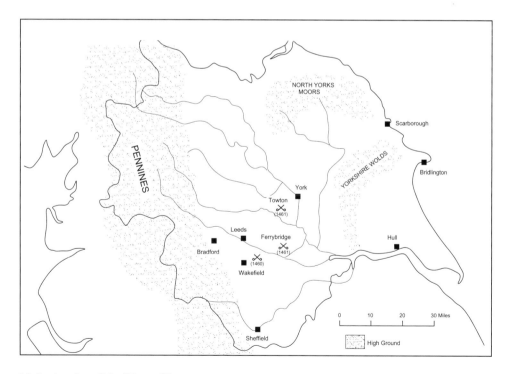

Major battles of the Wars of Roses

North, while, in the main, Richard, Duke of York's support came from the South and Midlands. The situation was not clear cut as the king had supporters in the South and South West, and the Duke of York had lands and supporters in Yorkshire. One of York's main supports was the Neville family, particularly Richard Neville, Earl of Warwick. The Neville family had large estates in North Yorkshire and were often at odds with the Percy family who were staunch Lancastrians and held much of the North East.

The modern name for the wars is a relatively recent invention – the term 'The Wars of the Roses' was first coined by Sir Walter Scott in the nineteenth century. It originates from a scene in William Shakespeare's *Henry VI*, where rival lords showed their allegiance by picking red and white roses in a garden. Although the scene is very dramatic it has no basis in history. It is far from certain whether people at the time considered the wars as a single entity, as we do today, or as just another series of disconnected campaigns.

Although troops raised in Yorkshire fought in most of the campaigns, actual military operations within the boundaries of the county took place over a very short period of time. In December 1460 the Duke of York marched north to Wakefield to oppose the Lancastrian forces gathering at Pontefract. In the subsequent battle he was defeated and killed. His eldest son, Edward Earl of March, gathered an army in the south and in March 1461 marched north to defeat the Lancastrians at the Battle of Towton, the largest battle of the Wars of the Roses, on Palm Sunday, 29 March 1461. Although armies continued to pass through the county throughout the wars, no more major actions were fought on her soil.

Background

England was a troubled nation in the middle years of the fifteenth century. A weak king, Henry VI, sat on the throne and was influenced by his nobles. Friction between two of these 'over mighty subjects' would lead to open warfare and a series of campaigns were fought over a thirty-year period. These campaigns have come down to us as the Wars of the Roses.

Henry VI had ascended the throne as an infant, after the untimely death of his warrior father, Henry V of Agincourt fame. As Henry grew into manhood it became obvious that he was more suited to the life of a scholar than that of a warrior, as his father and grandfather had been. Although he was married to Margaret of Anjou, a redoubtable woman whose commitment to his cause led directly to the battles of Wakefield and Towton, no heir to the throne had yet been born and this placed the house of Lancaster in a delicate situation.

Next in line of succession was Richard Plantagenet, Duke of York, who was one of the wealthiest men in England. His marriage to Cicely Neville, the Rose of Raby, brought him a rich dowry and a number of powerful allies. York was the king's lieutenant in France during the early part of the 1440s. At his own expense York had successfully defended the king's possessions on the continent, funding the campaigns with £38,000 out of his own pocket, an enormous sum at the time. During York's absence in France the king had found a new favourite, Edmund Beaufort, Duke of Somerset, and it was the rivalry that grew between the two dukes that became the root cause of the wars.

York continued to command in France until 1445, when, to add insult to injury, he was replaced by Somerset. To make matters worse York was then made Lieutenant of Ireland and he saw this as being one step short of exile. Somerset's time in command in France proved disastrous and by the time he returned to England in 1451 the king's continental possessions had shrunk to the area around Calais and the Hundred Years' War was virtually over. Throughout this period York remained in Ireland but his grievances against the king and his favourite continued to grow. While York had commanded in France money could not be found to fund his military operations so he had to use his own considerable resources, without any recompense from the king. When the king's favourite, Somerset, had assumed the mantle of command money suddenly became available and he received £25,000 to support his disastrous campaigns.

By late in 1451 the Duke of York had had enough and decided to return to England and reassert his rights as the king's successor and main advisor. York sailed from Ireland and began to gather forces in Wales and the marches. In February 1452 York began to move his army towards London with the intention of arresting Somerset and his supporters. The king immediately raised forces to oppose him and the two armies came close to confrontation at Blackheath on 3 March 1452. Messages passed between the king and York. The duke believed that Henry had agreed to arrest Somerset and receive York back into his favour but when York arrived at the king's encampment, with a small escort, and was shown into the king's tent he saw that Somerset was still standing at the king's right hand. Richard of York had badly misjudged the situation and instead of being accepted back as the king's valued advisor, he was immediately arrested. Fortunately, once the duke had given an oath of allegiance to the king and promises of good behaviour in the future, he was released and returned to his estates. Although bloodshed had been avoided the country was on an ever-quickening road to open warfare.

In 1453 York's precarious position suddenly reversed when King Henry had a mental breakdown. Many historians have tried to diagnose exactly what form this breakdown took but so far removed from events it is nigh on impossible to say what afflicted the king, although the main symptom of his ailment was mental and physical paralysis. York, who still had a lot of support among the nobles of the land, was proclaimed as protector during the king's illness. His first act was to have Somerset arrested and confined to the Tower of London. York's Neville in-laws took this opportunity to assert their claims to lands in Yorkshire and the North East and local skirmishing took place. The Nevilles' main rivals in the North were the Percy Earls of Northumberland. During York's protectorate the nobles of the land began to coalesce into two distinct camps, supporters of the House of York or the House of Lancaster. Another important event took place shortly after the king's breakdown – the birth of his son Edward. With the arrival of the Prince of Wales, York's position worsened. Although he was the power in the land, he was no longer the king's heir and if Henry recovered he would be in a very bad situation.

Early in 1455 Henry suddenly recovered and took over the reigns of power once again. As York's first act had been to arrest Somerset, Henry's was to release him. Somerset quickly formed an alliance with Henry Percy, 5th Earl of Northumberland, and Thomas, Lord Clifford, against York and his main supporters, Richard Neville, Earl of Salisbury, and his son Richard, Earl of Warwick. The battle lines had been drawn and the country moved rapidly towards war. At the prompting of his wife and Somerset, Henry called a meeting at Leicester for 21 May 1455. York was ordered to attend alone. York knew that if he did so the best he could hope for was imprisonment in the Tower and at worse execution as a traitor. Once again York decided that he would not surrender meekly and he would fight for his rights.

York gathered his forces and marched on London. At the same time Somerset, Northumberland and Clifford marched with the king to oppose him. The two armies clashed at a small town called St Albans on 22 May 1455 – it was not the first time and would not be the last time that this sleepy little town was the scene of military conflict. The Lancastrians defended the town and barricaded the streets leading into it. Initially, the Yorkists made little headway until a body of the Earl of Warwick's men broke into the town through some gardens and turned the Lancastrian defences, which rapidly crumbled. Somerset, Northumberland and Clifford all died during the battle or were executed immediately after the fighting ceased. York's main opponents were dead but their sons, who assumed their titles, were not and York would one day feel the wrath of their revenge.

The king was captured during the fighting and once again the House of York was in the ascendant. Although the duke continued with his illusion of allegiance to Henry and even returned him to London in a regal procession, York once again became the power of the land and was proclaimed Protector. This situation continued for ten months until, in late February 1456, the king, supported by his wife and the sons of his deceased supporters, dismissed York as Protector and reassumed his rule.

The status quo continued for three years with the Yorkists' position steadily worsening, while the Lancastrians grew in power and influence. In June 1459 things came to a head, when a Council was convened at Coventry, and York, Salisbury and Warwick were not invited. It was obvious to the Yorkist leaders what was about to happen and they decided to fight. York began to gather his army at his castle at Ludlow. Salisbury had to march his forces from Yorkshire and clashed with a Lancastrian force, commanded by Lord Audley, at Blore Heath near Newcastle-under-Lyme on 23 September 1459. It was not the custom for English men-at-arms to fight on horseback and Blore Heath is one of the few battles of the Wars of the Roses where this happened. Audley's mounted men-at-arms charged Salisbury's dismounted archers several times before accepting defeat and withdrawing from the field. Salisbury continued his march to Ludlow and combined with York and Warwick.

As the Yorkists gathered their forces at Ludlow the Lancastrians raised a larger force to oppose them, marching towards Ludlow and meeting their opponents at Ludford Bridge. The two armies faced each other and it seemed like a bloody clash could not be avoided on the following day. During the night events transpired that would cause the Yorkist leaders to abandon their army and flee the country. Warwick was the commander of the Calais garrison and had brought a number of men, all professional soldiers, from the garrison to the rendezvous at Ludlow. One of their commanders, Andrew Trollope, took his men over to the king's party during the night. Many authors have put this down as an act of base treachery, but this is questionable. Should Trollope's allegiance to Warwick have taken preference to his allegiance to his king? It is debatable, but Trollope's subsequent support for the king's cause showed that he was a true king's man.

Once Trollope's desertion became known to the Yorkist leaders they quickly abandoned their troops and fled: York and his second son, Edmund, Earl of Rutland, sailed for Ireland, while Salisbury, Warwick, and York's eldest son, Edward, Earl of March, took shelter in Calais. In November 1459 the Yorkist leaders were formally attainted (declared traitors) by a parliament held at Coventry.

From his safe base at Calais, Warwick carried out a sustained campaign of raiding and piracy and began to raise support for the Yorkist cause in the southern counties, particularly Kent. In March 1460 the Yorkist leaders gathered in Ireland to discuss their forthcoming operations. Warwick, Salisbury and March would sail from Calais and land in Kent. This would be followed by a march on London. The Yorkists landed at Sandwich on 26 June 1460 and successfully occupied London shortly afterwards. The Lancastrians gathered their forces quickly at Coventry and Warwick, in fact, so quickly that many of the king's main supporters did not have time to join him before the two armies clashed at Northampton on 10 July 1460.

The Lancastrians occupied a fortified camp on the south bank of the River Nene. After a Yorkist attempt to parley had been turned away, their army advanced on the Lancastrian fortifications. It looked like the Yorkists were in for a hard fight but as they approached the Lancastrian lines Lord Grey, the commander of the Lancastrian right wing, turned traitor and it is recorded that his men helped the Yorkist troops across the fortifications. The Lancastrian forces were quickly broken and the king captured. Warwick and Edward, Earl of March had ordered their men not to lay a hand on the king and to spare as many of the common folk as they could, but many of the Lancastrians were drowned as they tried to swim the river during the rout. The king was once again in Yorkist hands and the time was ripe for the Duke of York to return from Ireland.

York landed at Chester in early September 1460 and proceeded to London which he entered with his sword carried before him as though he was a king. He seems to have completely misunderstood the situation as Abbot Whethamstede of St Albans reported:

> *And coming there* [Westminster] *he walked straight on, until he came to the king's throne, upon the covering or cushion on which laying his hand, in this very act like a man about to take possession of his right, he held it upon it for a short time. But at length withdrawing it, he turned his face to the people, standing quietly under the canopy of royal state, he looked eagerly for their applause.*

He was to be sadly disappointed. The gathered lords and bishops stood in stunned silence until, at length, Thomas Bourchier, Archbishop of Canterbury, welcomed the duke and asked if he would 'come and see the king'. York refused. He had badly over-estimated how far people would support him.

On 24 October 1460 a compromise was reached with the Act of Accord. This stipulated that Henry would continue to rule and on his death York would be proclaimed king. This did not sit well with Margaret of Anjou who now saw that her son, the rightful heir, was in danger of losing his claim to the throne. Fortunately for Margaret, the Act of Accord was a purely Yorkist agreement and many of the king's supporters were of a similar mind to the queen. Margaret began to gather a large army at Hull, calling in her supporters from the North and the South West. As her army gathered she visited Wales to raise support and then sailed on to Scotland to negotiate for Scottish troops to support her. With Lancastrian forces gathering in Yorkshire and the Welsh Marches, the Duke of York took a bold, or, as events transpired, rash, decision to march into the North. His eldest son would be given his first independent command and would defeat the Welsh Lancastrian forces before heading into Yorkshire to join his father. Warwick would hold London and continue to gather support, while York and Warwick's father, the Earl of Salisbury, would lead a small force into Yorkshire. Events that would lead to the Battle of Wakefield had been set in motion.

The Wakefield campaign

There is some dispute in the contemporary and near contemporary accounts of the battle as to when the Duke of York left London, with dates between 2 and 9 December 1460 being given. One theory that has been put forward is that the bulk of the Duke's small force left on the 2nd while York, Salisbury and Rutland did not leave until the 9th and this is perfectly plausible. The bulk of the Yorkist force was infantry and would have marched steadily up the Great North Road and it would not have been a problem for York's mounted entourage to catch them before they got too far north.

What York's plan was at this time is difficult to ascertain. It is obvious that he was marching north to confront the growing Lancastrian army in Yorkshire but what is less obvious is where exactly he was heading towards. How much intelligence the Duke had managed to gather on the size and composition of the Lancastrian army is not mentioned, but it is likely that he did not realise how large a force the enemy had managed to gather at Hull and then Pontefract. If he did know of the size of the enemy force then it would have been sheer folly to divide his forces, as he had done, and march north with a small contingent. Contemporary writers tell us that he had received news from his Yorkshire tenants that they were being harassed by the Lancastrians and some modern authors have used this as a reason for his march north even though he had only a small force with him.

Was York heading towards Pontefract, where the Lancastrian army was encamped, or Wakefield where he could use his castle at Sandal as a base? One reason put forward for him marching towards Pontefract is that when he arrived at Sandal Castle it was ill provisioned, so York must have changed his destination part way through the march. This is reasonable, but there could be another reason for the lack of supplies at the castle and that is simply that the garrison was too small to send out foraging expeditions in the face of the Lancastrian army a few miles away at Pontefract.

If York had departed from London with the intention of marching directly to Pontefract, by the time his force reached north Nottinghamshire he had already changed his plan and was heading on a more westerly route, through Worksop and this road led in the direction of Wakefield. When York's vanguard reached Worksop they clashed with a large force of Lancastrian troops also heading north. The Yorkists were driven back incurring a number of casualties in a short, sharp fight and the Lancastrians continued on their way to Pontefract. These Lancastrians belonged to the contingents of the Duke of Somerset and several other nobles who held lands in the South West and had been recruited in the area before they had marched north to join with the northern Lancastrian troops.

York and his supporters continued their march to Wakefield and arrived at Sandal Castle between 21 and 24 December – once again the contemporary accounts give different dates. York and his nobles stayed in the castle, while many of his men were quartered in Sandal and Wakefield, the castle being much too small to accommodate the whole of his force. The Yorkists must have spent a miserable Christmas, miles from home and loved ones and short on supplies. York depleted his already small force by sending out foraging parties but it is unlikely that these would have alleviated his supply problems very much. The Lancastrians had the numbers to control the surrounding area and were close enough to exert pressure on the Yorkists and hinder their attempts to forage. The Yorkist situation was bad and continuing to deteriorate until, on 30 December 1460, the Lancastrian army appeared in the direction of Wakefield. Richard, Duke of York, gathered his forces and advanced from the high ground around the castle to meet his foes.

Longbow and billhook

The troops that fought for both sides at the battles of Wakefield and Towton were organised, recruited and equipped in a similar fashion. At times during the Wars of the Roses the two sides employed foreign mercenaries – Scots, French, Irish and Burgundians to name but a few – but the two battles fought in Yorkshire during the winter of 1460/61 were almost exclusively fought by Englishmen. This was bloody civil war.

The three main constituents of a Wars of the Roses army were the men-at-arms, bowmen and billmen and each contingent would have a varying number of each type, depending on the importance of their commander. The Wars of the Roses were fought at the end of the feudal period and the armies were still recruited in a similar way to a Saxon army 500 years earlier. Each man owed his allegiance to his lord right along the line until the king was reached, who, in theory, was owed allegiance by all his subjects. The peasant in the field owed his allegiance to the local squire and part of this debt was military service. The local squire, often a knight, had to provide a number of men, often including himself, to the noble who owned the area. In turn the noble had to provide troops for one of the great magnates of the land, the dukes and earls. Obviously, the more land a noble owned the larger his contingent would be and great nobles, such as the Earl of Warwick, could provide thousands of men if the situation required it.

At the time of the Wars of the Roses, England had a surfeit of experienced soldiers, veterans who had returned from the wars in France, and many of these were recruited

Men-at-arms prepare for battle. Although men-at-arms rode to battle they usually fought on foot (John Wilson).

Billmen march towards the battlefield (John Wilson).

into nobles' households. These professional soldiers would have formed a large proportion and the experienced core of each lordly contingent. Other troops could be raised by commissions of array, a charter given to an individual to raise troops within a particular geographic area and large numbers of troops could be raised in this fashion. Interestingly, King Charles I issued commissions of array to some of his nobles 200 years later, at the start of the English Civil Wars.

As has already been mentioned, each contingent was made up of three types of troop. The first was the men-at-arms. These were the armoured knights, equipped from head to foot in steel plate armour, the medieval equivalent of a tank! The knights and lords would be counted among their numbers, but many of them would have been professional soldiers who had attained enough wealth or rank to equip themselves with full plate armour and a horse. They used a variety of weapons – swords, poleaxes, war hammers or maces, depending on the individual's preference, and, if mounted, would charge with the lance.

The men-at-arms were supported by billmen and bowmen. The billman was equipped with a variation on a traditional farming implement, the bill hook. The bill was equipped with a chopping blade, similar to an axe, a point and a hook. It could be used as an axe, a spear, to hook a mounted opponent and pull him from his horse, or any combination. In the right hands it could be a deadly weapon and it should be borne in mind that most agricultural workers had been using a similar implement for their day-to-day work for most of their adult lives. The bowmen were armed with the deadly English longbow of Crècy and Agincourt fame. Many of them had been shooting bows from childhood, using progressively larger and heavier bows as they grew and developed. The longbow was no longer the battle winner it had been as developments in armour had rendered the men-at-arms nigh on impervious to the longbow except at close range. It could still cause carnage among the lesser armoured troops. Armour among the bill and bowmen would have varied greatly, with padded jackets and mail being predominant, along with bits and pieces of plate armour that the individual had collected along the way. A variety of helmets were worn, with the sallet being particularly fashionable. The lords' household troops would usually have been much better equipped than those raised by commission of array, who would have turned up with whatever equipment they had available, including the helmet that grandfather took off of a dead Frenchman at Agincourt fifty years ago!

It is obvious from the descriptions above that a major problem could occur on the battlefield, that of identifying who was on which side. To alleviate this problem both sides issued their troops with livery jackets. These were jackets, or tabards, in a lord's colour and with his armorial device on it. For example, the Earl of Warwick's men wore a red jacket with a white ragged staff, sometimes known as a crooked billet, while his uncle, Lord Fauconberg, used a blue and white halved jacket with a white fish hook. A derivative of the livery jacket is still used today for much the same reason – jockeys in horse races wear the owner's colours to allow the spectators to recognise them. The wearing of livery jackets did not always prevent confusion from occurring, particularly in foggy weather as happened at the Battle of Barnet in 1471.

A Wars of the Roses army was usually formed into three 'battles' – vaward, mainward and rearward. The vaward and rearward are sometimes referred to as vanguard and rearguard. Often the three battles were of a similar size as they would form the right, left and centre of the army when it deployed for battle. The three battles were also used when an army was on the march, with the vanguard leading the way, the main following them and the rearguard bringing up the rear, sometimes with several days between each battle.

Although a sizeable proportion of an English army would have been mounted, it would usually dismount to fight. Mounted charges are recorded at a couple of Wars of the Roses battles – Blore Heath and Bosworth – but the two battles we are interested in were bloody dismounted slogging matches. That said, at both battles horses would have been kept close to the fighting line and the victorious side would have mounted as many men as possible to take part in the pursuit after their opponents had broken and fled. The defeated men-at-arms would have also tried to reach their horses as riding gave them a much better chance of escape from the battlefield.

Some, but not all, battles began with an exchange of bow fire. The archers would step out in front of the fighting line and let fly. As both sides had archers the effect of the archery was nullified, with both sides incurring casualties. On occasion some external advantage made one side's shooting more effective than the other's and this was certainly the case at Towton where the Yorkists had the wind in their favour and were able to pound the Lancastrian line while the Lancastrian arrows dropped short. Because of advances in armour, bow fire was rarely decisive and at some stage one, or both, armies would advance to contact. At Towton this was the Lancastrian army which, unable to reply to the Yorkist archery, had no option but to advance.

The mêlée must have been a horrific experience. Most men were wearing helmets with very limited visibility, often merely a slit, with little if any peripheral vision. The noise would have been tremendous, with weapons clashing, men shouting and the cries of the wounded and dying. The weapons of the time could cause terrible wounds and even if a blow did not penetrate a man's armour, the shock wave could break his bones and cause internal injuries. As the lines closed the battle would begin to look like a gigantic rugby scrum and often the sides would be so closely packed together that the soldiers were unable to use their weapons effectively. As men in the front ranks fell they would be replaced by men from the rear and if the fighting was stationary a barrier of bodies would begin to build between the two lines, with men having to clamber over their dead and wounded comrades to get at the enemy.

The mêlée could go on for some time but eventually one side would begin to gain the ascendancy. At first the less stalwart of their adversaries would leave the line and head towards the rear and, hopefully, safety. Initially this would be a trickle but as the winning side pushed its advantage it would become a flood and then a rout with men fleeing in whatever direction they thought would take them to safety. Anyone who had a horse, both router and pursuer, would try to mount and the chase was on. This was the time of battle when most of the casualties occurred. Often the pursuit would go on until night fell and the bodies of the routers could stretch for miles. Although quarter was often given to common soldiers, a captured noble could expect short shrift from his captors and many battles, including Wakefield and Towton, were followed by executions.

The Battle of Wakefield

The Battle of Wakefield is one of the most enigmatic battles of the Wars of the Roses. The contemporary and near contemporary accounts are confusing and contradictory and this has been perpetuated by modern authors. The main stumbling block to most accounts is an attempt to explain why Richard, Duke of York, left the relative safety of his castle and marched down the hill towards Wakefield, into the clutches of a much larger army. A number of theories have been put forward including ambushes and treachery, or a combination of both – all have some basis in the contemporary accounts but little basis in reality. Let us consider some of these theories.

One of the most frequently cited theories is that of an ambush. The Lancastrians showed York only a small portion of their force, small enough for the duke to believe he could defeat them. Once the Yorkists had descended from the castle one or more ambush parties attacked the Yorkists, surrounding them and cutting them off from the castle. One of the ambush parties is often reported as coming from behind the castle having hidden in an area of woods during the night. Let us look at the practicalities of setting up this ambush. Firstly, the Lancastrian army would have had to leave Pontefract on the 29th to allow their ambush parties to get into position – no problem with that. Secondly, the ambush parties would have had to approach the castle and even move around to its rear without being detected. Several thousand men in steel armour and carrying metal weapons will inevitably make a noise as they move – it is still seen as a sign of well-trained and disciplined professional soldiers if they can move silently at night. Was the Yorkist army's security so lax that they didn't notice the Lancastrians closing to within a few hundred yards? It is pushing the boundaries of belief that an experienced campaigner like the Duke of York would have not taken adequate precautions. It is sometimes put forward that the two armies had come to an agreement not to fight during the Christmas period. This seems unlikely as the Lancastrian commanders were the sons of the lords killed or executed at the first Battle of St Albans and they wanted revenge. Their scouts would have apprised them of the size of York's army and they knew that they outnumbered it considerably. Why would they have come to an agreement with York when they had him exactly where they wanted him? If the ambushers had managed to get past the castle unseen, where would they have hidden? The only wooded area near the castle was a small deer park which was only large enough to keep thirty deer in. The castle had an unobstructed view all around and was surrounded by open ground and fields except for the deer park, which was too small and too close to the castle to be used as a hiding place. It seems highly unlikely that such an ambush took place.

Treachery is also used as a reason for York leaving the safety of Sandal Castle. Contemporary and near contemporary accounts talk of Lord Neville, brother of the Earl of Westmorland, requesting from the Duke a commission to raise troops for his cause. The sequence of events is quite clear in one of the accounts and states that Neville visited York after his arrival at Sandal Castle. This gives Neville no more than nine days to raise his troops and march them to Wakefield, if the earliest possible date for York's arrival is used. If York did not arrive at Sandal until the 24th, the date most often used by historians, Neville would have had only five days. On the day of the battle it is said that York saw a large body of men, 8,000 is the figure given, approaching the battlefield and flying friendly colours. It was this welcome reinforcement that prompted York to attack the Lancastrian army. One question that immediately springs to mind is how did Neville raise so many men in such a short time? The Lancastrian army contained the contingents of a number of very powerful nobles and had taken months to gather. It numbered 15,000 men, if the chronicles are to be believed, and Neville had managed to raise a force half as large in a matter of days. This seems very unlikely and smacks of the chroniclers using this as an excuse for York's subsequent defeat.

So why did the Duke of York lead his army from the safety of the castle into the clutches of the Lancastrian army? I will answer this with another question – did he

Wakefield. Looking towards the remains of the keep at Sandal Castle. It was from the keep that the Duke of York would have spotted the approach of the Lancastrian army.

have a choice? Sandal is a very small castle. During the First Civil War it was defended by a garrison of 100 men who were living in cramped conditions so would the Duke have been able to fit his army of several thousand men into the same area? It should also be taken into account that the castle had few supplies available and York had to send foraging parties out to try to keep his army supplied. With a small force he may have been able to stand a siege until reinforcements arrived but in December 1460 this was not an option. Many of his men would have been camped around the castle and others were quartered in Wakefield and the surrounding villages. Once the Lancastrian army hove into view he had three options: stand a siege, retreat or fight. Let us consider these options.

Standing a siege was not a viable option. York could not fit all his army into the castle and would have had to lock a large portion of his army outside the castle's gates, leaving them to the mercy of the Lancastrians. The small portion of his army that could have fitted in the castle would have soon been starved out, well before any reinforcements could have reached Yorkshire – the Earl of March was still on the Welsh border and Warwick was in London. Could York have fallen back towards the South? It is possible that the part of the Yorkist army around the castle could have begun a withdrawal but, once again, that would have meant leaving the men quartered in Wakefield. How far the retreat could have continued is debatable. York was heavily outnumbered and was falling back in the face of an enemy who was within a mile of him. It would not have taken long for the Lancastrians to bring him to battle.

One other point that is worth noting is that the road from Pontefract is on the far side of the ridge between Wakefield and Sandal Castle and is hidden from view for much of its length. One possible scenario is that York saw the Lancastrian vanguard arrive and deploy on the ridgeline between the castle and Wakefield. This force was of a similar size to his army and he decided to attack them. Unbeknown to the Duke, the rest of the Lancastrian army was still marching along the road and would have arrived close to or on his right flank, forcing the Yorkists towards the river and cutting them off from the castle. It is this scenario that I find most plausible.

The next question that needs addressing is the size of the two armies involved. Contemporary chronicles give a figure of 5,000 for the Yorkists and 15,000 for their opponents. Both of these numbers seem high. If the story of Lord Neville arriving with another 8,000 men is to be believed then this gives an implausibly high figure of 23,000 for the Lancastrian force. Chronicles of the time often give vastly inflated numbers for participants in battles, 100,000 men at Towton for example. It is difficult to calculate exact figures. It is probable that York, who had to despatch foraging

Wakefield. Looking from the keep of Sandal Castle towards Pontefract. Ferrybridge power station can be seen on the centre horizon. The Lancastrian army's approach was hidden by the nearest ridgeline.

Wakefield. Looking from the keep of Sandal Castle towards Wakefield. The battle was fought on the low ground in the middle distance. As can be seen from the photograph, most of the battlefield is now built over.

parties, had only 2,000–3,000 men remaining with him. The Lancastrian army heavily outnumbered him, so a conservative estimate of 10,000 may be close.

Standing at the castle today it is difficult to envisage how the battlefield looked at the time. As with many of our historical battlefields, Wakefield has been heavily built over, and little open ground remains. Initially the two armies deployed on two ridges, the Yorkists on the high ground where Sandal Castle lies and the Lancastrians on the ridge between Sandal and Wakefield. Although the ground in between would not have been built on, as it now is, it should not be thought that it was all open land. There is evidence of the land between the ridges being cultivated and broken up with small enclosures and remains of medieval ploughing can still be seen in the park opposite Manygates School.

It is likely that the Duke of York had prior knowledge of the approach of at least part of the Lancastrian army, although he would not have known how large a force was on its way. One of the tasks of an army's scouts, as well as finding the enemy, was to prevent the enemy from gaining information about their army. As the Lancastrian scouts heavily outnumbered York's it would have been a simple task for them to mask the size of the force approaching Wakefield. York would have had chance to gather his

Wakefield. Information board at Sandal Castle.

Wakefield. The monument to the Duke of York in the grounds of Manygates School, close to where the Duke lost his life.

Wakefield. A detail from the monument in the grounds of Manygates School. The figure is the Duke of York. At some point in the recent past a Lancastrian supporter decided to remove the Duke's head, much as his predecessors had done in 1460!

forces together on the castle ridge and would have seen the Lancastrian vanguard occupy the opposite high ground and deploy for battle. York then ordered his men to advance and would have quickly been in contact with the enemy.

Few details of the fighting at Wakefield are given in the contemporary chronicles and the battle seems to have been over fairly quickly. The Yorkists may have pushed their opponents back initially but as more Lancastrians arrived on the field, close to the Yorkist flank, the tide of battle turned and York's army was routed. The Duke fell in the battle. Tradition has it that he fell fighting with his back to a stand of willow trees which stood just below Manygates School. At least one contemporary account, *Whethamstede's Register*, speaks of the Duke being captured and executed on the field:

> *They stood him on a little anthill and placed on his head, as if a crown, a vile garland made of reeds, just as the Jews did to the Lord, and bent the knee to him, saying in jest, 'Hail King, without rule. Hail King, without ancestry. Hail leader and prince, with almost no subjects or possessions'. And having said this and various other shameful and dishonourable things to him, at last they cut off his head.*

Whether or not York died fighting or was executed, by the end of the day he had been beheaded, along with a number of his supporters.

One of the most famous scenes from Shakespeare's *Henry VI* is the murder of York's second son, the Earl of Rutland. Shakespeare, and many subsequent historians, tell of the Earl, a mere boy, being murdered by Lord Clifford in revenge for his father's

Wakefield. The chapel on the bridge. This is reputed to be the site where Lord Clifford murdered the Duke of York's son, Edmund, Earl of Rutland, in revenge for York having executed his father after the first battle of St Albans.

death at St Albans on a bridge with a chantry chapel. The bridge and chapel still exist to the right of the modern main road bridge into Wakefield. In fact Rutland was seventeen years old and fully armed and armoured. His tutor Sir Robert Aspall, described by Edward Hall as 'a priest', was actually his tutor in arms and both had taken an active part in the fighting and were captured in the rout. Although it is generally accepted that he was killed by Lord Clifford on the bridge, local tradition has it that he was captured above the bridge where an old building called 'Six Chimneys' stood until well into the last century. As the Earl and Aspall fled the field they tried to take shelter in a house, possibly the Six Chimneys, but had the door slammed in their faces. The pair were then captured, returned to the bridge and the Earl killed by Clifford; known afterwards as 'Butcher' Clifford.

Warwick's father, the Earl of Salisbury, survived the battle but was captured and sent to Pontefract Castle. Subsequent events are summed up in the *English Chronicle*:

> *The Earl of Salisbury was taken alive, and led by the said Duke of Somerset to the castle of Pomfret* [Pontefract], *and for a great sum of money that he should have paid*

had grant of his life. But the common people of the country, which loved him not, took
him out of the castle by violence and smote off his head.

There is some evidence that the Duke of Exeter's illegitimate son, the Bastard of Exeter as he is known in contemporary chronicles, was involved in Salisbury's demise.

By the end of the penultimate day in 1460 the Yorkist army in Yorkshire was shattered. York, Rutland, Salisbury and a number of York's supporters were beheaded and when the Lancastrian army returned to York to await the arrival of the Queen from Scotland, their heads were prominently displayed on the city's gates. Tradition has it that the heads of York, Rutland and Salisbury were displayed on Micklegate Bar, the main entrance into the city of York from the south.

The march to Towton

While York marched for Yorkshire his eldest son, Edward, the Earl of March, was despatched to the Welsh borders with an army. His objective was to destroy the Welsh Lancastrian forces that were gathering in preparation to join with the queen in Yorkshire. How quickly Edward heard of his father's demise is difficult to gauge but he decided to continue against his opponents in Wales, evidence of the single-minded determination he was to show throughout the campaign. He was to be rewarded on 2 February 1461 when he brought them to battle and defeated them at Mortimer's Cross near Hereford.

Early in January Queen Margaret had returned from Scotland with a sizeable force of Scots mercenaries. The Lancastrian commanders decided that the time was ripe to march south and recapture the capital and free the king. Once their army had crossed the Trent, the traditional border between the north and south, they unleashed a campaign of looting and pillaging, cutting a swathe thirty miles wide either side of the Great North Road. The Earl of Warwick, who was still in London, gathered what forces he could to oppose them. During the second week in February the Earl marched his force from London to St Albans, the scene of the Yorkists' first victory. Warwick deployed his army on a wide frontage as he was unsure from which direction the Lancastrians would approach. His left flank was stationed in St Albans itself while the remainder stretched from the town across the common land to the north. On 17 February 1461 the Lancastrian army attacked. First they turned Warwick's left flank and then rolled up the rest of his army. Andrew Trollope, who had changed sides to support the king at Ludford Bridge, played a prominent part in the battle and may have even been the tactical mind behind the Lancastrian victory. He was knighted on the field by the Prince of Wales. During the confusion of the Yorkist defeat King Henry, who had accompanied Warwick's army, was left behind and freed to be reunited with his wife and son.

Rather than retreating to London, Warwick decided to march his surviving force towards the Cotswolds, to join Edward's victorious army which was marching back towards London. In the meantime the Lancastrian army continued towards London which was now virtually defenceless. Fully aware of the looting and pillaging the Lancastrians had carried out on the way south the citizens of London refused the queen, Prince of Wales and the remainder of the Lancastrian nobles and commons entry to the city. Many of the queen's troops had returned to their homes, replete with the fruits of their pillaging and the victory at St Albans. With the gates of London closed firmly against them and a Yorkist army approaching from the west, a decision was taken to return to the heartland of Lancastrian support in the north.

On 26 February Edward, now Duke of York, and Warwick led their men into the capital, much to the joy of the Londoners. Events now began to move rapidly. Shortly after Edward's arrival a gathering of Londoners at St John's Field declared that he should be king and this was passed on to him by some of his supporters. On 4 March 1461 Edward was proclaimed King Edward IV in Westminster Abbey, although his coronation would have to wait until the Lancastrians in the north had been dealt with.

It was known that the Lancastrians had a large force in Yorkshire and it was now time for the Yorkist nobles to gather their men in the South and Midlands. Warwick left for the Midlands on 7 March and, at about the same time, the Duke of Norfolk left for his estates in East Anglia. On the 11th, Lord Fauconberg, Warwick's uncle, left London with the vanguard of the army, to be followed by King Edward and the main body on the 13th. By the 16th, the king had arrived at St Albans before moving on to Cambridge and Nottingham, which was reached on the 22nd. It is likely that this was where Warwick rendezvoused with Edward before they ventured across the Trent into the wolf's lair. During his recruiting drive in the Midlands Warwick's men had captured the Bastard of Exeter who, as has already been mentioned, was suspected of having caused Warwick's father's execution at Pontefract. In the climate of revenge and blood feud he had little chance of survival and Warwick had him beheaded.

The Yorkist army crossed the Trent and headed for Pontefract. It is difficult to ascertain whether Edward thought that the Lancastrian army was gathering at Pontefract, as it had before defeating his father, but he seems to have been intent on bringing them to battle as soon as possible. Edward arrived at Pontefract, which had been occupied without opposition by the vanguard, on the 27th. The rearguard was still some distance behind the rest of the army. The Duke of Norfolk was not a well man and this seems to have slowed the march of his East Anglian forces. The plan was for the van and main battles to cross the river on the 28th and push on towards the Lancastrians, now camped on the high ground between Saxton and Towton. Norfolk and his men would follow on at best speed.

The fight at Ferrybridge

During the 27th Edward despatched a small force commanded by Lord Fitzwalter to seize the bridge at Ferrybridge, the closest crossing of the River Aire and on the direct route to York. It is debateable whether or not the bridge was useable when Fitzwalter arrived but by the end of the 27th the bridge could be crossed. It is also not known whether the crossing was held by the Lancastrians when Fitzwalter arrived. A lack of any evidence of his having to fight for the bridge suggests that the Lancastrians had broken the bridge at some time before Fitzwalter's arrival and had withdrawn to the main army's position. Subsequent events show that the Lancastrian commanders were aware of Fitzwalter's arrival at Ferrybridge and probably had scouts watching the main crossings of the Aire at Ferrybridge and Castleford.

During the early hours of the 28th Lord Clifford led a body of 500 men, the 'Flower of Craven', to attack the Yorkist troops at Ferrybridge. Lord Fitzwalter was awoken by a commotion and thinking that a fight had broken out among his men descended into the street armed with a poleaxe to quieten them, as is reported by Edward Hall:

> *The Lord Fitzwalter hearing the noise suddenly rose from his bed and unarmed* [unarmoured], *with a poleaxe in his hand, thinking that it was an affray amongst his men, came down to appease the same, but before he could say a word, or knew what the matter was, he was slain, and with him the Bastard of Salisbury, brother to the Earl of Warwick, a valiant young gentleman, and of great audacity.*

Fitzwalter was cut down, along with many of his men, while the remainder fled back towards the main army at Pontefract Castle. The arrival of the remnants of Fitzwalter's force, crying that the enemy were coming, could have been a decisive moment in the

Ferrybridge. The site of the original bridge at Ferrybridge. In 1461 a much narrower wooden bridge was defended by Lord Clifford until he was outflanked and forced to retreat.

campaign, with a general rout setting in among the Yorkist troops. The Yorkist commanders rose to the occasion and Edward rode among his men steadying their nerve, while Warwick rode to the nervous troops, dismounted and then killed his horse, showing them that he would stand with them. This was a very theatrical act and, if looked at in a more cynical light, could have been an attempt to prove his courage after fleeing the field at the second Battle of St Albans. The Yorkist army steadied and prepared to move on Ferrybridge and recapture the bridge; it is reported that Edward gave a rousing speech to his men before they advanced.

Clifford had ordered his men to break the bridge again and then prepared to defend the north bank and delay the Yorkists crossing the river. A lengthy fight ensued with the Yorkists attempting to rebuild the bridge and force a crossing, while Clifford's men tried to prevent them doing so. Casualties were heavy on both sides – one account talks of 3,000 casualties – and it is reported that many men drowned in the freezing waters of the Aire. While the main Yorkist army tried to recapture the bridge, Edward had despatched a force of mounted archers under Lord Fauconberg to cross the river at Castleford and then outflank Clifford's men. It is difficult to ascertain at what point Edward despatched this force: either as the army advanced from Pontefract or due to its inability to seize the crossing. Fauconberg's flank march was completely successful, although Clifford's scouts reported the approaching Yorkist force and the Lancastrians were able to withdraw along the road towards Sherburn-in-Elmet and Tadcaster. Fauconberg's men set off in pursuit while the remainder of the Yorkist army began to cross the bridge.

Clifford continued his withdrawal through Sherburn-in-Elmet and Barkston Ash, hotly pursued by Fauconberg's mounted archers who forced the Lancastrians to turn and fight at Dintingdale, which lies close to the first turn off for Saxton, north of Barkston Ash. Here Clifford and his men were virtually annihilated. At some stage in the fight Clifford removed his gorget, an armoured collar which protected the neck, due to either heat or pain according to Edward Hall, a near contemporary writer. He was subsequently struck in the throat by an arrow, and Hall states that it may have been a headless arrow. This would have caused a devastating wound, akin to a modern hollow-point bullet, and the shock may have killed Clifford almost instantly.

It is difficult to understand why Clifford, who was now close to the Lancastrian encampment, was not supported. One reason that has been put forward by historians is jealousy. Comparisons had been made between Clifford and the Earl of Northumberland, another of the Lancastrian senior commanders, and the two vied with each other to show who was the better, braver, warrior. It is one reason given for Clifford's attack on Ferrybridge and may have been the cause for Northumberland not supporting Clifford. There could also be a much more mundane reason for Clifford's demise – the weather. It is known that the weather during the few days around the Battle of Towton was very cold and on the day of the battle heavy snow fell, blowing into the faces of the Lancastrians and blinding them. The Lancastrian army would have been camped on the northern end of the battlefield, close to Towton, hence the

Yorkists being able to deploy on the ridge above Saxton. They may have even been camped around the village and to the north of it. It is unlikely that the Lancastrians could see the fight at Dintingdale from the main encampment, but it is very likely that Lancastrian scouts were positioned on the ridge above Saxton with a clear view of the area to the south. Was their visibility so reduced by snow that they could not see the fight? One final possibility is that the Lancastrians did attempt to aid Clifford but this aid did not arrive before he had been overwhelmed. It would have taken some time for the Lancastrian scouts to reach the camp, a relief force be formed and then marched down to Dintingdale. All these possibilities are merely conjecture and we do not know why Clifford received no succour from the Lancastrian army. What we do know is that Clifford and most of his men died at Dintingdale.

As the fight at Dintingdale followed its course, the Yorkist army continued to march towards Tadcaster. It is possible that part of the army had crossed the Aire at Castleford, in the tracks of Fauconberg's force. By nightfall on the 28th the Yorkist army had begun to bivouac on the low ground around Saxton village, and their encampment would have stretched from the modern A162, through Saxton village, across to Led Church and the present day Crooked Billet public house. With the delay caused by Clifford at Ferrybridge it is very likely that many of the men did not arrive at their encampments until well after dark. It is easy to imagine that the scene in the Yorkist camp was similar to that of the English army on the night before Agincourt in Shakespeare's *Henry V*, with small groups of men huddled around fires, cold, tired and hungry – the Yorkist army had out-run its baggage train. Only the van and main battles had arrived and Norfolk's rearguard was still south of the Aire, almost a day's march behind the rest of the army. It is almost certain that Edward sent messengers galloping back down the road, urging Norfolk to push his men forward to arrive at the battlefield as early as possible on Palm Sunday, for there was little doubt that a battle would take place.

The Battle of Towton

With sunrise on Palm Sunday, 29 March 1461, the two armies began to form up. The Lancastrian army would have deployed in the traditional three battles. The Duke of Somerset and the Earl of Northumberland commanded two of the battles, but who commanded the third is not known, although it would have been one of the senior Lancastrian nobles. Some historians have shown the Lancastrians in only two battles and others have shown the Lancastrian battles formed up one behind the other, rather than side by side. I can find little evidence to support either of these alternatives and suggest that the Lancastrian army formed with its three battles in line. Due to the size of the Lancastrian force, which will be discussed shortly, and the width of the battle-field, it is likely that the battles formed up in a deeper formation than was usual.

The Yorkists, on the other hand, probably formed in only two battles as Norfolk and the rearguard were still some distance south of the battlefield and were marching

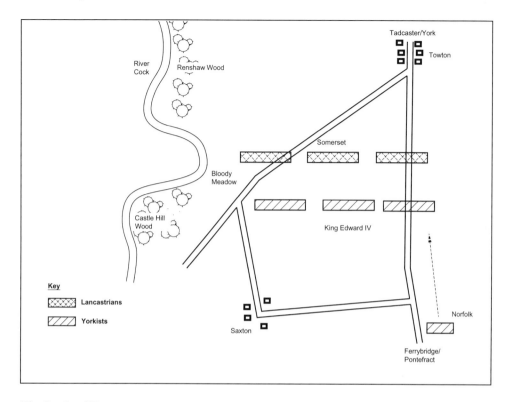

The Battle of Towton

north at their best speed. The two battles were commanded by Edward and Warwick. The Yorkists, with fewer men than the Lancastrians, would have formed a thinner line to cover the same frontage as their opponents.

The battle was fought on the high ground between the villages of Saxton and Towton. Immediately to the north of Saxton a ridge runs from west to east. At the western end of the ridge is a steep drop into the valley of the River Cock, or Cock Beck as it is known locally. The eastern edge of the ridge, close to the Sherburn-in-Elmet to Tadcaster road, the modern A162, has a much gentler slope. Standing on the ridge looking towards the east it is difficult to understand why the frontage of the battlefield was so narrow and the armies did not extend far beyond the road, but the ground to the east of the road was very boggy and unsuitable for deploying troops.

Looking north from the ridgeline above Saxton, the ground drops into a shallow valley before rising onto another ridge. The ground then falls gently towards the north until it reaches Towton. Although the valley between the two ridges is shallow and its slopes gentle for most of its length, its western end forms a steep re-entrant which descends into the valley of the Cock Beck and this re-entrant is overlooked by the only other terrain feature on the battlefield, Castle Hill Wood. The wood is at the western end of the ridge above Saxton and still exists today, although it does not extend as far along the ridge as it did at the time of the battle. The battlefield at Towton is one of the few Yorkshire battlefields that gives a good idea of what it looked like at the time of the battle. There are still no buildings on the battlefield itself, unlike some of our battlefields which have disappeared under brick-built estates or concrete and steel industrial complexes. The battlefield at the time was open, as it is now, with few obstructions to the deployment and operation of the armies which is probably the reason that the Lancastrians had encamped there and waited for the Yorkists to come to them.

Chroniclers at the time gave a figure of up to 100,000 men on the battlefield. In the nineteenth century some historians believed this figure and gave totals of 60,000 Lancastrians and 40,000 Yorkists, hence the battle has been acknowledged as the largest battle on British soil. More recently it has been recognised that these figures are vastly inflated and they have been revised accordingly. Andrew Boardman, in his book on the battle published in 1994 (see Further Reading section), discussed the strengths of the rival armies at length and came to a much more realistic figure of 25,000 Lancastrians and 20,000 Yorkists, with a further 5,000 Yorkists approaching the battlefield with the Duke of Norfolk's contingent. Even these revised figures could be a little high. The truth is we just do not know exactly how many men fought at the battle, although Boardman's figures are probably not too far out. What we do know is that Towton was an exceptionally large battle and was certainly the largest battle of the Wars of the Roses, if not the largest battle fought on these islands.

The Lancastrian army deployed along the northern ridge on which now stands Lord Dacre's Cross, a monument to the battle on the site where the Lancastrian Lord Dacre met his end. There is evidence that the Yorkists formed up to the north of Saxton but out of sight of the Lancastrians. Edward Hall tells us that when the Yorkists advanced onto the ridge above Saxton the two armies came into sight and 'when each party perceived each other they made a great shout'. He also adds that at the same time it began to snow. As the two armies stood on opposite ridges a few hundred yards apart, the priests gave their final blessing and the commanders said a few words to bolster their men's courage. At Wakefield the Lancastrian commanders were seeking revenge for the deaths of their fathers; at Towton the boot was on the other foot. Both Edward and Warwick had lost their fathers at Wakefield and their heads still adorned Micklegate Bar at York. Across the shallow valley were the men responsible. Edward declared the battle a no quarter battle and no mercy would be given by either side.

It is difficult to gauge how long the two armies stood opposite one another, yelling their defiance across the gap separating them. According to Edward Hall the two armies were deployed by nine o'clock and it was just after this time that the fighting commenced. Edward Hall reports that:

The Lord Fauconberg, which led the forward of King Edward's battle being a man of great policy and of much experience in martial feats caused every archer under his

Towton. Panoramic view of the Lancastrian lines taken from the Yorkist lines.

Towton. Panoramic view of the Yorkist lines taken from the Lancastrian lines at Dacre's Cross.

standard to shoot one flight and then made them stand still. The northern men [Lancastrians], *feeling the shoot, but by reason of the snow, not perfectly viewing the distance between them and their enemies like hardy men shot their sheaf arrows as fast as they might, but all their shot was lost and their labour in vain for they came not near the southern men by 40 tailors yards. When their shot was almost spent the Lord Fauconberg marched forward with his archers, who not only shot their own sheaves, but also gathered the arrows of their enemies and let a great part of them fly against their own masters, and another part they let stand in the ground which sore annoyed the legs of the owners when battle was joined.*

Fauconberg, Warwick's uncle and a wily old soldier, ordered the archers to step forward and shoot at the Lancastrians. Seeing the enemy shoot, the Lancastrian archers poured volley after volley towards their opponents but the wind, blowing from the south and directly into their faces reduced the range of their arrows which dropped well short of the Yorkist lines. Unable to see what was happening because of the heavy snow blowing directly into their faces, the Lancastrian archers continued to shoot until they had run out of arrows. As the Lancastrian fire slackened, Fauconberg ordered his men forward until they were well within range of the enemy and ordered them to commence a deadly rain of arrows into the enemy ranks. To add insult to injury, when the Yorkists were getting low on arrows they picked enemy arrows out of the ground and fired them back at their original owners.

Lancastrian casualties began to mount and they could not repay their enemy in kind. It is extremely difficult for an army to stand under unanswered fire and hold its ground. There are only two options – advance or retreat. The Lancastrian commanders chose the former and the whole Lancastrian army began to descend into the vale between the two ridges and then advance up the southerly ridge to come to grips with the enemy. All along the line men came into contact and the main event of the battle was on.

Having forced the Lancastrians to advance, the Yorkists were initially in an advantageous position. Their enemy had to advance up a slope towards them and the ground over which they had to advance was encumbered by arrows and made slippery by the falling snow. Few details have come down to us of the actual fighting. What we are told is that the fighting was savage and that it went on for some considerable time – up to ten hours in one account. As men fell dead or wounded, a pile of bodies began to form an obstruction between the two armies. Men would have found it difficult to keep their feet as the grounds became more and more slippery with snow and blood, and there was the ever present danger of tripping over a body lying on the ground. The noise and smell must have been horrific and most soldiers' visibility would have been very restricted, with the vision slits in their helmet giving only a narrow field of view to the front and little, if any, peripheral vision. The courage of the men, of both sides, in the fighting line is beyond doubt. The commanders would have rallied and cajoled their men into further efforts. Several accounts talk of King Edward's prodigious feats on the day and he seems to have appeared wherever the line was threatened most and often forced his way into the front line to block an enemy advance. The accounts that mention Edward's performance were pro-Yorkist so much of what was written may be pure propaganda, but Edward was a tall powerful man and had a reputation as a fighting man and commander, so there may also be a large grain of truth.

Slowly, but surely, Lancastrian weight of numbers began to tell and the Yorkists were gradually pushed back towards the edge of the ridge. At some stage in the fighting an element of the Yorkist left flank may have collapsed. This is often put down to an ambush or flank attack by a body of Lancastrian cavalry in the area of Castle Hill Wood. There is little evidence to support this ambush theory and the collapse of the extreme left flank of the Yorkist line, if indeed this did happen, could be attributed to a number of reasons: the death of a local commander or a body of newly raised troops breaking for example. If the Yorkist left flank did collapse, it was a localised event and had little effect on the outcome of the battle.

By mid-afternoon the Yorkists were in an unenviable position. The Lancastrians had pushed the Yorkists back almost to the edge of the ridge and if they were pushed onto the downward slope the Lancastrians, with the advantage of numbers and ground, would almost certainly prevail. King Edward's relief must have been great when he saw the head of Norfolk's column approaching the battlefield along the road from Sherburn. Polydore Vergil, writing some fifty years after the event, reported:

> *Thus did the fight continue more than ten hours in equal balance, when at last King Henry espied the forces of his foes increase, and his own somewhat yield, whom when by new exhortation he had compelled to press on more earnestly, he with a few horsemen removing a little out of that place, expected the event of the fight, but behold, suddenly his gave the back, which when he saw this he fled also.*

Vergil was probably in error when he mentions King Henry, who it is generally accepted was not on the field but at York. The Duke of Somerset commanded the Lancastrian army on Palm Sunday. It is also difficult to believe that a battle of such savagery could last for ten hours. What Vergil does convey admirably is the suddenness of the Lancastrian flight.

As Norfolk's men arrived on the field they initially bolstered the Yorkist right flank. As more men arrived they began to outflank the Lancastrian left which began to be forced back at an angle to the right and centre. Men in the front ranks would have had little idea of what was going on other than they were losing ground but men out of the fighting line would have been able to see what was happening and many of them began to head towards the rear and safety. As more men began to pull out of the line the Yorkists would have been able to drive the Lancastrian left back quicker and quicker until it broke and fled back towards Towton. The Yorkists would have then been able to roll up the enemy's centre and right wing which would have been unable to flee to the north and would have had to head towards the Cock Valley. In short order the

Towton. A view into the Bloody Meadow. When the Lancastrian army routed many men tried to flee down the steep slopes into the valley of the Cock Beck. Some accounts have stated that the river was in flood at the time and many Lancastrians drowned trying to cross it.

Lancastrian army was fleeing in an arc from north towards Towton to west, and it is easy to imagine, standing on the ridgeline, the fields below you covered in fleeing men, hotly pursued by their victorious enemy cutting them down as they ran.

In August 1996 a burial pit in the grounds of Towton Hall was excavated and the skeletal remains illustrated the savagery of the Yorkist pursuit. Although it cannot be proven for definite, it is likely that the bodies recovered were those of Lancastrian soldiers cut down in the pursuit or captured and executed. Many of the soldiers had been killed by blows to the top or back of the head and some had numerous wounds to the head. Several had diamond-shaped holes in the lower rear of the skull which initially were thought to be arrow wounds. Further analysis of the shape and angle of the wounds pointed towards these men having been executed by being stabbed in the back of the head with a dagger. A number of the skulls had scratch marks on the sides which were difficult to explain until someone put forward the idea that the victorious troops had been taking trophies by cutting the ears off the dead bodies. This period is often known as the Age of Chivalry but seeing the pitiful remains of these men who died at Towton it is difficult to see anything chivalric at all!

The pursuit continued until nightfall. Thousands of Lancastrian troops were cut

Towton. A view from Dacre's Cross towards Towton village. Late on the day of the battle this ground would have been covered with routing Lancastrian troops and their Yorkist pursuers.

down in the pursuit and many more were drowned in the Cock Beck and the River Wharfe – it was said that the Cock Beck could be crossed dry shod on the Lancastrian bodies. The number given by contemporary accounts for the total casualties in the battle vary with a figure of 28,000 being generally accepted. Of these 20,000 were Lancastrians, the majority of whom had been cut down in the pursuit. Any Lancastrian nobles captured were executed.

Edward had won a great victory and cemented his claim to the throne on the field of battle. Unfortunately, many of Edward's main opponents escaped the rout and lived to fight another day. King Henry, Queen Margaret and Edward, Prince of Wales, had all remained in York and had fled north to Berwick when they received news of their army's defeat and near annihilation at Towton. The Duke of Somerset and the Earls of Northumberland, Exeter, Devon and Wiltshire all escaped the field. Devon was subsequently captured in York and executed, while Wiltshire was captured at Cockermouth and taken to Newcastle to meet his end. Edward's two most resolute enemies, Somerset and Northumberland, escaped to continue the fight.

The aftermath of Towton

With the end of the Towton campaign, fighting in Yorkshire was over and no more large actions took place within the county. Initially, fighting moved north where the remnants of the Lancastrian army, supported by Scots troops, were defeated at

Hedgeley Moor (25 April 1464) and Hexham (15 May 1464). During this period King Henry was once again captured and imprisoned in the Tower of London. Relations between Edward and Warwick worsened over the subject of the king's choice of wife, Elizabeth Woodville, and Warwick's steadily lessening influence over the king.

In 1469 Warwick began to raise forces against the king and when an army marching from the Welsh Marches to support Edward was defeated at the Battle of Edgecote (26 July 1469), the king became Warwick's prisoner. Warwick, who gained the name 'Kingmaker', now had both the Yorkist and Lancastrian kings in his power. Edward bided his time and gained the ascendancy over Warwick, raising an army and defeating a rebel force, which supported Warwick, at Empingham (12 March 1470), a battle which was given the name 'Losecote Field' because of the speed with which the rebel troops shed their livery jackets and ran away. Warwick fled to the Continent.

Warwick returned in due course, now allied to the Lancastrians and Edward, in his turn, was forced to flee the country. In early 1471 Edward returned and the next phase of the Wars of the Roses began. Edward gathered a large army and marched to Barnet where he defeated Warwick on 14 April 1471; Warwick was killed at the battle. Edward then turned west and pursued another Lancastrian army along the Severn Valley until he brought it to battle at Tewkesbury on 4 May 1471. Once again, Edward was victorious and Queen Margaret and her son were captured. Edward, the Lancastrian Prince of Wales, was executed. Edward IV's youngest brother, Richard, Duke of Gloucester, had played a prominent part in both of his brother's victories and would go on to be one of the most controversial figures in English history.

King Henry was still a prisoner in the Tower but survived less than three weeks after the Battle of Tewkesbury, dying on 21 May 1471. Henry's death is suspicious, to say the least, following as quickly as it did the execution of his son, and Richard of Gloucester is often implicated.

Edward's victory at Tewkesbury was followed by twelve years of peace, although Edward descended into a life of drunken debauchery. When Edward passed away on 9 April 1483 he should have been succeeded by his son, Edward V. This never happened and the succession is still a topic for heated debate to this day. The story of the Princes in the Tower has had hundreds of books written about it and their 'wicked' uncle, Richard, is one of the most vilified characters in English history. It is beyond the scope of this book to enter into the debate. All that needs to be said is that Edward was never crowned and Richard of Gloucester came to the throne as Richard III.

Although the house of Lancaster no longer had a surviving claimant to the throne, Richard's short reign was far from peaceful. Shortly after his coronation another pretender to the throne, Henry Tudor, and a number of his English supporters, including the Duke of Buckingham, attempted to raise a rebellion against the king. Tudor attempted to sail from the Continent but was unable to land and his supporters in England were quickly dispersed and Buckingham was captured. Buckingham, who had been a close ally of Richard, met his end in Salisbury marketplace, where he was beheaded at the order of the king.

In mid 1485 Henry Tudor once again attempted a landing, this time successfully. Landing in Wales with a small force of English supporters and foreign mercenaries, Henry marched up through the Marches and the Midlands gathering forces as he went. Richard had also gathered an army and the two clashed at Bosworth, west of Leicester, on 22 August 1485. Henry was victorious and Richard died on the field, leading a last-ditch charge against his opponent. In due course Henry was crowned as the seventh king of that name.

The Wars of the Roses were coming to an end but Henry's early reign was disturbed by two Yorkist risings. The first of these resulted in the final battle of the Wars of the Roses at Stoke Field (16 June 1487), south of Newark. With the Yorkist defeat at Stoke Field and the defeat of the short-lived Perkin Warbeck rebellion, the Wars of the Roses came to an end. England would see almost 150 years of peace until the onset of the English Civil Wars in the 1640s and it is to these campaigns that we now turn.

CHAPTER FIVE

ROUNDHEADS
AND CAVALIERS

Background

The English Civil Wars, 1642-1651, were different from any war that had gone before. In the past large areas of the country had been left untouched by conflicts unless an army had passed close by or a lord had raised recruits in the area. Kings had come and gone, lords had changed but the daily grind had continued. If a raiding or pillaging army attacked a town, the next town often went untouched. After the Battle of Wakefield in 1460 the victorious Lancastrian army cut a swathe of devastation along the Great North Road thirty miles wide but beyond this corridor life went on as normal.

A good gauge of this is some of the medieval chronicles. An event now considered to be of national importance, for example a major battle such as Towton, is summed up in a few sentences or, on occasion, a few words, while a very local event, such as the exorcising of a demon from a local villager – an actual event recorded in the *Croyland Chronicle* – goes on for pages.

This was certainly not the case during the Civil Wars. Many libraries have collections of Civil Wars material, ranging from news pamphlets to personal memoirs and letters. Although we have substantially more contemporary information about the various actions that took place, they need to be treated with care, particularly some of the news pamphlets. I have a copy of one published in London only two days after the Battle of Marston Moor which categorically states that the Scots and Parliamentarian army lost the battle. The news had been carried to Hull by some of Lord Fairfax's fleeing horsemen and then by ship to London. It was several days before the true story of the battle reached the city, much to the relief of Parliament.

The Civil Wars, particularly the First Civil War, were a nationwide event and the whole of the kingdom was affected, from Cornwall to Kent and from Sussex to Northumberland. Even if fighting did not take place in an area the people were still taxed and recruits were drawn from the area. Many towns, castles and large houses were garrisoned and these garrisons subjected the surrounding area to enforced contributions, conscription and raiding. Pity the poor village that came under the sway of two opposing garrisons! Although we often refer to the period as the English Civil Wars, it should really be known as the British Civil Wars. Fighting took place throughout the British Isles with armies campaigning for and against the King in Scotland and Ireland as well as England.

On a more local level, very few places in Yorkshire were not affected by the wars or were the site of a skirmish, siege or battle. The village I was brought up in was the site of a skirmish in 1642 and close to where I work is a battlefield. It is this immediacy that gives the Civil Wars their appeal – many shoppers in Wakefield, Leeds, Bradford and York do not realise that they are walking through the scene of a battle. To write a complete account of every skirmish, battle and siege that took place in the county between 1642 and 1645 would fill volumes. My intention in this chapter is to give a brief account of the campaign between Lord Fairfax and the Earl of Newcastle for control of the county, with detailed accounts of the two main battles – Adwalton Moor and Marston Moor. In addition, to give a flavour of the other sorts of action that took place, I will include details of the storming of a town and a siege.

The causes of the Civil Wars were numerous and space precludes going into a lengthy account of the background to the wars. King Charles I had ruled the kingdom without recourse to parliament from early in his reign. A monarch's main source of income was through parliament and Charles looked for other means of financing his government. This included the sale of monopolies, titles and positions, and the extension of Ship Money, a tax normally levied on coastal counties, to the whole country, to name but two of the methods used by the King for raising funds. This led to dissatisfaction among many of the King's subjects.

Another source of discontent was Charles' meddling in religious affairs. From the time of Elizabeth I England had been a Protestant country. Many non–conformist sects, often referred to as puritans, had appeared and the King's religious reforms were not to their liking. This led to a steady stream of emigration to the New England colonies. To many staunch Protestants the reforms smacked of Catholicism and the fact that the Queen was a practising Catholic, and had great influence with the King, only reinforced this.

Charles was also King of Scotland and it was his attempts to impose his religious reforms on the mainly Calvinist Scots that would lead to the first open opposition to his rule. In 1639 Charles' attempts to force the Scots into a new form of worship led to the First Bishops War. Charles needed to bring his rebellious Scots subjects back into line by force and this would require the raising of an army. Obviously, this would cost money and although the King's money-raising schemes had allowed him to rule without a parliament, they were not sufficient to fund his campaign against the Scots. He had no choice but to call a parliament and ask them for funds. Although both sides raised armies the conflict was resolved peacefully. Parliament had been obstructive to the King's cause and he very quickly dissolved it once he had come to terms with the Scots, hence the parliament being known as the Short Parliament.

Never one to learn from his mistakes Charles continued to try to foist his reforms onto the Scots and, in 1640, this led to the outbreak of the Second Bishops War. This time the disagreement did come to armed conflict when the Scots defeated the English army at Newburn and captured Newcastle. With the situation deteriorating in the North, Charles had no choice but to call Parliament once again. This parliament would become known as the Long Parliament. Charles' poor financial position prevented him from dissolving this parliament as he had done the previous one and allowed its members to bring pressure to bear on the King for social and economic reforms. Slowly, but surely, the breach between the sovereign and Parliament grew.

Opposition to the King was on both political and religious grounds. A good example of this is the Hothams, a pair who will figure prominently in the story of the Civil War in Yorkshire. Sir John Hotham opposed the King on political grounds and, it has to be said, for purely personal reasons. He felt that he had been slighted when he was not appointed as the governor of Hull, a position he coveted. His son, Captain John Hotham, on the other hand, had puritanical leanings and he opposed the King's religious reforms. Although the Hothams fought on the same side, many families were divided and friends found themselves on opposite sides.

York. The King's Manor. This was King Charles' headquarters during the last few months before he marched south to raise the Royal Standard at Nottingham, an event that is taken by many to be the start of the Civil Wars.

On 4 January 1642 the King attempted to carry out a pre-emptive strike against his main opponents in Parliament. Entering the Commons with an armed escort, he tried to arrest five members of the House: John Pym, John Hampden, Denzil Holles, Sir Arthur Haselrig and William Strode. Unfortunately, to use the King's words, 'the birds had flown'. The five members had fled to the City of London where they were hidden. Charles had shown his hand and while Pym and his colleagues triumphantly returned to Parliament, the King left for Windsor. The next time he would see his capital he would be on trial for his life.

Events began to move rapidly. On 31 January Sir John Hotham arrived at Hull and assumed its governorship, having been appointed by Parliament and having sworn to hold the town at all costs. On 23 February the Queen set sail for Holland with many of the crown jewels, the sale of which would provide the King with much needed funds to purchase arms and ammunition. Once his wife was on her way the King moved to his northern capital, York, arriving there on 19 March.

In the seventeenth century Hull was a very important town. It was one of the main arms magazines in the north and its possession would be a great boon to the King's cause. On 22 April the King sent his son, James, Duke of York, to visit the town and Sir John Hotham received him with the utmost courtesy. On the following day the King, escorted by a large entourage, arrived before the town's Beverley Gate. Hotham, true to his word, refused the King entry into the town and on the 24th a Royal Herald

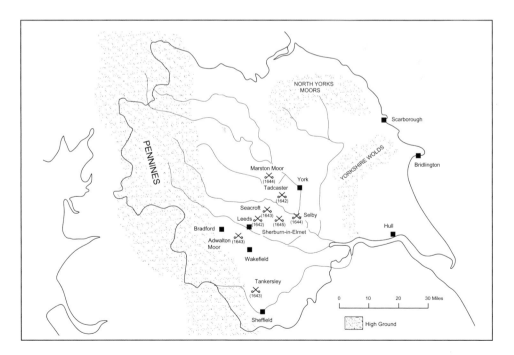

Major battles of the English Civil Wars

declared Sir John a traitor. Even this turn of events did not prompt Hotham to open the gates.

Both sides continued to recruit troops throughout the late spring and early summer of 1642 as the nation slipped inexorably towards war. On 2 July the King received another piece of unwelcome news: the fleet had declared its support for Parliament. It was around this time that the King decided to make another attempt on Hull. A Parliamentarian warship captured a small vessel that was then taken into Hull. On board, disguised as a Frenchman, was Lord George Digby, a staunch Royalist and high on Parliament's list of the King's 'wicked advisers'. Digby seems to have come to an agreement with Hotham that, if the King laid siege to the town, he would surrender it. Fortunately for Parliament, as the King moved his forces into place on 10 July, Sir John Meldrum, an experienced Scots soldier, arrived with 500 reinforcements and the town remained firmly in Parliament's hands.

Leaving the siege in the less-than-capable hands of the Earl of Newport, and taking many of the troops raised in Yorkshire, the King moved south towards Nottingham, where he raised his standard on 22 August. Many historians have marked this act as the start of the Civil Wars but, as can be seen above, fighting had broken out in Yorkshire well before this date. In late July Meldrum led a foray against the Royalist siege lines and drove the enemy back as far as Beverley, thus breaking the siege.

After the King's departure both sides in the county continued to raise troops and vied for control of her towns. Command of the Royalist forces devolved on the Earl of Cumberland, a senior Yorkshire nobleman but no soldier, as he readily admitted. The main Royalist army was based around York. Cumberland was opposed by three Parliamentarian forces. In the West Riding Lord Fairfax raised troops and controlled a number of mill towns such as Bradford and Halifax. From Hull the two Hothams controlled much of the East Riding and Sir Hugh Cholmley commanded the garrison of Scarborough. Possession of Hull and Scarborough gave Parliament control of most of the east coast of Yorkshire. The Queen was due to arrive in the North East with a cargo of arms and ammunition and her options would be severely limited.

After the King had departed, a period of relative calm began but as autumn came things began to warm up. The three Parliamentarian forces began to exert pressure on the Royalist army at York from three directions and Cumberland was having difficulty in holding the enemy at bay. On 26 September the Yorkshire Royalists wrote a letter to the Earl of Newcastle asking him for assistance.

William Cavendish, Earl of Newcastle, had been given a commission by the King to raise troops in the four northernmost counties: Cumberland, Westmorland, Northumberland and Durham. He had managed to raise and equip a substantial force at his own expense – he was a very wealthy man. On the 30th Newcastle replied with a number of propositions to which the Yorkshire gentry quickly acquiesced. He also told them that the King had given him the task of ensuring that the Queen arrived safely and was escorted south with her precious consignment of weapons. This would be his primary objective.

Newcastle did not move immediately and completed the training of his army before he marched for York. On 1 December the Earl's army entered Yorkshire. Sir Hugh Cholmley attempted to stop the Royalist advance at Piercebridge but was quickly brushed aside. Further south, Lord Fairfax, with a substantial force, had advanced out of the West Riding towards York. News of Cholmley's defeat at Piercebridge brought him to a halt at Tadcaster. His son, Sir Thomas Fairfax, was at Wetherby where he was attacked by a Royalist force from York but successfully drove it off.

On 3 December Newcastle arrived at York with a well-trained and well-equipped force of 6,000 men, which considerably outnumbered the local Parliamentarian forces. The situation in the county had changed completely. Now it was not the Royalists who were under pressure but the Parliamentarians. Fairfax found himself out on a limb at Tadcaster and Newcastle quickly took the opportunity to advance on the town and defeat one of the enemy forces in detail.

Pike and shot

During the Civil Wars troops were recruited by a number of methods. In the early stages of the wars many nobles and gentlemen were given commissions to raise regiments of foot or troops of horse. These were raised from their retainers or from volunteers. Later, when the stream of volunteers had reduced to a trickle, both sides resorted to conscription. Another source of manpower was from enemy prisoners, who would be given the choice of imprisonment or fighting for their captors. Often the second was the preferable option. Sometimes they had no option and were forced to fight – this happened to Parliamentarian prisoners captured at Rotherham in 1643, who were forced to join the Royalist army.

Foot regiments usually comprised ten companies, although some regiments, the Earl of Newcastle's for example, could be up to double strength. On paper a regiment of foot numbered 1,200 men, with each of the seven captains' companies having a strength of 100. The strength of the major's, lieutenant colonel's and colonel's companies increased with the rank of their commander. These strengths were rarely achieved and, on occasion, several weak regiments had to be combined to make a viable fighting unit.

Each company was divided into two elements – pike and shot. In theory there should have been one pikeman for every two musketeers – this was the ideal ratio but was not always achieved. The company was an administrative unit and the regiment was divided into pike and musket blocks when they deployed to fight. All the pikemen were gathered in the centre of the unit in a single block, while the musketeers were divided into two blocks which deployed on each flank of the pike. When the tactical situation warranted it the pike and shot could operate independently.

The manuals of the day show the pikeman to be very well armoured. This was good in theory and on the parade ground but pikeman's armour was not easy to come by and heavy to carry. Most pikemen would have quickly discarded their armour and

A regiment of foot prepares to advance. The pike block in the centre would normally be flanked by two wings of musket (John Wilson).

been equipped with an iron pot helmet at most. Similarly, the pike should have been sixteen feet long but was often trimmed down by several feet to make it easier to handle and provide a ready source of firewood! Pikemen were also issued with swords which were mass produced and of very low quality. They were more suited to chopping firewood than to killing an opponent.

Musketeers were usually equipped with a matchlock musket – flintlocks, or firelocks as they are sometimes known, were the preserve of specialist troops such as artillery train guards who operated in close proximity to barrels of gunpowder, where a match, a slow burning cord, would have been a major liability. Musketeers were also equipped with swords but tended to use the butt end of their muskets when in close combat.

The ideal horseman, known in the manuals as a harquebusier, was protected by a long-sleeved, thick, buff leather coat. Over this he wore a breast and back plate and on his head he wore a lobster pot helmet, given its name for the resemblance of its articulated neck guard to a lobster's tail. His legs were protected by thigh-length leather boots. For weapons he carried a good quality sword, a pair of pistols and a carbine. This was the ideal but many troopers would have come nowhere near this level of equipment. Many would have been in their everyday clothes and armed only with a sword.

The horse was formed into troops of sixty men, although troop strengths could vary greatly. A number of troops then formed a regiment and, once again, this varied from regiment to regiment. At the start of the First Civil War both sides adopted different cavalry tactics. Parliamentarian horse depended on firepower to overthrow the enemy, basing their tactics on the Dutch school of thought. The Royalists, on the other hand, followed Swedish tactics and charged the enemy at the gallop with swords drawn; using their pistols only in hand-to-hand combat. This is a sweeping generalisation and, as always, there were exceptions to the rule. Lord Fairfax's horse fought in a similar fashion to their Royalist opponents, charging in with the sword. This may not have been a tactical choice but a necessity due to a lack of firearms. By the time of Marston Moor the Eastern Association horse, commanded by one Oliver Cromwell, had also adopted the charge. Unlike the Royalist charge at the gallop, Cromwell's men attacked at a good round trot, in a compact formation.

Dragoons formed the third element of a Civil Wars army. These were the jack-of-all-trades, who rode to battle and dismounted to fight. They were equipped in a similar fashion to musketeers and could be used in a number of roles, including scouting and supporting the horse on the battlefield. Dragoons were usually organised into companies, although some troops of horse had a number of dragoons attached. The companies could operate independently or be formed into regiments.

The final element was the artillery which included the full gamut from small, highly mobile, field guns to massive siege guns. They seem to have had little effect on the battlefield and are often not even mentioned in accounts of actions even though they are listed as being captured.

Having had a brief look at the different elements of a Civil Wars army, it is now time to consider how the army fought. In a set piece battle the foot would form in the centre of the army, usually in two lines with the regiments of the second line covering the gaps in the first. Normally the foot, both pike and shot, would be deployed six ranks deep, although this could be lessened if an army was badly outnumbered and

The fog of war. A small body of musketeers have just fired and are covered by a cloud of smoke. Imagine the amount of smoke produced by several thousand muskets, cavalry pistols and cannon at a battle such as Marston Moor (John Wilson).

had to cover a wider frontage than normal. Interspersed with the foot would be the artillery, not in massed batteries as was the norm in later periods, but in ones or twos to supplement the fire of the musketeers. To either side of the foot the horse was deployed, three ranks deep and in two lines. On occasion the horse was interspersed with small bodies of musketeers detached from the regiments of foot. These are often referred to as 'commanded' musketeers. The companies or regiments of dragoons would form the outer flanks of the army and operate in support of the horse.

Battle commenced with the horse of both sides trying to overthrow their opponents, while the foot advanced to firing range and then often to 'push of pike'. The objective of the horse was to drive off their opponents then fall on the flank of the enemy foot. All too often this was not the case, as the victorious horsemen would gallop off in pursuit. If the horse did not intervene, the fighting between the foot often ended in a stalemate. Some of the most decisive victories were gained by the side which kept enough of its horse in hand to intervene in the infantry fight. Marston Moor and Naseby are prime examples of this.

Every Civil War battlefield was different and the armies soon learnt to suit their tactics to the terrain presented to them. Actions in Yorkshire during the period range from a full-scale set piece battle, to a large battle fought in enclosed terrain, to the storming of towns. Many of the commanders were very inexperienced in 1642 but learnt their new trade quickly and became capable soldiers. Some even became great commanders.

Opening moves

The Earl of Newcastle quickly decided on a course of action. The bulk of his army would advance on Tadcaster from the east, along the main road from York, and attack Lord Fairfax's army at Tadcaster. Newcastle's Lieutenant-General, the Earl of Newport, would advance towards Wetherby and then attack Tadcaster from the northwest. Fairfax's force would be trapped between the two forces and destroyed.

Lord Fairfax was well aware of his isolated and precarious position. He gathered as many troops as he could at Tadcaster and made preparations to defend the town by building a redoubt on the crest of the hill above the east bank of the River Wharfe. This fortification defended the town from any attack from the direction of York. There were several houses close to the redoubt and these may also have been fortified, although contemporary accounts make no mention of it. Another possibility is that these houses were demolished and their rubble used in the construction of the earthwork.

During 6 December the Royalist forces began their advance. Late in the day Lord Fairfax called a Council of War. The Parliamentarian commanders decided that their position was untenable. Sir Thomas Fairfax, Lord Fairfax's son, gives a figure of only 900 men for the force his father had available and these were opposed by over 6,000 well-equipped Royalist troops a few miles to the east. Newcastle was advancing with the main body of the army, which comprised the foot, artillery and a few troops of horse: some 4,000–4,500 men. Newport's flanking force was formed from the bulk of the army's horse and amounted to about 1,500 men, although one Royalist account numbers them at 15,000 – obviously a zero too many!

Lord Fairfax decided that the only course of action was to withdraw his army towards the west, in the direction of Leeds. On the morning of 7 December, a large proportion of Fairfax's men were formed up on Tadcaster's main street ready to march, when firing broke out on the opposite bank. Fairfax had left a rearguard to defend the redoubt and this was now being attacked by Newcastle's foot. Withdrawal was no longer an option and Fairfax had to stand his ground. Reinforcements were rushed across the bridge to support the earthwork's defenders and the Royalist attack was brought to a halt. A second Royalist attack developed from the north along Mill Lane and succeeded in capturing a house close to the bridge and cutting off the defenders of the redoubt. A Parliamentarian counterattack recaptured the house and drove the Royalists back along Mill Lane. To prevent the Royalists repeating their attack a number of houses were set on fire. For the remainder of the day the battle degenerated into a long-range musketry exchange.

Although Newcastle's prompt attack had prevented the Parliamentarians from withdrawing, the second half of his plan did not come to fruition. Why did the Earl of Newport not strike the town from the northwest as he had been ordered? The probable reason is that his force was accompanied by a pair of light guns and these, in combination with the state of the roads in December, conspired to slow him so much that he was unable to reach the battlefield. In Drake's *History of York* a much more interesting reason is given. Drake states that Captain John Hotham despatched a letter to Newport, under Newcastle's signature, ordering him to halt and await further instructions. If there is any truth in this it would have been a brilliant stroke by Hotham but would have meant that the Parliamentarians would have had to be aware of Newport's flank march.

Although Lord Fairfax had held his ground, he was still in a dangerous position. In a letter to Parliament he asserted that he could have continued to hold Tadcaster had he not been low on gunpowder – a curse of armies throughout the Civil Wars. Without powder his musketeers could not oppose the enemy and Fairfax had no choice but to withdraw. It is interesting that Fairfax decided to withdraw to Selby, while Captain Hotham withdrew to Cawood. This seems a little strange as it was taking Fairfax away from his main area of support in the West Riding but it moved him closer to Hull which, as has already been mentioned, was a major magazine and a ready source of supply for him.

On the morning of the 8th the Royalists occupied Tadcaster. Newcastle then moved his army south and garrisoned Pontefract Castle. He also set up several other small garrisons, including one at Ferrybridge, which effectively cut off Fairfax from the West Riding. Elements of the Royalist army, under Sir William Saville, captured Leeds and on Sunday 18 December moved on to attack Bradford. Heavily outnumbered by the Royalist troops, the ill-equipped citizens of Bradford held their ground around the church and, once they had been reinforced by a body of men from the Halifax area, drove the Royalists off and sent them scurrying back to Leeds. During the action a Royalist officer had asked for quarter but the citizens who were attacking him did not understand what the term meant and cut him down. This led to the ominous term 'Bradford quarter'.

Several days after the attack on Bradford Sir Thomas Fairfax arrived at the town with reinforcements. He immediately put out a call for volunteers to carry out an attack on Leeds. By the morning of the 23rd he had gathered 1,200-1,300 musketeers and horse and a substantial body of clubmen – ill-armed local volunteers – possibly as many as 2,000. The town was defended by Sir William Saville who had 1,500 foot and five troops of horse and dragoons.

The course of the storming of Leeds is straightforward to trace on the ground. At the time Leeds comprised three main streets: the Headrow, Briggate and Kirkgate. All of these streets still exist. At the bottom of Briggate a bridge crossed the River Aire and the road continued on to Hunslet. All the exits to the town had been barricaded and an earthwork ran from close to St John's church, across the Headrow and then down to the river.

Fairfax's force approached the town along the Headrow and summoned Saville to surrender. When this summons was refused Sir Thomas began his assault. Fairfax attacked along the Headrow while Sir William Fairfax attacked the area around St John's church. Neither of these attacks made much progress. Sergeant-Major-General Forbes had been despatched to attack the enemy earthwork where it approached the river, while Captain Mildmay had been sent on a more circuitous route to approach the town from the far side of the Aire and prevent any enemy escaping in that direction. Forbes, supported by musket fire from Mildmay's men, managed to break into the town and was soon reinforced by Mildmay's men who had stormed the defences of the bridge. The combined force then attacked up Briggate towards the Market Place which stood at the top of Briggate close to the Headrow. The success of this attack allowed the Fairfaxes to force their way into the town and Sir Thomas led a cavalry charge along the Headrow into the Market Place. Many of the Royalist garrison were killed or captured and some were drowned trying to swim the Aire. The survivors continued on to Wakefield but their arrival seems to have panicked the garrison of that town which promptly withdrew to Pontefract. A force of Parliamentarian troops from Almondbury, near Huddersfield, occupied Wakefield on 24 January 1643.

In the aftermath of the loss of Leeds and Wakefield, Newcastle pulled the bulk of his army back to York. Before he could turn his attention fully on defeating Lord Fairfax he had two tasks to carry out. The first was to escort an ammunition convoy from Newcastle-upon-Tyne and the Earl despatched James King, his Lieutenant-General, with a body of horse to carry out this mission. Sir Hugh Cholmley attempted to intercept the convoy at Yarm in North Yorkshire on 1 February. Cholmley was defeated and King moved on to deliver the precious gunpowder to the army at York.

Cholmley's defeat may have been one of the main contributory factors to his subsequent change of sides.

Newcastle's second task was to secure the Queen after her impending arrival and aid her march to join her husband at Oxford. The Queen arrived at Bridlington Quay – the town and harbour were separate at this time – on 22 February. Newcastle immediately set off with a large force to escort the Queen to York but while she was awaiting his arrival she was still in danger. Several Parliamentarian ships arrived and began a bombardment of the town and the Queen and her ladies had to take shelter in a ditch. Help was at hand when the Dutch admiral, van Tromp, who had escorted the Queen's ship from the Continent, threatened the Parliamentarian commander that his ships would engage if the Parliamentarian ships did not withdraw. This had the desired effect and Newcastle was able to escort the Queen to safety at York on 7 March.

On 25 March Sir Hugh Cholmley changed sides. His defeat at Yarm and the Queen's arrival finally decided him on this course of action. His defection was a great boon to the Royalist cause and gave them control of much of the East Coast of Yorkshire. It also seems to have had an effect on the Hothams who began a correspondence with the Earl of Newcastle and became very uncooperative with Fairfax.

Fairfax found himself in an unenviable position. The main Royalist army was at York and considerably outnumbered his own force. The East Riding was now under Royalist control and, to his rear, the Hothams had withdrawn their troops into Hull and were refusing to cooperate with him. His main base of support was in the West Riding, around the mill towns and he took a decision to withdraw to Leeds. His first action was to call his son, Sir Thomas, from Leeds with a small force of horse and musketeers and a large body of clubmen. His plan called for Sir Thomas to carry out a diversionary attack on Tadcaster with the troops he had brought from the West Riding, while his father with the main force marched directly from Selby to Leeds. On the morning of 30 March the Fairfaxes put this plan into action.

The plan worked well. Lord Fairfax and his men arrived safely at Leeds while Sir Thomas drove the garrison of Tadcaster out of the town. He may have exceeded his father's orders at this point, which may have been to demonstrate against the town, not to capture it. Unfortunately, Sir Thomas tarried in Tadcaster for too long and as he began to march up onto Bramham Moor a pursuing body of Royalist horse came into sight. The Royalists, under Colonel George Goring, comprised twenty troops of horse and dragoons, some 1,000 mounted men. To oppose them Fairfax had only three troops of horse, amounting to around 150 troopers. The rest of his force was made up of musketeers and a large body of clubmen. When attacked by horse it was usual for the pike to provide protection against them for the musketeers. As Fairfax had no pikemen with him his force was in considerable danger from the Royalist horse, particularly as they had to cross two large areas of open moor-land before they reached the safety of Leeds.

As Fairfax ascended the road onto Bramham Moor he had to pass through an area of enclosures. This was ideal terrain for his horse to hold up the larger enemy force, while his foot crossed the first area of open ground and reached the shelter of the next area of enclosures. Having held the enemy for what he deemed to be a sufficient amount of time, Fairfax pulled back his horsemen and set off in pursuit of his foot. Imagine his surprise when he found his foot were waiting for him and had not yet crossed the open ground. The Parliamentarian force continued to march westwards and Fairfax spotted the enemy horse on a parallel road several hundred yards to the north. The Parliamentarians successfully reached the next area of enclosures and continued onto the open ground beyond – Seacroft Moor. By now Fairfax's men were beginning to straggle and Goring timed his attack perfectly. Although the pitifully small force of Parliamentarian horse attempted to protect the foot, the force was quickly broken as Goring's horsemen mounted an unstoppable charge. Fairfax and most of his troopers were able to escape to Leeds but most of the foot were killed or captured. Sir Thomas summed up the action as 'the greatest loss we ever received'.

The storming of Wakefield

After the defeat at Seacroft Moor, Lord Fairfax concentrated his men into two garrisons: Bradford and Leeds. It was during this period that one of the most mysterious battles of the Civil War in Yorkshire took place, at Tankersley, just off junction 36 of the M1. Little is written about this action, either by contemporary or modern authors, but it was a sizeable affair with up to 4,000 men taking part. A force of Derbyshire Parliamentarians marched north and were intercepted and defeated by a force of local Royalists. These Royalist troops may have been the advance guard of a planned advance into the south of the county.

The Earl of Newcastle still had one major task to perform before he turned his attention fully to defeating Lord Fairfax – the safe despatch of the Queen to the south. His first move was to lay siege to Leeds, but after a few days the Royalist army moved to Wakefield, where Newcastle left a garrison of 3,000 men, before moving into South Yorkshire. On 4 May Newcastle captured Rotherham. Accounts of the siege are contradictory – the Duchess of Newcastle's account states that the town was taken by storm, while a letter from Lord Fairfax to Parliament states that the town held out for two days and then yielded. Fairfax goes on to state that the Royalists then plundered the town and forced many of the prisoners to join their army.

Two days after the capture of Rotherham the Royalist army moved on Sheffield but found that the town and castle had been abandoned by the garrison. Newcastle installed Sir William Saville as governor of the town and gave him orders to use the local iron foundries to produce cannon. The Royalists then spent the next two weeks consolidating their position in the south of the county until, on 21 May, Newcastle received startling news – Wakefield and the bulk of its garrison had fallen to the Parliamentarians.

Wakefield is one of the best examples of the storming of a town and is worth looking at in detail. Newcastle's march into the south of Yorkshire presented the Fairfaxes with an ideal opportunity to strike back. Sir Thomas Fairfax gives the reason for the attack on Wakefield as an attempt to capture Royalist troops to exchange for the prisoners taken at Seacroft Moor. Prisoner exchanges of all ranks were a common occurrence during the Civil War. A good example of this is the case of Colonel George Goring. As will be described shortly, Goring was captured at Wakefield and remained a prisoner for almost twelve months. He was exchanged during the spring of 1644 in time to take part in the Marston Moor campaign. Many of the Parliamentarian troops captured at Seacroft Moor were not soldiers but clubmen – ill-armed local volunteers. On a number of occasions – Bradford, Leeds, Seacroft Moor and Adwalton Moor – Lord Fairfax used clubmen to supplement his limited supply of regular troops. As these men were agricultural workers and tradesmen their imprisonment had a major effect on the local economy of the areas from which they came. One of the reasons that Wakefield was chosen as a target was that Lord Fairfax had received intelligence that it was held by only 800-900 men, a serious underestimation of the garrison's actual strength.

During the evening of 20 May a force of 1,500 men gathered at Howley Hall, near Batley, from the garrisons of Leeds, Bradford, Halifax and the hall itself. It comprised 1,000 foot, probably all musketeers, and eight troops of horse and three troops of dragoons. The mounted troops were divided equally between Sir Thomas Fairfax and Sir Henry Foulis, while the foot was commanded by Sergeant-Major-General Gifford and Sir William Fairfax. There is no mention of any artillery being present, which is hardly surprising as this was a raiding force. Sir Thomas Fairfax had overall command.

The Parliamentarian force moved on Wakefield via Stanley, where they attacked the small garrison, capturing twenty-one prisoners in the process. They then moved on to Wakefield where, alerted by survivors from the Stanley garrison, the Royalist horse and musketeers were waiting for them, as Sir Thomas Fairfax reported:

> *About four a clock in the morning we came before Wakefield, where after some of their horse were beaten into the town, the foot with unspeakable courage, beat the enemies from the hedges, which they had lined with musketeers into the town.*

The Parliamentarians first encountered a strong patrol of horse from the town which they quickly drove back. They then found 500 musketeers manning the enclosures outside the town and again, after a short fight, these were driven back. With the approaches to the town cleared the Parliamentarians could put their plan into action. It should not be imagined that Wakefield was a fortified town. Its defences were formed by the hedges and walls of the houses along its four main streets – Kirkgate, Westgate, Warrengate and Northgate. The end of each street was barricaded. Fairfax's plan was to attack along two of these streets: Northgate and Warrengate. No account states who attacked along which street but it can be surmised from subsequent events that Sir Thomas Fairfax and Gifford attacked Warrengate while Foulis and Sir William Fairfax attacked Northgate. The reasoning behind this is that Sir Thomas and Gifford were the first to reach the Market Place and the route along

Warrengate is shorter, and that Gifford was able to plant a captured gun in the churchyard to fire on the Market Place. If he had attacked down Northgate he would have had to cross the Market Place, which was full of Royalist troops, to get to the churchyard.

The Royalist defences held out for some considerable time: one and a half to two hours are mentioned by contemporary accounts. Sir Thomas Fairfax wrote two accounts of the action, one immediately after the battle and one in his memoirs many years later. In his memoirs he reports that:

After 2 hours dispute the foot forced open a barricade where I entered with my own troop. Colonel Alured and Captain Bright followed with theirs. The street which we entered was full of their foot which we charged through and routed, leaving them to the foot which followed close behind us. And presently we were charged again with horse led by General Goring, where, after a hot encounter, some were slain, and himself [Goring] taken prisoner by Captain Alured.

The account written shortly after the action is very much in agreement:

When the barricades were opened, Sir Thomas Fairfax with the horse, fell into the town, and cleared the street where Colonel Goring was taken, by Lieutenant Alured, brother to Captain Alured, a Member of the House.

It is interesting to note the difference in the ranks of the Alured brothers given in the two accounts. The first gives their ranks at the close of the Civil Wars while the second gives their ranks at the time of the action.

After a lengthy dispute, Gifford's foot managed to break into the end of Warrengate and open the barricade. This allowed Fairfax to lead his four troops in a charge down the street which was packed with enemy foot. These were quickly dispersed. Fairfax was then counterattacked by a body of horse led by George Goring. The Royalist horse was defeated and Goring captured by Lieutenant Alured. During this phase of the fighting Sir Thomas became separated from his men:

And here I cannot but acknowledge God's goodness to me this day, who being advanced, a good way single, before my men, having a Colonel and a Lieutenant Colonel (who had engaged themselves as my prisoners) only with me, and many of the enemy now between me and my [men] I light on a regiment of foot standing in the Market Place. Thus encompassed, and thinking what to do, I spied a lane which I thought would lead me back to my men again; at the end of this lane there was a corps du guard of the enemy's, with 15 or 16 soldiers which was, then, just quitting of it, with a Sergeant leading them off; whom we met; who seeing their officers came up to us. Taking no notice of me, they asked them what they would have them do, for they could keep that work no longer, because the Roundheads (as they called them) came so fast upon them. But the gentlemen, who had passed their words to be my true prisoners, said nothing, so looking upon one another, I thought it not fit, now, to own them as so, much less to bid the rest to render themselves prisoners to me; so, being well mounted, and seeing a place in the works where men used to go over, I rushed from them, seeing no other remedy, and made my horse leap over the works, and so, by good providence, got to my men again.

Sir Thomas's bravery can never be doubted but sometimes his common sense can be. This would not be the last time his impetuous courage would leave him stranded on his own in the midst of the enemy.

Gifford had continued his attack along Warrengate, bringing the captured cannon with him. As he reached the Market Place he realised that it contained three troops of enemy horse and a regiment of their foot, as Fairfax reported:

Yet in the Market Place there stood three troops of horse, and Colonel Lampton's Regiment [foot], to whom Major General Gifford sent a trumpet with offer of quarter, if they would lay down their arms, they answered they scorned the motion; then he fired a piece of their own ordinance upon them, and the horse fell in upon them, beat them out of the town.

In his memoirs Fairfax mentions that Gifford set the cannon up in the churchyard. Having given the Royalist troops an opportunity to surrender, Gifford ordered his men to open fire and then ordered Fairfax's rallied troopers to charge the enemy. This was the last straw. Those who could, escaped; the remainder threw down their arms and surrendered. By nine o'clock Wakefield was firmly in Parliamentarian hands. Accounts do not give figures for the dead and wounded but do give a list of captured men and material: thirty-eight named officers, 1,500 common soldiers, four cannon, twenty-seven foot colours and three horse cornets, along with weapons and a large amount of powder, ball and match. The weapons, powder and ammunition were a great boon to the Parliamentarian cause. In a letter to Parliament Lord Fairfax summed up the victory:

And truly for my part I do rather account it a miracle, than a victory, and the glory and praise to be ascribed to God that wrought it, in which I hope I derogate nothing from the merits of the Commanders and Soldiers, who every man in his place and duty, showed as much courage and resolution as could be expected from men.

How had this 'miracle' taken place? The Parliamentarian victory at Wakefield flies in the face of military wisdom. The victors had taken a town garrisoned by twice their number and had captured more prisoners than they had soldiers. There are a number of reasons for the Parliamentarian victory. Firstly, they attacked the barricades at the end of the streets, which meant that only a limited number of Royalist troops could defend at any given time. Once the attackers had penetrated the barricades, the enemy troops, packed in the streets behind, were unable to defend themselves, as was also the case with the troops packed into the Market Place. There also seems to have been a breakdown in the Royalist command structure, with troops standing still instead of reacting to the changing situation. One possible reason for this is given by Dr Nathaniel Johnstone, a contemporary who left the following anecdote:

> *There was a meeting at Heath Hall upon the Saturday, at a bowling, and most of the officers and the governor were there, and had spent the afternoon in drinking, and were most drunk when the town was alarmed. It was taken fully by nine o'clock in the morning, and more prisoners were taken than the forces that came against it. It seems probable that Sir Thomas Fairfax had notice of their festivities at Heath, and perceived the advantage which they might afford him.*

It has been reported that Goring had arisen from his sick bed to lead the mounted counterattack but Johnstone's account may give another reason for Goring being seen reeling in his saddle – he was still drunk. His later record would point to this being a strong possibility.

Whatever the reasons for the Royalist defeat, Sir Thomas and his men had won a remarkable victory. They had no plans to remain in the town and expected a rapid response from Newcastle. Sir Thomas led his men out of Wakefield and back to their garrisons, complete with the spoils of their victory. The Fairfaxes had their prisoners for exchange but we do not know whether this ever took place.

The Battle of Adwalton Moor

The Earl of Newcastle's reaction to the storming of Wakefield must have been of considerable concern to the Fairfaxes. It must have come as a great surprise when Newcastle tamely withdrew his army to York. The Earl's main task was still the protection of the Queen and her safe despatch to the south. In early June Newcastle put his plan into operation. On the 4th his army, accompanied by the Queen and her arms convoy, left York and marched to Pontefract. A Council of War was then held to decide on the next course of action. The main question was: should Newcastle and his whole army escort the Queen? Many of Newcastle's officers were Yorkshire men and did not like the idea of leaving the county in the possession of the Parliamentarians. A decision was made for the bulk of the army to remain in the county while the Queen, with a strong escort, travelled to Newark, where she arrived safely on 16 June.

With the departure of the Queen, Newcastle was now free to move against Lord Fairfax in the West Riding. The Earl spent a number of days at Pontefract, gathering his forces and recruiting and training replacements for the troops that had accompanied the Queen. Newcastle first moved his troops to Wakefield in preparation for an advance on Bradford, where Fairfax's main army was stationed. On 21 June he captured Howley Hall but was unable to carry on his advance due to the unseasonal heavy rain. By 30 June the roads had dried enough to allow him to begin his approach march to Bradford.

While Newcastle waited for a change in the weather at Howley Hall, Fairfax gathered his commanders, and troops, at Bradford and tried to come to a decision. The town was untenable. Bradford sits in a bowl and is overlooked from all sides. It was also unfortified and would take a lot of men to defend. If Fairfax could gather enough men he would not be able to supply them, so defending the town was discounted. He could attempt to skirt around the Royalist army and head for Hull but, as the Hothams were becoming less and less cooperative, this was not an attractive option. A withdrawal into Lancashire, a Parliamentarian stronghold at this time, seems to have been discounted. This left one course of action – to fight. The success of the attack on Wakefield may have caused the Parliamentarian command to have a 'rush of blood to the head'. They had defeated twice their number at Wakefield; could a surprise attack on the Royalist encampment at Howley Hall not have the same success? A decision was made and on 30 June the Parliamentarian army left Bradford. Both armies were now marching along the same road towards each other. A clash was inevitable.

The old road between Bradford and Wakefield ran along a narrow ridgeline, running from north-west (Bradford) to south-east (Wakefield). As Lord Fairfax's army marched towards Wakefield, the road began to rise up the north-west side of a hill, known locally as Whiskett, or Westgate Hill, whose crest stood at about 700 feet. About three-quarters of a mile south-east of the main crest of Whiskett Hill was a second crest, slightly lower at 650 feet, which formed the military crest of the hill for an army marching from Bradford. It was not until the top of this hill was reached that Adwalton Moor could be seen, as the ground gently drops into a shallow bowl between the two crests. About half a mile further on is the edge of Adwalton Moor. The north-west edge of the moor had a series of hedged enclosures, and a substantial ditch along it, and further enclosures encroached onto the southwest corner of the moor. A couple of hundred yards from the edge of the moor the land begins to rise again and climbs to 650 feet at the top of Hungar Hill, which formed the south-east edge of the battlefield. On either side of the ridge the ground falls away quite steeply.

As Lord Fairfax's army left Bradford it was divided into a number of bodies. First came the Forlorn Hope, or advance guard, which was a combined arms force of six companies/troops of horse, foot and dragoons, although it is not certain what proportion each type provided, but it would have had a total of 300-350 men. It was commanded by Captain Mildmay, who seems to have been a trusted officer, more than capable of operating independently, as had been shown at Leeds when he was detached with a substantial force to attack the town from the south side of the River Aire.

The vanguard was commanded by Sergeant-Major-General Gifford and comprised 1,200 men from the Leeds garrison. Lord Fairfax himself commanded the main battle, which was made up of 500 men from the garrisons of Halifax, and its surrounding towns, and 700 Lancashire foot, divided into twelve companies. Sir Thomas Fairfax had command of the horse, which was formed from thirteen troops, for a strength of about 650-700 men. The horse was divided into two wings of five troops each, which points to the remaining three troops being part of the Forlorn Hope. Thomas Stockdale, a close associate of Lord Fairfax, stated that the Parliamentarian army was 'not full 4,000 men horse and foot armed'. Taking into account the troops already listed this gives a total of about 500-600 men for the Bradford garrison, divided into seven companies, which formed the rearguard, commanded by Lieutenant-Colonel Forbes. Thomas Stockdale also mentions a substantial number of clubmen being present, although he does not give an exact number.

The strength of the Royalist army is much more problematic and little detail is given in any of the contemporary accounts of the battle. Thomas Stockdale stated that the Royalist had 15,000 foot and 4,000 horse, almost certainly a highly inflated figure, although his total for the horse may be close. Sir Thomas Fairfax puts the Royalist strength at between 10,000 and 12,000 men, and this is probably very close to the truth. The two Royalist accounts that give any clue to their strength are the Duchess of Newcastle, who writes that 'My Lord's forces, which then contained not above half so many musketeers as the enemy had; their chiefest strength consisting in horse', and the Earl of Newcastle himself who reports the enemy having 'a greater number of foot than we'. It is probable that the Royalist army was close to Sir Thomas Fairfax's lower total of 10,000 men, with an almost equal split of horse and foot at about 5,000 men each. Newcastle also had a substantial artillery train, as his objective was to lay siege to Bradford.

The first shots of the battle were fired on the north-west slopes of Whiskett Hill, when the two Forlorn Hopes clashed with each other. No contemporary account gives a time for this first clash, but Sir Thomas Fairfax provides a clue:

> *My father appointed 4 o'clock the next morning, to begin to march; but Major-General Gifford, who had the ordering of the business, so delayed the execution of it,*

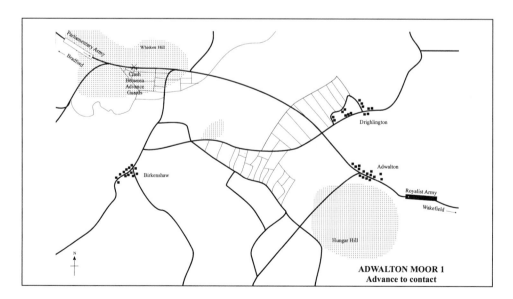

Adwalton Moor 1 – Advance to contact

that it was 7 or 8 before we began to move; and not without much suspicion of treachery in it.

If Sir Thomas is correct and the Parliamentarian army had covered four miles, then the first clash must have been between nine and ten o'clock on the morning of 30 June 1643.

Three accounts give details of the initial clash between the Forlorn Hopes. Sir Henry Slingsby writes:

The fortune [forlorn] *hope of his excellency's army met unexpectedly with the van of the enemy. They skirmish and are put to retreat. He encouraged his men and put the enemy to a stand. They come on fiercer, and beat the enemy from one hedge, from one house to another; at last they are driven to retreat and we recover the moor.*

Thomas Stockdale reported:

Upon Atherton Moor they planted ordnance, and ordered their battalia, but they manned diverse houses standing in the enclosed grounds between Bradford and Atherton Moor with musketeers, and sent out great parties of horse and foot by the lanes and enclosed ground to give us fight. Our forlorn hope beat back the enemy's out of the lanes and enclosed ground, killing many and taking some prisoners.

Finally, Sir Thomas Fairfax writes:

For when we were near the place we intended, the whole enemy army was drawn up in battalia. We were to go up a hill to them, which our forlorn hope gained by beating theirs into their main body, which was drawn up half a mile further, upon a place called Adderton Moor [locals still sometimes refer to Adwalton as Adderton]. *We being all up the hill drew into battalia also.*

*Adwalton Moor.
Looking back towards
the moor from Whiskett
(Westgate) Hill.*

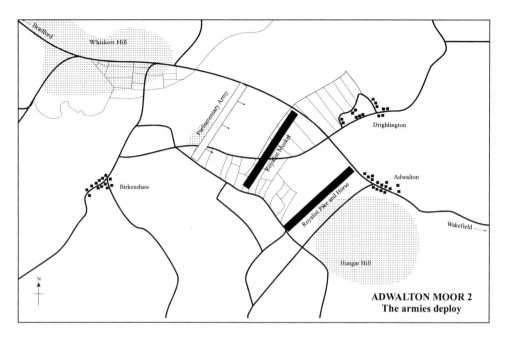

ADWALTON MOOR 2
The armies deploy

Adwalton Moor 2 – The armies deploy

There seems to be some discrepancy between these accounts as to the state of the Royalist army at the start of the action. Enough information is given to work out the course of events.

Captain Mildmay led his forlorn hope up the northwest side of Whiskett Hill, where they clashed unexpectedly with the Royalist vanguard. The Royalists were driven back from Whiskett Hill to the second, lower ridge, where they were rallied by the Earl of Newcastle and the Parliamentarian forlorn hope was brought to a stand. Reinforced, the Parliamentarians renewed their attack, driving the Royalists back into the enclosures at the foot of the hill and here, once again, the Royalists made a stand.

By this time the Royalist army had begun to deploy onto the moor, and a large number of musketeers, supported by horse, had been sent into the enclosures to reinforce their retreating forlorn hope. The main Parliamentarian army had reached the top of the lower crest, overlooking the moor, and began to form into line of battle. There would have been a pause while both armies continued to deploy.

The Parliamentarian army split into two wings and a reserve. Major-General Gifford commanded the left wing, with his five troops of horse deployed close to the Bradford-Wakefield road, and to their right 1,200 foot, mostly musketeers. Continuing the line was a similar sized body of foot and then another five troops of horse completed the Parliamentarian line. The right half of the Parliamentarian front line was commanded by Sir Thomas Fairfax. Somewhere within this line were

Adwalton Moor. Looking from the lower part of the moor towards the Royalist lines.

Adwalton Moor. Looking from the Royalist line across the moor towards Whiskett Hill.

deployed three light cannon, the only guns Lord Fairfax had with him. The remainder of Lord Fairfax's troops formed a reserve, and this comprised about 600 regular foot, possibly the men from the Bradford garrison, and the clubmen, and, as they are not taken into account elsewhere Captain Mildmay's weary forlorn hope.

On the moor the Royalists were in the process of deploying into a similar formation, with horse on the flanks and foot in the centre. As most of Newcastle's musketeers had been deployed into the enclosures on the edge of the moor, the foot in the centre would have comprised, in the main, blocks of pikemen and these would have been interspersed with cannon, most of which were still in the act of deploying onto the moor. The troops of horse on the Royalist left flank had problems deploying due to a number of coal pits dotted around the southern half of the moor, the remains of which can still be detected today. The Royalist right flank may well have extended beyond the Bradford-Wakefield road, which was open ground at the time of the battle, but any advance they made would be affected by a continuation of the enclosures bordering the moor. It is difficult to ascertain how far forward on the moor the Royalists had deployed but, as several accounts write of the Royalists coming down towards the Parliamentarian troops and Parliamentarian troops going up towards the Royalists, it is a fair assumption that the main Royalist line was deployed part way up the north-west slope of Hungar Hill.

Once their deployment was complete the Parliamentarian army began to roll forward towards the enclosure at the bottom of the hill. After a sharp fight the Royalist musketeers were driven from the enclosures, withdrawing towards their main body, and the Parliamentarian troops closed up to the edge of the moor. Sir Thomas Fairfax's five troops of horse had occupied an enclosure running along the south-west edge of the moor and some of his musketeers were deployed in another enclosure at right

angles to the first. The only entrance to the field in which Sir Thomas's horse was deployed was through a narrow opening, or gateway, which was flanked by his musketeers, the whole forming a very useful defensive position. Sir Thomas needed this as the enemy horse opposing him vastly outnumbered his five troops. It was not long before a body of Royalist horse began to move forward to attack him, sweeping around the end of the enclosure to force an entry through the gateway. Sir Thomas reports the results of this attack:

Adwalton Moor. Looking across the lower slope of Whiskett (Westgate) Hill. The Parliamentary army drove the Royalist musketeers through this area.

Ten or 12 troops of horse charged us in the right wing. We kept the enclosure, placing our musketeers in the hedges in the moor, which was a good advantage to us who had so few horse. There was a gate, or open place to the moor, where 5 or 6 might enter abreast. Here they strove to enter, and we to defend; but after some dispute, those that entered the pass found sharp entertainment; and those that had not yet entered, a hot welcome from the musketeers that flanked them in the hedges. All, in the end, were forced to retreat, with the loss of one Colonel Howard, who commanded them.

The Duchess of Newcastle gives similar details to Sir Thomas but states that the gateway would only allow access to two men at a time. Outnumbered two to one, the importance of Sir Thomas's position was proven and his men not only held their ground but drove off the enemy.

Shortly after the repulse of the first cavalry attack, another large body of Royalist horse descended the hill and almost succeeded in breaking into the enclosure, as Sir Thomas Fairfax reports:

The horse came down again and charged us, being about 13 or 14 troops. We defended ourselves as before, but with much more difficulty, many having gotten in among us; but were beaten off again, with loss; and Colonel Herne who commanded that party was slain. We pursued them to their cannon.

Sir Thomas goes on to describe an act of divine retribution which took place just after this attack:

And here, I cannot omit a remarkable passage of divine justice. While we were engaged in the fight with the horse that entered the gate, 4 soldiers had stripped Colonel Herne naked, as he laid dead on the ground (men still fighting around about him), and so dextrous were these villains, that they had done it, and mounted themselves again before we had beat them off. But after we had beaten them to their ordnance (as I said) and now returning to our ground again, the enemy discharged a piece of cannon in our rear; the bullet fell into Captain Copley's troop, in which these 4 men were; two of them were killed and some hurt, or mark remained on the rest, though dispersed into several ranks of the troop which was the more remarkable, we had not martial law among us, which gave me a good occasion to reprove it, by showing the soldiers the sinfulness of the act, and how God would punish when man wanted power to do it.

It is quite a surprise that after ten months at war the Parliamentarian army in Yorkshire does not seem to have had any articles of war.

The Parliamentarians were exerting pressure right along the line and began to advance onto the moor itself, driving the Royalist musketeers before them. Joseph Lister, an inhabitant of Bradford, writes that the Parliamentarian foot:

Charged them so warmly, that they beat them off their great guns, and turned them against the enemy and they began to run.

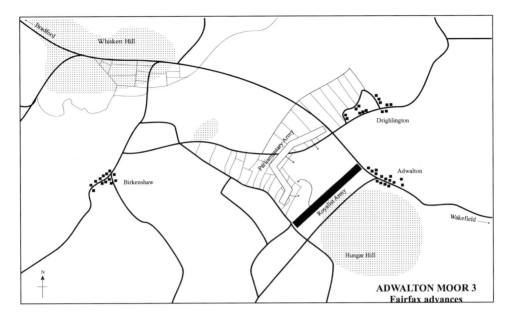

Adwalton Moor 3 – Fairfax advances

There is no evidence to support Lister's mention of the Royalist guns being captured and turned on their original owners, but several other accounts talk of Lord Fairfax's foot almost reaching the Royalist guns. Sir Henry Slingsby wrote:

There the enemy had like to have gained our cannon; but was manfully defended by a stand of pikes.

While the Duchess of Newcastle said that:

In the meanwhile the foot of both sides on the right and left wings encountered each other, who fought from hedge to hedge and for a long time together overpowered and got ground of my Lord's foot, almost to the environing of his cannon.

By this time the action had been going on for two hours and it must have been around noon. The Royalist musketeers had been driven back to their gun line, the horse of their left wing had been driven back twice by Sir Thomas Fairfax's men – the Royalist right wing does not seem to have taken a great part in the action – and their guns were in danger of capture. Sir Philip Warwick sums up the Royalist situation:

When the day seemed lost on his side [Newcastle's], *and many of his horse and foot standing doubtful and wavering; a stand or body of pikes, which being not useful, where the two armies were strongest engaged, came up to the defence of their foot, and charged by Fairfax's horse, repelling them, gave leisure to rally horse and foot.*

Sir Thomas Fairfax takes this a little further:

> *This charge and the resolution that our soldiers showed in the left wing, made the enemy think of retreating. Orders were given for it, and some marched off the field.*

Outnumbered by almost three to one, the Parliamentarian army was on the verge of winning a stunning victory. Although the intervention of some of the Royalist pikes had halted the enemy's advance temporarily, the Royalist army was in some disarray and Newcastle issued orders to withdraw. Battles can sometimes swing on the actions of one man and Adwalton Moor was a prime example of this, when a Royalist colonel changed the whole course of the action, as Sir Thomas Fairfax reports:

> *While they were in this wavering condition, one Colonel Skirton, a wild and desperate man, desired his General [Newcastle] to let him charge once more, with a stand of pikes, with which he broke in upon our men, and not relieved by our reserves, commanded by some ill affected officers, and chiefly, Major-General Gifford (who did not his part as he ought to have done) our men lost ground; which the enemy seeing, pursued their advantage by bringing on fresh troops. Ours being herewith discouraged, began to flee, and so were soon routed.*

This turn of events is also mentioned by the Duchess of Newcastle:

> *At last the pikes of my Lord's army having had no employment all the day, were drawn against the enemy's left wing, and particularly those of my Lord's own regiment, which were all stout and valiant men, who fell so furiously upon the enemy, that they forsook their hedges, and fell to their heels.*

Colonel Skirton, who was probably Colonel Posthumous Kirton, requested Newcastle's permission to carry out one last attack against the enemy and this turned the course of the battle. Closing rapidly with the enemy musketeers, Kirton's pikemen broke in among them and drove them back into the enclosures. Other bodies of foot joined in this attack and the situation of Lord Fairfax's left wing deteriorated rapidly. Sir Thomas Fairfax states that Gifford was responsible for the defeat, as he did not deploy the reserve promptly. This hardly seems justified. It was no more Gifford's responsibility to deploy the reserve than it was Sir Thomas's and his statement seems to be trying to find a scapegoat for the officer whose responsibility it was – his father Lord Ferdinando Fairfax.

With the enemy being forced back into the enclosures, General King, Newcastle's Lieutenant-General, led forward the horse of the Royalist right wing. This was the last straw for Fairfax's left wing and in short order they were streaming back towards Bradford with the Royalist horse in full pursuit. Due to the lie of the land and the mass of powder smoke blowing across the battlefield, Sir Thomas Fairfax was unaware of the disaster on the left flank. Newcastle now turned his attention to Sir Thomas's men, the only surviving formed bodies of Parliamentarian troops on the battlefield. The Duchess of Newcastle writes:

> *At which very instant my Lord caused a shot or two to be made by his cannon against the body of the enemy's horse, drawn up within cannon shot, which took so good effect,*

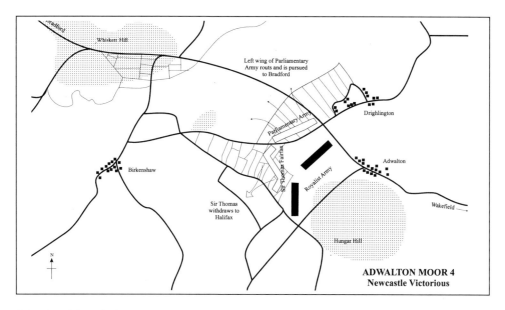

Adwalton Moor 4 – Newcastle Victorious

that it disordered the enemy's troops. Hereupon my Lord's horse got over the hedge, not in a body (for that they could not), but dispersedly two on a breast; and as soon as some considerable number was gotten over, and drawn up, they charged the enemy, and routed them. So that in an instant there was a strange change of fortune, and the field totally won by my Lord.

Sir Thomas mentions the enemy guns opening fire on his men as they withdrew to the enclosure they had so stoutly defended and this continued once they had arrived there. The reason for Sir Thomas's withdrawal was almost certainly the repulse of Gifford's men by Kirton's attack and, finding his men facing the whole Royalist left wing, he had no option but to pull back. Sir Thomas goes on to describe the closing moments of the battle:

The horse also charged us again. We not knowing what was done in the left wing, our men maintained their ground, until a command came for us to retreat having scarce any way now to do it; the enemy being almost round about us, and our way to Bradford cut off; but there was a lane in the field we were in which led to Halifax, which, as a happy providence, brought us off without any great loss, saving one Captain Talbot and 12 more which were slain in this last encounter.

So there is a discrepancy between the Duchess's account and that of Sir Thomas. The Duchess asserts that Fairfax was driven from the field, while Sir Thomas states that he withdrew from the field after receiving an order, probably from his father. Sir

Thomas's story has the ring of truth about it, as he brought virtually all of his men off the field in good order, something he certainly would not have been able to do had he been driven from the field. Local tradition has it that the lane along which Sir Thomas withdrew was Warren Lane, which still exists today, although it follows a slightly different course, passing through the grounds of Oakwell Hall, just to the south of the battlefield.

By early afternoon the Fairfaxes were in full retreat, Sir Thomas to Halifax and the remainder of the army towards Bradford. Accounts of both sides' losses in the battle are sparse and contradictory. For example Sir Thomas Fairfax puts the Parliamentarian losses at 'about 60 killed, and 300 taken prisoners', while the Duchess of Newcastle writes:

> In this victory the enemy lost most of their foot, about 3,000 were taken prisoner, and 700 horse and foot slain, and those that escaped fled into their garrison at Bradford, amongst whom was also their General of Horse [Sir Thomas Fairfax].

Both of these accounts were written a long time after the battle and give vastly different figures, one too low and one too high. A third account giving more realistic figures is attributed to the Earl of Newcastle and was written soon after the battle:

> So we pursued them, killing and taking them to Bradford town end, which was more than two mile [old English miles, nearer four modern miles], in which chase was slain (as is supposed) about 500 of the enemy's, and about 1400 taken prisoners, amongst which many officers, together with three field pieces, and all their ammunition there, which was not much. We had many soldiers hurt, two colonels of horse slain, Heron and Howard, and some officers hurt, as Colonel Throckmorton, Colonel Carnaby, and Captain Maison, all recoverable, and not above twenty common soldiers slain.

This account gives more reasonable figures for the Parliamentarian losses, although the figure for the Royalist dead seems a little low. That said, most of the Parliamentarian dead would have been killed during the pursuit after the battle. With the enemy in rout Newcastle was able to continue his march to his original objective – Bradford.

During the night Sir Thomas Fairfax was able to march from Halifax to Bradford where he joined the remnants of his father's army. Sir Thomas sums up their situation:

> I found my Father much troubled, having neither a place of strength to defend ourselves in; nor a garrison in Yorkshire to retreat to. (For the Governor of Hull [Sir John Hotham] had declared himself, that if we were forced to retreat thither, he would shut the gates against us.) But while he was musing on these sad thoughts, a messenger was sent from Hull to let him know that the townsmen had secured the Governor, and if he had any occasion to make use of that place (for they were sensible of the danger he was in) he should be readily and gladly received. Which news was joyfully received, and acknowledged as a great mercy of God to us.

The Hothams had continued their correspondence with Newcastle and were on the verge of changing sides. Fortunately for Parliament, the citizens of Hull took matters into their own hands and arrested Sir John on 29 June. He managed to escape but was pursued and recaptured at Beverley. His son had also been arrested and the two were transported to the Tower of London on the ship *Hercules*. The pair were tried, convicted and executed on Tower Hill: Captain John on 1 January 1644 and his father on the following day. With the arrival of the news from Hull, Lord Fairfax decided to withdraw what he could of his army to Leeds and then on to Hull.

Leaving his son to defend Bradford with 800 foot and sixty horse, Fairfax safely reached Leeds early on 1 July. During the previous evening the Royalists had moved their artillery into position to bombard Bradford. This bombardment commenced on the morning of the 1st. Having given the defenders a taste of what was to come, Newcastle called for a parley. If Parliamentarian accounts are to be believed, Newcastle did not intend to come to an agreement with the defenders but used the time to surround the town. A decision to break out was taken by the Parliamentarian officers and they attempted to carry this out during the night of the 1st/2nd. While many of the horse were able to break out most of the foot were driven back into the town. Sir Thomas Fairfax clashed with a force of enemy horse and during the exchange his wife was captured. The Earl of Newcastle showed that he was a real gentleman by returning Sir Thomas's wife in his own coach. Sir Thomas reached Leeds safely.

Newcastle had ordered his men to storm Bradford on the morning of the 2nd and they were to show no quarter. Local tradition has it that Newcastle, who was spending the night at Bolling Hall, was awoken by a spirit imploring him to 'Pity poor Bradford' several times during the night. Whether or not there is any truth in this tradition, by the morning of the 2nd Newcastle called off the assault and occupied the town peacefully.

Within two hours of his arrival at Leeds, Sir Thomas Fairfax was on the road again, this time marching for Hull and safety. The Parliamentarians' first objective was to cross the Ouse at Selby and several bodies of Royalist horse had been sent to intercept them. While his father and the bulk of his surviving troops crossed the Ouse, Sir Thomas turned on one of the Royalist forces, attacking it in the streets of Selby. During the fight Sir Thomas was wounded in the wrist but his men sent the Royalist troopers on their way back to Cawood Castle. Unfortunately, Fairfax and his men were unable to cross the Ouse and follow his father. Crossing the Trent they rode along the south bank of the Humber, pursued by the Royalists, until they came to Barton-on-Humber where they were picked up by a ship and taken to Hull. During the pursuit Fairfax had to leave his young daughter, who was ill, behind. His relief must have been great when she was subsequently brought safely to Hull.

The immediate aftermath of the Battle of Adwalton Moor was that, with the exception of Hull, the Royalists had control of the whole of Yorkshire. This meant that Newcastle was now able to move his army to the south and reinforce the King. Not for the first time, the Yorkshire gentry bridled against leaving the county while an enemy force existed. On 2 September the Royalists once again laid siege to Hull. Lord Fairfax's horse were of no use during a siege, so they were ferried across the Humber. This force, led by Sir Thomas Fairfax, joined with the cavalry of the Eastern Association commanded by Oliver Cromwell.

The siege of Hull progressed slowly. Lord Fairfax opened the floodgates along the River Hull and inundated the land around the town, seriously inhibiting the Royalist attempts to commence a bombardment. On 11 October Newcastle received two pieces of bad news. At Hull a major sortie by the garrison had driven his men back and on the 12th the siege was raised. In Lincolnshire a large body of his horse had been defeated by Fairfax and Cromwell at the Battle of Winceby. These two events, both taking place on the 11th, seem to have brought Newcastle to a decision to go into winter quarters at Welbeck and the fighting in Yorkshire came to a close for 1643.

Although Adwalton Moor had given control of Yorkshire to the Royalists it had a much more profound effect on the course of the war. In the immediate aftermath of the battle Thomas Stockdale, a close associate of Lord Fairfax, had written from Halifax to the Speaker of the House of Commons, William Lenthall, summing up the day's events and the magnitude of Fairfax's defeat. This letter was read to the House on 5 July and galvanised Parliament to follow a course it had been considering for some time – an alliance with the Scots. On 25 September Parliament ratified an agreement with the Scots, known as the Solemn League and Covenant. Although this agreement contained political and religious clauses, it was its military implications that would have the greatest effect on the Civil War in Yorkshire and, indeed, the rest of the country. The Scots would invade northern England with an army of 20,000 men in support of Parliament. Due to some minor disagreements this part of the treaty was not completed until November 1643. The Scots began to gather their forces and would be ready to invade the North in January 1644.

All roads lead to York

On 19 January 1644 the Scots army crossed the River Tweed into Northumberland. It comprised twenty-one regiments of foot and seven regiments of horse, some 18,000 men. Sir Thomas Glemham had only 2,000 men with which to oppose them and all he could do was retreat before the Scots, breaking bridges as he went. By the 25th the Scots had reached Alnwick and arrived at Morpeth two days later. On 1 February the Scots began their final march to Newcastle-upon-Tyne, although due to the weather they did not arrive before the town until the 3rd. The town was immediately summoned to surrender and the Scots' surprise must have been great when they received a refusal from the Marquess of Newcastle himself – he had been promoted in the peerage for his victory at Adwalton Moor as had his lieutenant general, James King, as Lord Eythin.

On 15 January Newcastle had returned to York. For the next two weeks he gathered his forces to move north against the Scots and put plans for the defence of Yorkshire into place. On the 29th he set off north with 5,000 foot and 3,000 horse. Newcastle's army arrived at Newcastle-upon-Tyne on 3 February, a few hours before the Scots army approached from the north, having taken only five days to complete the march.

With their summons refused the Scots were in a poor situation. They had intended to seize Newcastle-upon-Tyne and use it as a supply base. At this early part of the year the roads back to Scotland were in very poor condition and could not be used to supply such a large army. The obvious solution was to supply the army by sea but this needed a decent sized port. The coast of Northumberland was sadly deficient in such ports. The Marquess of Newcastle was aware of the precarious Scots position and his main objective became the defence of the line of the River Tyne. The Scots army sidestepped towards the west in an attempt to find an undefended crossing, as well as covering Newcastle-upon-Tyne. As the Scots army spread out, Newcastle was presented with an ideal opportunity to strike at them. On 19 February two Royalist columns crossed the Tyne and attacked the Scots' quarters at Corbridge. In a hard-fought action the Scots were driven back with loss and their commander, Alexander Leslie, Earl of Leven, concentrated the whole army close to Newcastle to prevent a repetition.

Although Newcastle had successfully held the Tyne his army was exhausted and in need of rest. With this in mind, Newcastle withdrew his army to Durham. This presented Leven with an ideal opportunity, which the canny old soldier did not let pass. On 28 February the Scots crossed the Tyne and marched for Sunderland which was occupied on 4 March. The Scots now had their supply base and spent the next four weeks gathering supplies in preparation for their next move. On several occasions Newcastle tried to draw the Scots out of Sunderland to fight him in open ground. Leven realised that although his army outnumbered Newcastle's, the veteran Royalist horse could be decisive. Leven refused to be drawn and several inconclusive actions were fought among the enclosures surrounding Sunderland. By the 25th Newcastle had realised that the Scots would not be drawn out on to ground of his choosing and pulled his troops back into Durham. On the 31st the Scots marched in pursuit of Newcastle and by 8 April had occupied Quarrington Hill, to the east of the town, effectively cutting Newcastle off from Hartlepool, his main supply port.

Things began to move rapidly. On the 12 April Newcastle received news that his Yorkshire army had been defeated at Selby and York was in danger of falling. During the early hours of the 13th Newcastle's army set off for York, with the Scots in close pursuit. The Royalists arrived at York on the 19th, in the nick of time. The Scots and Lord Fairfax's armies joined at Tadcaster on the 20th. In a matter of days the whole situation in Yorkshire had changed.

The storming of Selby

When Newcastle had marched north in January he had left Yorkshire under the command of Colonel John Belasyse. His original intention had been to leave Sir William Saville in command but Saville had died prior to Newcastle's departure.

Belasyse had been left with 3,000 foot and 1,500 horse and continued to recruit, for both his own army and for Newcastle's in the North.

By the end of February Belasyse was coming under pressure from several directions. From Hull, Lord Fairfax launched a cavalry raid commanded by Sir William Constable. This raid reached as far north as Pickering before returning to Hull. Belasyse sent several columns of cavalry to intercept Constable, but he managed to evade them all, even carrying out a surprise attack on one of them. In Nottinghamshire a large force of Parliamentarian troops, commanded by Sir John Meldrum, had laid siege to Newark and was threatening south Yorkshire. Over the winter Sir Thomas Fairfax, after fighting alongside Cromwell, had been despatched into Lancashire with his troopers. His orders were to gather what forces he could and then relieve the town of Nantwich, which was under siege. On 25 January Fairfax decisively defeated the besiegers and lifted the siege. Sir Thomas then returned to Lancashire and continued to raise troops in preparation for a return into his home county. By 6 March Bradford had been reoccupied by Fairfax's vanguard, under Colonel John Lambert.

In response to these Parliamentarian threats, Belasyse reorganised his troops into three main bodies: one at Leeds to cover the West Riding, one at Malton to cover the East Riding and one at York to cover the north of the county. He had also deployed garrisons of foot at Halifax, Doncaster and Stamford Bridge. His main force held a central position at Selby, from where any of the other three forces could be supported. The total Royalist forces in the county probably numbered 1,500 horse and 5,000 foot. Belasyse had been ordered to adopt a defensive stance and, in the light of this, his deployment makes sense.

On 21 March Prince Rupert, the King's nephew, carried out a surprise attack on the forces besieging Newark, forcing them to surrender. This allowed 1,000 Royalist horse, commanded by Sir Gervase Lucas and Colonel George Porter, to reinforce Belasyse who ordered an immediate attack on Lambert at Bradford on, or about, the 25th. In a confused fight, first Lambert's men withdrew from the town, then the Royalists, who were short of powder, withdrew to Leeds and Lambert reoccupied the town. Belasyse blamed Porter for the debacle. Porter took exception to this and returned to Newark with his men.

On 1 April the Committee of Both Kingdoms, a committee of English and Scots representatives responsible for the day-to-day running of the war, issued orders to both the Fairfaxes. They were to combine their forces and march north to assist the Scots but by the time these orders had arrived another plan had been put into action. On the 9th the Fairfaxes had combined their forces at Ferrybridge and on the 10th they advanced to Selby.

Lord Fairfax had a force of 2,000 horse and 2,000 foot with which to attack Selby on the 11th. In defence of the town Colonel Belasyse could muster 1,500 horse and 1,800 foot, although this figure may be a little high as Sir Thomas Fairfax gives the Royalist force a total strength of only 2,000 men.

Although Selby was not a fortified town its defences were formidable. Most of the town was surrounded by water obstacles of one form or another. To the north was the River Ouse, which was crossed by a bridge of boats. Between Ousegate and Brayton Lane a stream and a series of fishponds belonging to the Abbey prevented access to the town from the east. To the west was Selby Mill Dam and between Brayton Lane and Gowthorpe was a ditch, dug by Lord Fairfax's men during their stay at the town in early 1643. The only points that could be attacked were the three main streets into the town. There was a fourth entrance, Mill Lane, but this was so narrow that it was not an option.

The main Parliamentarian attack took place along Ousegate, while Brayton Lane and Gowthorpe were attacked by smaller forces. Lord Fairfax wrote of the attack:

The enemy received us with much courage, and made strong resistance for two hours or thereabouts; but in conclusion, my own foot regiment forced a passage by the river side, and my son with his regiment of horse rushed into the town, where he encountered Colonel Belasyse, and the enemy's horse; but they being beaten back, and Master Belasyse himself wounded and taken prisoner, and our foot entered the town on all sides of the town, the enemy was wholly routed, and as many as could saved themselves by flight, some towards Cawood [along Mill Lane], some towards Pontefract, and the rest towards York, over the river by a bridge of boats laid by themselves. We pursued them every way, and took in the town and chase, the prisoners, ordnance, arm ammunition, and colours mentioned in the list enclosed.

His son's account is very much in agreement:

The enemy within defended themselves stoutly, a good while; our men, at length, beat them from the line, but could not advance further, because of the horse within. I getting a barricade open, which let us in between the houses and the river, we had an encounter with their horse. After one charge they fled over a bridge of boats to York. Other horse came up and charged us again, where my horse was overthrown, being single, a little before my men, who presently relieved me, and forced the enemy back, who retreated also to York. In this charge we took Colonel Belasyse, governor of York. By this time the foot had entered the town, and also took many prisoners.

This is another example of Sir Thomas finding himself cut off among the enemy! The fighting lasted for some time before the Parliamentarian troops managed to break in along Ousegate – in one Royalist account this is put down to the treachery of a Royalist officer. Sir Thomas Fairfax led a charge along the street and was promptly counter-attacked by Belasyse and unhorsed as his men were driven back. The Parliamentarian horse promptly rallied and routed the enemy, wounding and capturing Belasyse in the process.

The Royalist army had been smashed and most of the foot captured. Lord Fairfax reports the capture of eighty named officers, 1,600 common soldiers, large quantities of powder and ammunition, four brass cannon, 2,000 arms, seven barrels of powder and sixteen bundles of match. Once again the arms and ammunition were a great boon to the Parliamentarian army.

Newcastle's rapid march from Durham to York has already been mentioned, as has the combining of the Scots and Parliamentarian armies at Tadcaster on 20 April. The combined army arrived before the walls of York on the 22nd. It was obvious to Newcastle that he was about to stand a siege and he decided to despatch his horse to the south. This makes perfect sense. His troopers and their horses would be extra mouths to feed and they would be of limited use behind the walls of York. They would be of much more use out in the open where they could form part of a relieving force. On the 23rd the Allied force began to dig its siege lines and the siege of York had begun.

The siege of York

The Allies moved into their assigned zones, with the Scots covering the south and west sides of the town. Lord Fairfax was still short of infantry and several regiments of Scots foot, under Sir James Lumsden, were despatched to reinforce him on the eastern side of York. Although the Allied force heavily outnumbered the Royalist defenders, they were still too few to cover the whole circuit of the town's defences. The area to the north of the town, between the Ouse and the Fosse, was covered only by cavalry patrols. Until this gap was sealed the Royalists would be able to bring supplies and reinforcements into the town, thus making the Allied task much more difficult.

It was obvious that the Allies needed more troops but where were they to come from? As it happened another force was within easy reach of York. In East Anglia the Earl of Manchester's Army of the Eastern Association had captured Lincoln on 5 May, finally clearing the Royalists from his assigned area of responsibility. A deputation, including the Scots Earl of Crawford-Lindsey and Sir Thomas Fairfax, was despatched to talk to Manchester, who readily agreed to bring his troops to York. Manchester's army began its march on the 24th and moved into position to the north of York on 3 June. The city was now fully surrounded and the siege began.

West of the Pennines, Prince Rupert was beginning his move to relieve York. To try to prevent this Sir John Meldrum had been sent to Manchester with two regiments of foot, including one Scots regiment. The bulk of the Allied horse had been sent to cover the passes through the Pennines – Cromwell is mentioned as visiting Penistone to cover the Woodhead Pass and Otley to defend the road from Skipton.

On 5 June Lord Fairfax put a plan into action to raise a battery against Walmgate Bar. To mask this move the Scots and Eastern Association troops formed up as though they were going to attack. While the defenders' attention was drawn to the other side of the town, Fairfax made his move, capturing the suburbs outside the gate and raising a five-gun battery within 200 yards of the gate. Newcastle had made a mistake by not destroying the suburbs outside the town as these covered the enemy advances against the town's weak points: its gates. It also gave the Allies defensible positions should the Royalists sally out of the town. Realising his mistake, Newcastle tried to rectify the situation on 8 June by burning down the buildings outside Bootham Bar. The attempt was unsuccessful and the fire raisers captured. In return, Manchester's men tried to set fire to Bootham Bar's wooden gates but this attempt was also unsuccessful.

Newcastle had received news of Prince Rupert's advance into Lancashire. It is thought that this communication was carried out by signal fires from Pontefract Castle. At this stage of the war Prince Rupert had a reputation for invincibility and his northward march had put fear into the hearts of the Committee of Both Kingdoms. Several letters from the Committee to the commanders at York prompted them to divide their armies and send a substantial force over the Pennines. Leven, Fairfax and Manchester stuck to their task, telling the Committee that a division of their force would lead to disaster.

On 8 June Newcastle decided to open communications with the Allied commanders, more in an effort to waste time rather than a desire to come to an agreement. For one week the two sides exchanged messages and held discussions until, on the 15th, Newcastle peremptorily refused to accept the Allies' surrender terms. It now became obvious that the previous week's parleys had been a time wasting measure and Newcastle had no intention of surrendering the town. On the 16th the first attempt to storm the town took place.

Sir Henry Vane, a representative of the Committee of Both Kingdoms with the army at York, was sitting in his room writing a letter to the Committee, reporting the completion of two mines and the repair of a massive siege gun. Mines were a method of breeching defensive walls that had been used from ancient times. A tunnel was dug until it reached the walls and then a chamber was dug. Originally, a fire had been set in the chamber which burnt through the tunnel's supports, causing the ground above to collapse, bringing the walls down with it. By the time of the Civil War the chamber was filled with gunpowder which was then exploded, blowing the wall above, and any defenders standing on it, into the air. Sir Henry was disturbed part way through writing his letter by a loud explosion. When he returned to his correspondence he added some important news:

> *Since my writing thus much Manchester played his mine with very good success, made a fair breach, and entered with his men and possessed the manor house* [King's Manor], *but Leven and Fairfax not being acquainted therewith, that they might have diverted the enemy at other places, the enemy drew all their strength against our men, and beat them off again, but with no great loss, as I hear.*

A mine had been exploded under St Mary's Tower. Much of the tower and its adjacent walls had collapsed – the damage can still be seen today.

With the wall breached, Lawrence Crawford, Manchester's Sergeant-Major-General of foot and a professional Scots soldier, ordered his assault force to attack. The attack by Manchester's men seems to have caught the other commanders by surprise and the Royalists were able to concentrate on repulsing the attack. Newcastle took part in the defence, leading a party from his own regiment. The

Parliamentarian force was repulsed with considerable loss – Manchester mentions, in a letter to the Committee of Both Kingdoms, losing 300 men in the assault, including 200 prisoners.

It is difficult to understand why Manchester carried out this attack without support from the other Allied commanders. Sir Thomas Fairfax gives one possible reason:

Till, in my Lord Manchester's quarters, approaches were made to St Mary's Tower; and soon came to mine it; which Colonel Crawford, a Scotchman, who commanded that quarter, (being ambitious to have the honour, alone, of springing the mine) undertook, without acquainting the other Generals with it, for their advice and concurrence, which proved very prejudicial.

Another interesting point is the location of the attack. St Mary's Tower forms one corner of the defences of the King's Manor, which is outside York's main defensive walls. Even if Manchester's men had captured the Manor they would still not have breached the main defences, although their approach to Bootham Bar would have become much easier – any approach could be flanked by musket fire from the manor. What had happened to the second mine? Lord Fairfax had attempted to mine Walmgate Bar and Sir Henry Vane had reported its completion. Why had this mine not been exploded? Sir Henry Slingsby, one of the Royalist defenders, gives the reason: the mine had flooded. Simeon Ashe, the Earl of Manchester's chaplain, gives this as the reason for Crawford blowing the mine when he did, rather than his ambition, as Sir Thomas Fairfax asserts.

The attack on the King's Manor was the only attempt by the Allied commanders to assault the town. For two weeks after the failed assault things quietened. Both sides were holding their breath and waiting for Prince Rupert's next move. On 30 June news reached the Allied commanders that the Prince had arrived at Knaresborough, within a day's march of the town. They had no choice but to leave their siege lines and gather the army to oppose the Prince's advance. Early on 1 July the Allies marched west from York and formed line of battle on Hessay Moor. This position blocked the Prince's direct route from Knaresborough, via Wetherby.

It is now time to go back several weeks and briefly look at Prince Rupert's advance into Lancashire and his approach march to York. On 16 May Rupert began his march to the north. His first move would be into Lancashire which, early in the war, had been a fertile recruiting ground for the Royalist cause. After the Battle of Sabden Brook, in May 1643, the county had come under Parliamentarian control, although many of its inhabitants still had Royalist leanings. Only one position still held out for the King, Lathom House, and one of Rupert's objectives was to relieve it.

By 23 May Rupert's growing force had reached Knutsford. He had been joined on the march by Sir John Byron's Cheshire forces. The Royalists were confronted by the River Mersey which had only three crossing points between Manchester and the sea: Hale Ford, Warrington and Stockport. Hale Ford was covered by the defences of Liverpool and Warrington had been garrisoned. This left Stockport as Rupert's choice of crossing point and he successfully brushed aside the locally raised garrison and continued into Lancashire on the 25th.

The immediate effect of Rupert's entry into Lancashire was the raising of the siege of Lathom House. The besiegers withdrew into Bolton and this was Rupert's next target. On 28 May Rupert's army stormed the town in, if Parliamentarian news sheets are to be believed, one of the bloodiest episodes in the Civil War. That said, there is little evidence beyond Parliamentary propaganda to support the wholesale slaughter reported.

On the 30th the Royalists moved on to Bury, where they were joined by Newcastle's cavalry, the Northern Horse, commanded once again by George Goring after his exchange, and several other small forces from Derbyshire. With the arrival of these reinforcements Rupert's force had grown to 7,000 horse and 7,000 foot.

Rupert's next target was Liverpool which would provide the Royalists with a good arrival port for Irish reinforcements. Leaving Bury on 4 June, the Royalists arrived before Liverpool on the 7th, having marched via Bolton and Wigan. Rupert summoned the town to surrender but its commander, Colonel Moore, refused. Between the 7th and 9th the town was bombarded and by the morning of the 10th a large enough breach had been made in the town's defences to allow an assault. Although the attack was repulsed, Colonel Moore realised that his men could not hold out for much longer. During the night the defenders were evacuated onto the ships in the harbour and the Royalists occupied the town on the 11th.

While he was at Liverpool Rupert received a letter from his uncle, the King. This letter is one of the most controversial documents to have come out of the Civil War and historians are still disputing its correct interpretation. Rupert believed it was a direct order to fight the Allied forces besieging York and, after his defeat at Marston Moor, carried it with him for the rest of his life as proof of why he fought the battle.

On 20 June the Royalist army left Liverpool and began its approach march to York. By the 23rd they had reached Preston and then crossed the Pennines to Skipton by the 26th. After resting for several days the Royalists continued their march, arriving at Knaresborough on the 30th. On 1 July Rupert caught the waiting Allied commanders by surprise by not taking the direct line from Knaresborough to York but taking the longer route along the north bank of the River Ouse. By nightfall the Prince's army was encamped in the Forest of Galtres, north-west of the city, and York had been relieved.

The Battle of Marston Moor

By nightfall on 1 July the two armies lay within a few miles of each other, separated by the River Ouse. In the Allied camp a Council of War was held during the night to decide what should be done on the morrow and Thomas Stockdale reported its results in a letter to Parliament:

Upon this the generals and principal field officers held another consultation upon Monday at night, wherein it was resolved the next morning to rise from thence, and march to Cawood, Tadcaster, and those parts, from whence they could not only safe-guard the forces from Cheshire etc, but also prevent the marching of Prince Rupert southwards, and likewise (by the help of a bridge of boats then at Cawood) to stop all provisions going to York either from the West or East Riding, and so in time necessi-tate him to draw out and fight.

Sir John Meldrum was on the march from Manchester with a sizeable force; at least 4,000 horse and 4,000 foot. By withdrawing to the south the Allied army would cover this force's crossing of the Pennines and receive a major reinforcement. The Allied commanders were also working under the impression that Prince Rupert's force was at least 25,000 men strong and equalled if not exceeded their own combined force. In fact, Rupert had only about 14,000 men. The Prince's reputation and the supposed size of his army, which could now be reinforced by Newcastle's men, brought the Allied commanders to a decision to withdraw, although this decision may not have been unanimous, as Sir Thomas Fairfax reported:

We were divided in our opinions what to do. The English were for fighting them; the Scots, for retreating, to gain (as they alleged) both time and place of advantage.

Sir Thomas makes this sound like a minor strategic disagreement, but another source, Thomas Fuller, shows that these disagreements may have gone much deeper:

Such were the present animosities in the Parliaments Army, and so great their mutual dissatisfactions when they drew off from York, that (as a prime person since freely confessed) if let alone, they would have fallen foul amongst themselves, had not the Prince preparing to fight them, cemented their differences to agree against a general enemy.

If the Allied army had been left alone, according to Fuller, they would have fallen out and separated but Rupert was not the type of commander to tamely allow an enemy to withdraw, particularly when he had a direct order to fight; all the excuse he needed.

No such prevarications existed among the Royalist command. Rupert had decided to advance across the Ouse using the bridge of boats his men had captured and a nearby ford. He also sent peremptory orders into York, commanding Newcastle to meet him on Marston Moor at first light, with all his men. This must have rankled as Newcastle had been an independent commander since the start of the war. In reality, Prince Rupert was senior to Newcastle in the Royalist hierarchy and was within his rights to give the Marquess orders but, as a sop to Newcastle's sensibilities, George Goring, who had been the commander of Newcastle's horse until his capture at Wakefield, carried the order.

Early on the morning of 2 July the Allied army began its march towards Tadcaster, having left a body of 3,000 horse and dragoons, commanded by Oliver Cromwell, Sir

Thomas Fairfax and David Leslie, Leven's Lieutenant-General, to form a rearguard. The Royalists were also on the move early on the 2nd and the waiting Allied rearguard, posted on the ridge above Long Marston village, soon noticed large bodies of enemy horse deploying onto the open moor below them, which were quickly followed by regiments of foot and the whole began to form for battle. Thomas Stockdale writes:

> *Where about 9 o'clock in the morning they discovered that the enemy had drawn over a great part of their army by a bridge they surprised the night before, and a ford near to it. Whereupon the generals gave present order to call back the foot with the ordnance, ammunition, and carriages.*

Unfortunately, by the time the recall order was issued the vanguard of the Scots foot had almost reached Tadcaster, and the army would take some considerable time to return to the field and deploy.

On the moor Prince Rupert was having similar problems. Newcastle had been ordered to arrive, with all his infantry, by four o'clock but at nine there was still no sign of him. While Rupert waited he decided to attempt to gain an advantage over his opponents by capturing the western end of the ridge upon which the Allied rearguard was deployed. Captain William Stewart, a Parliamentary officer, reported the results of this skirmish:

> *In the meanwhile, the enemy perceiving that our cavalry had possessed themselves of a corn hill, and having discovered near unto that hill a place of great advantage, where they might have both sun and wind of us, advanced thither with a regiment of Red Coats and a party of horse; but we understanding well their intentions, and how prejudicial it would be unto us if they should keep that ground, we sent out a party which beat them off, and planted our left wing of horse.*

The area of the skirmish was almost certainly Bilton Bream, above Tockwith village, as it was in this area that the Allied left wing, commanded by Oliver Cromwell, were deployed later in the day.

At about this time the Earl of Newcastle arrived on the field with his newly raised bodyguard troop, formed of 'gentlemen of quality which were in York', but none of his foot. The Prince expressed his regret that Newcastle's men had not arrived and Newcastle explained that his men had been busy pillaging the abandoned enemy siege lines and could not be gathered in time to march. His Lieutenant-General, James King, Lord Eythin, was busy gathering them together and would arrive in due time. This could have not inspired Rupert with much confidence, as Rupert and King had crossed each other's paths several years earlier, during the Thirty Years' War in Germany. At the Battle of Vlotho Rupert had led the Protestant horse in an unsuccessful attack and had been captured and imprisoned. Rupert blamed King for his imprisonment as King had not supported Rupert's horsemen with his foot soldiers and King blamed Rupert for his impetuous charge. There was no love lost between the pair.

By two o'clock both armies were deployed ready for battle, although there is some evidence that Newcastle's foot did not arrive from York until nearer four. At two o'clock the first shots of the battle were fired by the Allied artillery.

The battlefield lay between two villages: Long Marston in the east and Tockwith in the west. A road now runs between the two villages and to its south the ground rises quite steeply to a ridge, 38 metres high at its highest point. Most of the ridge stands at about 30 metres and it was from this ridge that the Allied rearguard watched Rupert's army deploy onto the moor below and along it that the Allied army initially formed its battle lines. At the western end of the ridge, close to Tockwith, is Bilton Bream, which included a hedged rabbit warren – this provided the people of Tockwith with a supply of meat throughout the year. As the Eastern Association horse deployed into this area pioneers were tasked with clearing these hedges, which would restrict the horse's ability to deploy and its movement once battle had been joined.

The ridge between the two villages was covered in a large cornfield which ran beyond the road to the edge of the moor. Between the cultivated land and the moor lay an obstacle, variously described as a ditch or a hedge, which varied in extent along its length. Towards Tockwith, in front of Cromwell's Eastern Association horse, the obstacle seems to have comprised a small ditch and bank. Next in line were Lawrence Crawford's Eastern Association foot and the obstacle here was negligible, if it existed at all. A hedge or a ditch – a hedge in front of Lord Fairfax's foot and a ditch in front of the Scots – faced the rest of the Allied infantry front line. In front of Sir Thomas Fairfax's wing the cultivated land ended in a six feet high bank, dropping down onto the moor, which also seems to have been more rugged, with 'whins and ditches', causing Fairfax's men much disorder. As can be seen from the description, the obstacle

Marston Moor. Looking through the Royalist lines towards the ridge.

Marston Moor. Looking from the Allied lines towards the Royalist positions.

does not seem to have formed one continuous unbroken line, with some areas being easier to cross than others. There is also evidence that a number of small enclosures existed along the ditch/hedge line.

The Royalist army deployed on the uncultivated land to the north of the obstacle. This was ideal terrain to fight a battle: level and gently sloping – the moor only drops eight metres in 1,000 from the bottom of the ridge across the moor. To the rear of the Royalist position was a large wood which still exists today: Wilstrop Wood. This marked the northern edge of the battlefield.

Several tracks ran across the field. Moor Lane, which still runs north from the monument, crosses the ditch after about 400 metres and then continues for 600 metres further until it comes to a crossroads. Turning east at this point the track continued towards Hessay and then on towards York – it is probable that this was the route taken by Newcastle's foot as they marched to the battlefield from York and was the escape route for many of the routing Royalist troops at the end of the day. Local children still dare each other to venture down this lane at night. From the crossroads another track continued north, although this track no longer exists. Sugar Hill Lane runs west from the crossroads for about 600 metres until it reaches a small field called White Syke Close. For a long time this close has been identified as the location of one of the battle's most poignant events, which will be discussed later, but this close did not exist at the time of the battle and did not come into existence until the moor was enclosed during the late eighteenth century. Another track, Atterwith Lane, ran north across the moor from the western edge of Long Marston.

Having briefly discussed the terrain, it is now time to look at how the two armies were deployed. Initially, the Allied army formed on the ridge between Long Marston

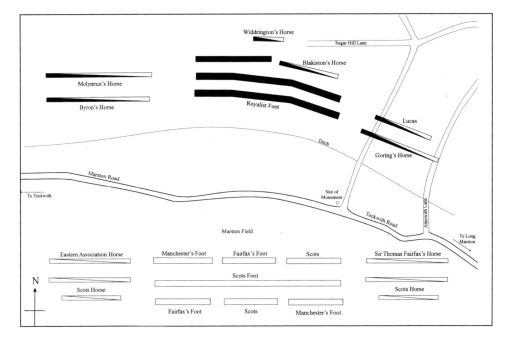

Marston Moor Deployment

and Tockwith, with two wings of horse and the foot in the centre. Sir Thomas Fairfax commanded the right wing of horse which comprised 3,000 horse and 500 dragoons from Lord Fairfax's Northern Army, 500 commanded musketeers and 1,000 Scottish horse, in three regiments. Sir Thomas commanded the first line in person and this was divided into five bodies of approximately 300 men each, interspersed with small bodies of commanded shot with about fifty musketeers in each. The second line was of a similar size and composition and was commanded by John Lambert. In reserve were the three regiments of Scots horse, each approximately 300 men strong, commanded by the Earl of Eglinton; from left to right: Balgonie, Eglinton, and Dalhousie. Balgonie's regiment was unique on the battlefield as half its men were armed with lances and the regiment fought as two squadrons; one of lancers, the other as normal troopers.

Massed in the centre of the Allied line were the regiments of foot, 15,000–16,000 strong. The first line was made up of five brigades, each formed of two bodies, or in the case of the Scots, regiments. The right of the line was formed by two brigades of Scots, the first made up of the regiments of Maitland and Crawford-Lindsay and the second of Rae and Hamilton. Next, forming the centre of the line was a brigade of Lord Fairfax's Northern foot. Identification of the regiments that made up the two bodies is problematic to say the least. Many of Fairfax's regiments were well under strength and the two bodies comprising this brigade could have been formed from several regiments each. The left of the first line was formed by two brigades of the Earl of Manchester's Eastern Association foot, commanded by Lawrence Crawford, each of two bodies. Once again it is difficult to allocate individual regiments.

The Allied second line comprised four brigades, all of them formed from Scots regiments. From right to left these were: Loudon, Buccleuch, Cassillis, Kilhead, Dunfermline, Coupar, Livingstone and Yester. The third line was once again made up of four brigades. As with the first line, this line had units from all three armies, with a brigade of Manchester's foot forming the right, a Scots brigade in the centre, comprising the regiments of Dudhope and Erskine, and two brigades of Lord Fairfax's foot on the left. Finally, two late-arriving Scots regiments formed a short fourth line, although the names of these regiments are not known.

The Allied left wing of horse was commanded by Oliver Cromwell and comprised 3,000 of the Earl of Manchester's horse, 1,000 Scots horse, 500 commanded musketeers and at least 500 dragoons. Cromwell commanded the first line of five bodies of horse, approximately 300 men each, interspersed with bodies of fifty commanded shot. At the western end of this line was Frazer's regiment of Scots dragoons. Colonel Bartholomew Vermuyden commanded the second line, again comprising five bodies of horse interspersed with musketeers. The Eastern Association is known to have had a regiment of dragoons, five companies strong, commanded by John Lilburne. This regiment is not mentioned in contemporary accounts of the battle but probably formed on the left of Vermuyden's second line and operated in support of Frazer's Scots dragoons. Finally, David Leslie, the Earl of Leven's lieutenant general, formed a third line with the regiments of Balcarres, Kirkcudbright and his own.

As can be seen from the above description, the Allied army was formed in the textbook manner, with infantry in the centre and cavalry on the wings. This does not seem to have been the case with the Royalist army.

John Byron commanded the Royalist right wing which comprised 3,000 horse and 500 commanded musketeers. Byron commanded the first line which was formed from his own regiment and those of Sir John Urry, Sir William Vaughan and Colonel Marcus Trevor. Lord Molyneux commanded the second line which was formed from his own regiment, Sir Thomas Tyldesly's, Colonel Thomas Levenson's and Prince Rupert's. Between the two lines of horse was Colonel Samuel Tuke's regiment, whose mission was to protect the open right flank of the Royalist horse. Between Vaughan and Trevor's regiments was a sizeable gap. Filling this gap, but not part of Byron's command, was a brigade of foot formed by Prince Rupert's blue-coated regiment and Byron's regiment. It is difficult to establish why this brigade was positioned well away from the remainder of the Royalist foot. There are three possible reasons. First, these regiments had supported the Royalist horse's attempt to take the Bilton Bream during the morning and had not been pulled back to form up with the rest of the foot. Second, the brigade had been moved forward to support some Royalist guns, which could have been a contributory factor to the battle starting when it did. Finally, the brigade may have been positioned deliberately to protect a gap in the hedge-and-ditch line through which, in due course, Crawford led his men. Whether any one of these reasons, or a combination, is correct, the brigade was out on a limb with little support once the battle started.

The Royalist centre was formed of a mixture of horse and foot – Rupert may have been forced to deploy several units of horse to support his thin infantry line while he awaited the arrival of Newcastle's foot from York. The centre comprised approximately 10,000 foot and 1,200 horse. The first line was formed from a number of the regiments Rupert had brought from Lancashire; from right to left: Warren, Tyldesly, Broughton, Erneley and Gibson (two weak regiments forming one body) and Tillier, the whole commanded by Colonel Henry Tillier, a veteran of the wars in Ireland. Initially, only the left half of the second line was formed, with space on the right for Newcastle's men to fill once they arrived. Once again, the regiments forming the left half of the second line all belonged to Prince Rupert's army and were formed of the regiments of Cheater and Chisenhall, with a small body of Derbyshire foot in between. Newcastle's foot then filed into position to the right of the line, with three bodies of foot forming part of the second line and four further bodies forming a short third line. It is very difficult to ascertain which regiments were involved as Newcastle's 3,500 foot was made up of many small, under strength regiments.

Behind the centre of the Royalist foot was Sir William Blakiston's brigade of horse; about 500 men strong. Further to the rear was another brigade of horse, about 400 men, commanded by Sir Edward Widdrington. Close by was Prince Rupert's Lifeguard and a small body of horse commanded by George Porter. One final body of horse was somewhere in this area; the Marquess of Newcastle's Lifeguard, formed that morning from gentlemen volunteers in York. Although it is not known exactly where this troop was deployed, it certainly fought in this area of the battlefield.

Colonel George Goring, a brilliant if somewhat erratic commander, led the Royalist left wing. Marston Moor was to prove one of his better days. It had a similar strength to the Royalist right wing, approximately 3,000 horse and 500 musketeers. Its front line was formed from the regiments of Colonels John Frescheville and Rowland Eyre and Sir Marmaduke Langdale's brigade, and was commanded by Goring in person. Sir Charles Lucas commanded the second line, which was formed from Sir Richard Dacre's brigade of horse. Finally, Colonel Francis Carnaby's regiment was deployed between the two lines to protect their flanks, much as Tuke's regiment was on the right flank. The Royalists also deployed small bodies of musketeers along the length of the ditch and hedge to provide warning of an Allied advance and oppose their crossing of the obstacle.

At about two o'clock the first shots of the battle were fired, as Leonard Watson, Manchester's scoutmaster wrote:

About two of the clock, the great ordnance of both sides began to play, but with small success to either; about five o'clock we had a general silence on both sides, each expecting who should attack first.

Other contemporary writers agree with Watson as to the start time of the bombardment and its general lack of effect. The slow, steady, bombardment continued until about five o'clock when silence fell once again over the field. Few casualties are reported, but several individuals are named. For example, Sir Henry Slingsby reports the death of Captain Haughton, son of Sir Gilbert Haughton, and this occurred early enough in the bombardment for Haughton's body to be returned to York for burial. Oliver Cromwell also reported the death of his nephew, Captain Valentine Walton, to his father:

> *Sir, God hath taken away your eldest son by a cannon-shot. It broke his leg. We were necessitated to have it cut off, whereof he died.*

Simeon Ashe also reports an incident related to him by Lord Grandison, a Royalist officer captured after the battle:

> *Before the fight, while the cannon was playing on both sides, a trooper hearing the singing of psalms in our several regiments* [Manchester's]*, came three times to his Lordship with bloody oaths and fearful execrations in his mouth, telling him, that the Roundheads were singing psalms, and therefore they should be routed that day, and that himself should be slain. His Lordship did reprove him, and cane him for swearing and cursing, but he proceeded in his wickedness; and as these words, God damn me, God sink me, were in his mouth, a drake bullet* [cannonball] *killed him.*

The Allied troops singing psalms is also reported by Sir Henry Slingsby, who wrote that they 'in Marston fields falls to singing psalms'.

Neither of the armies seemed to be keen on starting the battle and a long pause ensued. During this pause a discussion took place between the Royalist commanders, James King, Lord Eythin, having arrived from York. As has already been mentioned, there was no love lost between Rupert and King, and Sir Henry Slingsby reported their discussions:

> *The Prince demanded of King how he liked the marshalling of the army, who replied he did not approve of it being drawn too near the enemy, and in a place of disadvantage, then said the Prince 'they must be drawn to a further distance.' 'No Sir' said King 'it is too late.' It is so, King dissuaded the Prince from fighting, saying 'Sir your forwardness lost us the day in Germany, where yourself was taken prisoner,' upon the dissuasions of the Marquess and King and that it was near night, the Prince was resolved not to join battle that day, and therefore gave order to have provisions for his army brought from York, and did not imagine the enemy durst make any attempt; so that when the alarm was given, he was set upon the earth at meat a pretty distance from his troops, and many horsemen were dismounted and laid on the ground with their horses in their hands.*

The Duchess of Newcastle also reports these discussions and adds that her husband was in his coach resting when the Allied attack commenced.

At some time between five and seven the Allied army had descended from the ridge to within musket shot, a couple of hundred yards, of the Royalist manned hedge and ditch. At about half past seven the whole Allied army began to advance. Why did Leven decide to attack so late in the day, with only two to three hours light left? Sir Hugh Cholmley gave one possible reason:

> *The reason why they fell thus suddenly upon the Prince, as many conjecture, is that a Scottish officer amongst the Prince's horse, whilst the armies faced one another, fled to the Parliament army and gave them intelligence; and it was further observed that Hurry a Scotchman having the marshalling of the horse in the Prince's right wing, his own troop were the first that turned their backs; yet I have heard the Prince in his own private opinion did not think Hurry capable of infidelity.*

There seems to be little evidence to support this claim and Prince Rupert did not believe Hurry capable of such base treachery.

A much more convincing reason is that given by Edmund Ludlow who wrote that Cromwell:

> *Engaged the right wing of the enemy commanded by Prince Rupert, who had gained an advantageous piece of ground upon Marston Moor, and caused a battery to be erected upon if, from which Captain Walton, Cromwell's sister's son, was wounded by a shot in the knee. Whereupon Colonel Cromwell commanded two field pieces to be brought in order to annoy the enemy, appointing two regiments of foot to guard them; who marching to that purpose, were attacked by the foot of the enemy's right wing, that fired upon them from the ditches. Upon this both parties seconding their foot, were wholly engaged, who before had stood only facing each other.*

This is a very plausible reason and quite a few battles throughout history have been started by an over-active subordinate, against the wishes of their commander. The Royalists had placed several guns in an advantageous position and had opened fire on Cromwell's horse. Cavalry is hard pushed to stand under artillery fire, so Cromwell ordered a pair of guns forward to engage the enemy cannon. He supported this with two regiments of foot, which were probably from Lawrence Crawford's command. These regiments were engaged by enemy foot, possibly Rupert's and Byron's regiments. As more troops began to be drawn into the fighting Leven decided to order the whole army forward and at about half past seven the general advance began. Simeon Ashe described the Allied advance: 'Our Army in its several parts moving down the hill, was like unto so many thick clouds'. As late in the day as it was, both armies prepared to lay on. Leonard Watson also described the opening of the action:

> *About half an hour after seven o'clock at night, we seeing the enemy would not charge us, we resolved by the help of God, to charge them, and so the sign being given, we marched down to a charge. We came down the hill in the bravest order, and with the greatest resolution that was ever seen.*

It must have been an awe-inspiring sight; 24,000 men advancing with colours flying and drums beating.

Initially, the Battle of Marston Moor split into three separate actions, as did many English Civil Wars' battles, with the horse on each wing engaging each other and the opposing foot closing in the centre. Only when the cavalry actions on the wings were resolved did the remaining horse intervene in the infantry fight. Each sector will be detailed in turn.

On the Allied right Sir Thomas Fairfax and his troopers were faced by a formidable obstacle in the form of a steep bank, almost the height of a man, down which they had to descend onto the moor. They had little scope for manoeuvre as to their right was Long Marston and to the left were the advancing Allied foot. As well as the bank, the cultivated land was separated from the moor by a ditch and a hedge, either side of Atterwith Lane, and both of these obstacles were lined with George Goring's commanded musketeers. Sir Thomas Fairfax, while recounting the lack of success on his wing, describes the terrain and its effects:

> *By reason of the whins and ditches which we were to pass over before we could get to the enemy, which put us into great disorder.*

Both Goring and Fairfax had commanded musketeers in support of their mounted men but, while Goring fully exploited his, Fairfax nullified their support by advancing quickly to the attack and outpacing his musketeers. On the Allied left flank Cromwell and David Leslie used their dragoons, Frazer's and Lilburn's, to clear the Royalist musketeers from the ditch which then allowed the horse to advance unimpeded. Sir Thomas Fairfax seems to have made no such effort on his wing.

As Sir Thomas's men advanced they were met by a heavy concentration of musket fire from Goring's musketeers, as is evidenced by recent artefact finds: hundreds of musket balls have been recovered from the ground over which Sir Thomas had to attack. The Royalist musketeers were able to fire for a longer period than would have been normal because of the slowing effect of the terrain. Once the Parliamentary Horse had crossed the obstacle they halted to reform their ranks but were caught while doing so by the advance of Goring's first line and had to fight their opponents while they were still in disorder. Sir Thomas takes up the story:

> *Notwithstanding, I drew up a body of 400 horse. But because the intervals of horse in this wing only, was lined with musketeers (which did much hurt with their shot) I was necessitated to charge them. We were a long time engaged one with another till, at last, we routed that part of their wing. We charged and pursued them a good way towards York. Myself, only, returned presently, to get the men I left behind me; but that part of the enemy which stood (perceiving the disorder they were in) had charged them, and routed them before I could get to them; so that the good success, we had at first, was eclipsed much by this bad conclusion.*

Sir Thomas is in error when he states that only his wing was faced by commanded musketeers and was possibly using it to excuse his defeat. The success of the body under Sir Thomas's command is also mentioned by Captain Stewart, who writes:

> *Sir Thomas Fairfax, Colonel Lambert, and Sir Thomas's brother with five or six troops charged through the enemy and went to the left wing of horse.*

It seems likely that Sir Thomas's immediate command, almost certainly on the right of the line which was a position of seniority, struck Colonel Francis Carnaby's regiment which was deployed to protect the Royalist flank. If he had attacked Goring's first line he would have then had to face Sir Charles Lucas and the second line, before his men could pursue the routing Royalist troopers towards York. Striking Carnaby's regiment would also have given him some protection from the Royalist musketeers. There is also evidence that Fairfax's men struck the enemy in a more compact and ordered body than the rest of his front line. One possible reason for this is that Atterwith Lane gave them access to the moor without crossing the bank and ditch.

Stewart seems to have been in error when he reported Lambert being with Sir Thomas and going to Cromwell's wing of the army. Sir Thomas states that 'Colonel Lambert who should have seconded us, but could not get to us charged in another place' and he is also clear that the men who charged with him continued towards York, while he returned to the battlefield alone. Yet again Sir Thomas found himself cut off from his men and surrounded by the enemy:

> *But I must not forget to remember with thankfulness God's goodness to me this day, for having charged through the enemy, and my men going after the pursuit, returning back to go to my other troops, I was gotten in among the enemy, which stood up and down the field in several bodies of horse. So, taking the signal out of my hat, I passed through them for one of their own commanders, and got to my Lord Manchester's horse, in the other wing; only with a cut in my cheek, which was given in the first charge; and a shot which my horse received.*

The signal Sir Thomas speaks of was a field sign worn by the Allied army, a piece of white paper or handkerchief in the hat band, to differentiate them from the Royalists, the dress and equipment of both sides being so similar. There is evidence, quoted above, to show that Colonel John Lambert and some of his men reached Cromwell's flank but separately to Sir Thomas.

Fairfax had led his men forward and, after a sharp fight, had broken Carnaby's men, pursuing them towards York. Before Sir Thomas could return to the field the remainder of his first line, and the bulk of Lambert's second line, had been driven from the field by George Goring's men. Lambert had managed to avoid the general rout, possibly by following Fairfax through the gap he had created. Sir Thomas returned to the field and found the rest of his wing in shambles. At this point he decided to make for the left flank, arriving safely, although he may have left the field shortly after. Simeon Ashe, writing of Sir Thomas's courage, mentions his withdrawal from the field:

For he stayed in the field until being dismounted and wounded, he was brought off by a soldier. The hurt which Sir Thomas Fairfax received is in his face, but (God be thanked) we fear no danger.

Unhorsed and wounded, Sir Thomas was escorted from the field.

While Fairfax and Lambert had been fighting their way through the Royalist lines, what had been happening to the rest of their men? George Goring had bided his time well, waiting until his musketeers and the terrain had disordered the Parliamentary horse, before he launched a shattering counter charge. Sir Philip Monkton, one of Goring's regimental commanders, describes his experiences during this attack:

At the battle of Hessay Moor [another name for the battle] *I had my horse shot under me as I caracoled at the head of the body I commanded, and so near the enemy that I could not be mounted again, but charged on foot, and beat Sir Hugh Bethell's regiment of horse, who was wounded and dismounted, and my servant brought me his horse. When I was mounted upon him the wind driving the smoke so as I could not see what was become of the body I commanded, which went in pursuit of the enemy.*

It is of interest that Sir Philip speaks of charging the enemy on foot as his horse had been shot, a very brave, or foolhardy, action. In the time it took him to get remounted his men had disappeared into the distance in pursuit of the broken enemy, which points to the fighting being of very short duration. Robert Douglas, the Earl of Leven's chaplain, also reports the brevity of the cavalry action on the Allied right flank, writing 'in the same instant, all Fairfax 3,000 horse fled at once, our horsemen upon that had stood till they were disordered'. Here Douglas gives another possible reason for Sir Thomas's success, and the failure of the remainder of his wing. While Sir Thomas led the 400 men with him into a charge without waiting to reform, the remainder of the first line did halt to regain their order and were struck by Goring's men while they were still stationary, a recipe for defeat.

As the two lines of Parliamentary horse were routed, the three regiments of Scots horse to their rear also had a hard fight of it, as Captain Stewart reports:

The two squadrons of Balgonie's regiment being divided by the enemy each from the other, one of them being lancers charged a regiment of the enemies foot, and put them wholly to rout, and after joined with the left wing of horse, the other by another way went also to the left wing. The Earl of Eglington's regiment maintained their ground (most of the enemies going in pursuit of the horse and foot that fled) but with the loss of four lieutenants, the lieutenant-colonel, the major, and Eglington's son being deadly wounded.

Dalhousie's regiment was caught up in the general rout, while Eglington's stood its ground, suffering heavy losses, particularly in officers. The two squadrons of Balgonie's both made it to the left wing horse; the lancer squadron having broken a regiment of enemy foot on its way. It is likely that this enemy foot was in fact a body of Goring's commanded musketeers, not one of the foot regiments from the centre. These were covered by the charges of Sir Charles Lucas's men, which will be discussed in due course.

Goring had completely shattered the enemy's right wing which would play no further part in the battle. While Goring and his first line pursued the enemy from the field, Sir Charles Lucas prepared to lead his men into the exposed flank of the Allied centre. Casualties among Fairfax's men were high and Sir Thomas gives details of the casualties among his officers:

> *In which charge also many of my officers were slain, and hurt. The Captain of my own troop was shot in the arm. My Cornet had both his hands cut, which rendered him ever after unserviceable. Captain Micklethwaite, an honest stout man, was slain; and scarce any officer, which was in this charge, which did not receive hurt. But Colonel Lambert who should have seconded us, but could not get to us charged in another place. Major Fairfax who was major to his regiment had at least 30 wounds, whereof he died, after he was abroad, again, and good hopes of his recovery. But that which nearest of all concerned me, was the loss of my brother, who being deserted of his men, was sore wounded, of which, in 3 or 4 days he died. So as, in this charge, as many were hurt, and killed, as in the whole army besides.*

Sir Thomas's statement that as many of his men were lost in this one charge, as were killed in the rest of the army during the whole battle, brings home the horror of the action. With the defeat of the Allied right, it is now time to turn to the infantry fight in the centre.

As the Allied foot advanced towards the ditch the Earl of Manchester's regiments, led on by Lawrence Crawford, were the first to make contact. To their front, covering a gap in the ditch, were Prince Rupert and Byron's regiments of foot. Leonard Watson states that Manchester's foot came on at a 'running march' and that 'in a moment we were past the ditch', which supports Stewart's description of the terrain that 'between the Earl of Manchester's foot and the enemy there was a plain', indicating that the obstacle at this point of the line was negligible. Simeon Ashe describes the clash between the two forces:

> *Upon the advancing of the Earl of Manchester's foot, after short firings on both sides, we caused the enemy to quit the hedge in a disorderly manner, where they left behind them four drakes.*

The Royalist foot was out on a limb, some distance from its nearest supports, and outnumbered, as is described by Thomas Fuller, who writes 'impressed with unequal numbers, and distanced from reasonable succour, became prey to their enemy'. Their only close support was Colonel Marcus Trevor's regiment of horse which, by this time, had become involved in the general cavalry mêlée against Cromwell's men. The Royalist foot were soon driven from the meagre shelter of the hedge, in some disorder, leaving four guns behind. This then allowed Crawford to exert pressure on the flank of the Royalist foot to his right, which in turn allowed Lord Fairfax's foot to cross the obstacle to their front.

To the right of Crawford's men was a brigade of Lord Fairfax's northern foot and Simeon Ashe writes of their initial success:

> *The Lord Fairfax his brigade on our right hand did also beat off the enemy from the hedges before them, driving them from their cannon, being two drakes and one demi-culverin.*

As Fairfax's men threw back the enemy infantry they were counterattacked by a unit of Newcastle's foot, as Simeon Ashe goes on to describe:

> [They were] *received by the Marquess of Newcastle's regiment of foot, and by them furiously assaulted, did make a retreat in some disorder.*

Newcastle's men, possibly his own regiment, drove Fairfax's brigade back beyond the hedge in some disorder. To the right of Fairfax's brigade were two brigades of Scots, which formed the right of the Allied foot's first line. They too had managed to cross the obstacle against tough opposition, as William Stewart writes:

> *In this ditch the enemy had placed four brigades of their best foot, which upon the advance of our battle* [centre] *were forced to give ground, being gallantly assaulted by the Earl of Lindsay's regiment, the Lord Maitland's, Cassillis, and Kilhead's.*

Marston Moor. Looking along the ditch from Moor Lane towards Tockwith. Close to this spot two Scots foot regiments held their position against several attacks by horse and foot. This was the pivotal moment in the battle.

> *General Major Crawford having overwinged the enemy set upon their flank, and did good execution upon the enemy, which gave occasion to the Scottish foot to advance and pass the ditch.*

By this stage the whole of the Allied first line had crossed the obstacle and were fighting on equal terms on the moor beyond. The only setback had been the repulse of Fairfax's men by Newcastle's and it was at this moment disaster struck.

As Lord Fairfax's foot attempted to reform after their repulse they were struck by a body of Royalist horse, in all probability part of Sir William Blakiston's brigade. Thomas Stockdale describes the effect of this attack on Fairfax's men and on some of the Scots:

> *The Lord Fairfax's foot and Scots that were joined with them pursuing their advantage were charged by the enemy's horse and so disordered that they were forced to fly back and leave our ordinance behind them.*

Simeon Ashe supports this statement, as he writes about the repulse of Fairfax's foot, where he adds that 'This advantage espied by a body of the enemy's horse, they charged through them to the top of the hill'. Robert Douglas reports several Scots regiments from the second line joining in, what was in danger of becoming, a general rout:

> *In this meantime, some of the enemies horse charged the battle, Fairfax brigade of foot fled, the Edinburgh and Artillery regiment followed, first the Chancellor and*

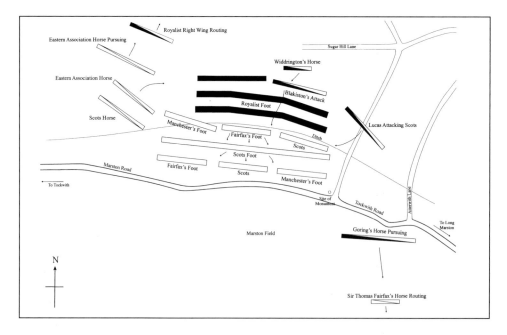

Marston Moor Opening Moves

Maclaines fled, some levy of all the horsemen of the enemy charged up where they were fleeing.

It is sometimes difficult to build a sequence of events for a large battle, for example, the relationship between the collapse of the Allied centre and the rout of Sir Thomas Fairfax's horse of the Allied right wing. In this instance it is possible to follow a sequence, as Robert Douglas gives a clue after writing of the collapse of the Allied foot:

General Leslie [Earl of Leven] *came up for horse to beat them in, and went towards the rescue of horse; in that same instant, all Fairfax's 3,000 horse fled at once, our horsemen upon that hand stood till they were disordered.*

So, if Douglas's sequence of events is to be believed and there is no reason for it not to be, Blakiston's counterattack had broken through Lord Fairfax's foot, with several Scots regiment getting caught up in the rout. Leven, having seen this, rode towards the right flank to bring up some horse to counter Blakiston's attack and as he was doing so the Allied right wing horse broke.

There is also some evidence pointing towards the Marquess of Newcastle having abandoned his post as an army commander and led his bodyguard troop forward with Blakiston's men, as his wife reports:

In this confusion my Lord (accompanied only with his brother Sir Charles Cavendish, Major Scott, Captain Mazine, and his page), hastening to see in what posture his own regiment was, met with a troop of gentlemen volunteers, who formerly had chosen him their captain, notwithstanding he was general of an army; to whom my Lord spoke after this manner 'Gentlemen,' said he, 'you have done me the honour to choose me your captain, and now is the fittest time I may do you service; wherefore if you will follow me, I shall lead you on the best I can, and show you the way to your own honour.' They being as glad of my Lord's proffer as my Lord was of their readiness, went on with the greatest courage; and passing through two bodies of foot, engaged one with each other not at forty yards distance, received not the least hurt, although they fired quick upon each other; but marched towards a Scots regiment of foot, which they charged and routed; in which encounter my Lord himself killed three with his page's half-leaden sword, for he had no other left him; and though all the gentlemen in particular offered him their swords, yet my Lord refused to take a sword of any of them. At last, after they had passed through this regiment of foot, a pikeman made a stand to the whole troop; and though my Lord charged him twice or thrice, yet he could not enter him, but the troop despatched him soon.

As the broken Allied foot continued to rout towards their baggage train, Blakiston was supported by other bodies of horse and foot and there was a danger of the Allied army being split in two; but help was at hand and Simeon Ashe reports that a body of the Earl of Manchester's foot 'did wheel on their right hand, upon their flank, and gave them so hot a charge, that they were forced to fly back disbanded into the moor'.

Marston Moor. Looking from the ditch towards the initial positions of Goring's horse. Sir Charles Lucas led the Royalist second line of horse in an attack on the Scots foot across the ground illustrated, towards the camera.

The action of Manchester's foot quite probably staved off immediate defeat but the Allied army was still in grave danger. The survivors of Thomas Fairfax's wing were either pursuing the enemy towards York or trying to cut their way through to the left wing of the army, while much of the Allied centre's first line, and part of the second, were fleeing southwards. Crawford's men were still making progress against the Royalist foot but there was then a large gap to the two remaining Scots regiments in the first line; Maitland and Crawford-Lindsay's. These two regiments were in an unenviable position, with enemy foot to their front and their right flank exposed by the rout of Sir Thomas Fairfax's men to the remaining Royalist horse, commanded by Sir Charles Lucas, and the Royalists, both horse and foot, began a protracted assault on the two regiments. Sir James Lumsden, who commanded the Scots foot in the second line, wrote of their extraordinary stand:

> *They that fought stood extraordinary well to it, whereof my Lord Lyndsay, his brigade commanded by himself was one.*

Captain William Stewart gives more details:

> *Sir Charles Lucas and General Major Porter having thus divided all our horse on that wing assaulted the Scottish foot upon their flanks, so that they had foot upon their front, and the whole cavalry of the enemy's left wing to fight with, whom they encountered with so much courage and resolution, that having interlined their musketeers with pikemen they made the enemy's horse, notwithstanding for all the assistance they had of their foot, at two several assaults to give ground; and in this hot dispute with both they continued almost an hour, still maintaining their ground; Lieutenant-General*

Baillie, and Major-General Lumsden (who both gave good evidence of their courage and skill) perceiving the greatest weight of the battle to lie sore upon the Earl of Lindsay's and Lord Maitland's regiment, sent up a reserve for their assistance, after which the enemy's horse having made a third assault upon them, had almost put them in some disorder; but the Earl of Lindsay, and Lieutenant Colonel Pitscottie, Lieutenant Colonel to the Lord Maitland's regiment, behaved themselves so gallantly, that they quickly made the enemy's horse to retreat, killed Sir Charles Lucas his horse, took him prisoner and gained ground upon the foot.

The stand of Lindsay's brigade is one of the pivotal moments of the battle, if not the whole First Civil War. If these 1,000 Scots had not held their position Lucas's horsemen could have crashed into the flank of the already shaken Allied centre. Baillie and Lumsden eventually led four regiments forward to support Lindsay and as these regiments advanced Lucas led his troopers forward for the third and final time, during which he was unhorsed and captured.

At this stage of the battle the Royalists had definitely had the better of the fighting, which is reflected by the fact that all three of the Allied commanders, Leven, Fairfax and Manchester, had left, or were in the process of leaving, the field. Leven had withdrawn to either Leeds or Bradford – witnesses mention both – and Fairfax had gone to Cawood Castle, near Selby. Manchester was in the process of leaving the field when he was confronted by Robert Douglas:

My Lord Manchester was fleeing with a number of Scots officers. God used me as an instrument to move him to come back again; for I was gathering men a mile from the place, and having some there he drew that way, and having purpose to go away, and some of our officers, as Colonel Lyell, was persuading him to go away, but I exhorted him before many witnesses to go back to the field, and he was induced; we came back about 5 or 600 horse; he only of all the generals was on the field.

All three of the Allied commanders had left the field, although Manchester did return, and would be the only one of the five commanders, on either side, to be on the field at the close of the day. The final phase of the battle would be commanded by the lieutenant generals and, fortunately for the Allies, the lieutenant generals commanding their left wing, Oliver Cromwell and David Leslie, were up to the task and it was left to this pair to pull victory from the closing jaws of defeat.

As Cromwell and Leslie descended from the Bilton Bream, they faced a similar problem to that faced by Sir Thomas Fairfax, over a mile to their east, although the ditch to their front was not as great an obstacle as that faced by Sir Thomas. They would still have to cross the ditch in the face of John Byron's commanded musketeers and face Byron's counter charge while still disordered. To counter this, Colonel Frazer's dragoons, possibly supported by Lilburn's, were sent forward to clear the enemy musketeers from the area of the ditch, a task they carried out with few problems, as Captain Stewart reports:

The Scottish dragoons that were placed upon the left wing, by the good managing of Colonel Frizell [Frazer] acted their part so well, that at the first assault they beat the enemy from the ditch, and shortly after killed a great many, and put the rest to rout.

Frazer's action cleared the way for the Allied horse to cross the ditch unopposed but before they had opportunity fate, and John Byron, took a hand. Rather than waiting for the enemy to cross the ditch Byron led his first line forward, crossing the ditch himself, as Thomas Fuller reports:

Besides a right valiant Lord, severed (and in some sort secured) with a ditch from the enemy, did not attend till the foe forced their way unto him, but gave his men the trouble to pass over that ditch: the occasion of much disorder.

Although Fuller was not an eyewitness, and wrote his account some time after the event, he asserts that he got his information from 'a prime person' who 'since freely confessed'. Although no other source mentions the crossing of the ditch by the Royalist horse, it could easily account for their rapid defeat. Why did Byron commit himself so quickly? One possible explanation is the effect of the Allied artillery fire on his men which has already been mentioned. With the start of the action the artillery fire would have intensified and horse found it very difficult to stand under such fire. The advance of Cromwell's horse gave Byron's troopers an excuse to advance and get clear of the artillery fire.

The clash between the two front lines seems to have been over very quickly, although evidence is a little contradictory. Sir Henry Slingsby reports:

Marston Moor. Looking from White Syke Close towards Wilstrop Wood. Early in the battle this area would have been full of routing Royalist horse, crossing from left to right.

Cromwell having the left wing drawn into 5 bodies of horse, came off the Coney [rabbit] warren, by Bilton Bream, to charge our horse, and upon their first charge routed them; they fly along by Wilstrop woodside, as fast and as thick as could be.

Oliver Cromwell himself commented that 'we never charged but we routed the enemy', once again pointing to a fairly limited duration to the fighting on his wing. Leonard Watson, on the other hand, reports Cromwell's own unit as having 'a hard pull of it', being charged in the front and flank by some of Prince Rupert's best troopers, although 'at last (it so pleased God) he brake through them, scattering them before him like a little dust'. Cromwell was slightly wounded during this 'hard pull' and may have left the field for a short time to have his wound dressed, or so Robert Douglas, and local tradition, report.

Several other pieces of evidence point to the whole fight on the Allied left being of short duration. The Duchess of Newcastle writes:

Where upon he [Newcastle] immediately put on his arms, and was no sooner got on horseback, but he beheld a dismal sight of His Majesty's right wing, which out of a panic fear had left the field, and run away with all the speed they could; and though my Lord made them stand once, yet they immediately betook themselves to their heels again, and killed even those of their own party that endeavoured to stop them.

When Newcastle heard the start of the Allied advance he immediately armed himself and in the time it took him to do this and mount his horse, a matter of minutes, part of the Royalist right wing were routing past him, not to be rallied.

Byron's second line, commanded by Lord Molyneux may have put up a better performance, and there is evidence that David Leslie's Scots horse had a part in their defeat, as Captain Stewart reports:

He [Leslie] charged the enemy's horse (with whom Lieutenant-General Cromwell was engaged) upon the flank, and in a very short space the enemy's whole cavalry was routed, on whom our fore-troops did execution to the very walls of York; but our body of horse kept their ground.

Cromwell and Leslie kept a major portion of their troops in hand to fall upon the flanks of the enemy's foot, much as Sir Charles Lucas had done on the other side of the battle-field, where he had been fought to a standstill by Lindsay's brigade of Scots foot. Unfortunately for the Royalists, no such stand would occur until late in the day, when it was too late.

While the fight on the Royalist right was going on, Prince Rupert armed himself and returned to the field. Sir Hugh Cholmley describes the sight that greeted him:

Upon the alarm the Prince mounted to horse and galloping up to the right wing, met his own regiment turning their backs to the enemy which was a thing so strange and unusual he said 'swounds, do you run, follow me,' so they facing about, he led them to a charge, but fruitlessly, the enemy having broken the force of that wing, and without

any great difficulty, for these troops which formerly had been thought unconquerable,
now upon a panic fear, or I know not by what fate, took scare and fled, most of them
without striking a stroke, or having the enemy come near them, made as fast as they
could to York.

Swounds indeed! Sir Hugh was not an eyewitness, but spoke to senior survivors of the
battle the day after when they arrived at Scarborough, and makes a very interesting
point when he states that many of the Royalist horse fled without striking a stroke or
being approached by the enemy. The defeat of Byron's first line may have swept much
of his second line away with it. The attempt to rally his own regiment, which was part
of Byron's second line, seems to have been Prince Rupert's only contribution to the
battle, other than hiding in a bean field, if Parliamentary propaganda sheets are to be
believed, which also take great pleasure in reporting the death of Rupert's favourite
dog during the battle. Whatever Rupert's movements were during the remainder of
the battle, he had returned to York by eleven o'clock that night.

With the demise of the Royalist right wing, the climax of the battle had been reached
and while Sir Charles Lucas was been held at bay by Lindsay's men, Cromwell,
Crawford, and David Leslie prepared to fall on the exposed flank of the Royalist
centre. There seems to be some debate as to exactly what happened next. Many
modern authors have Cromwell leading his men right around the Royalist army to
confront George Goring's returning troopers, before falling on the flank of the
Royalist infantry. This seems very unlikely and several contemporary accounts are
clear on the course of events. James Somerville writes:

These two commanders of the horse upon that wing, Leslie and Cromwell wisely
restrained the great bodies of their horse from pursuing these broken troops, but
wheeling to the left [right] *hand, falls in upon the naked flanks of the Prince's main*
battalion of foot, carrying them down with great violence.

Sir Hugh Cholmley is in agreement:

Those that gave this defeat were most of them Cromwell's horse to whom before the
battle were joined David Leslie, and half the Scottish horse; and who kept close
together in firm bodies, still falling upon that quarter of the Prince's forces which
seemed to make most resistance, which were the foot who fought gallantly and main-
tained the field three hours after the horse had left them.

Oliver Cromwell himself gives the final piece of evidence:

The left wing, which I commanded, being our own horse, saving a few Scots in our
rear, beat all the Prince's horse. God made them stubble to our swords. We charged
their regiments of foot with our horse, and routed all we charged.

The attack into the Royalist right flank by Cromwell, Crawford and Leslie's men
seems to have carried all before it and Leonard Watson describes them 'dispersing the

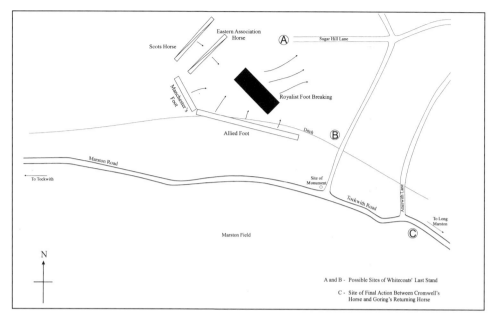

Marston Moor Final moves

enemy's foot almost as fast as they charged them'. This dispersal of the Royalist foot had one famous exception – the Whitecoats. Newcastle's men brought the Allied advance to a temporary halt, as is described by James Somerville:

> *Neither met they with any great resistance, until they came to the Marquis of Newcastle his battalion of white coats, who first peppering them soundly with their shot when they came to the charge stoutly bore them up with their pikes, that they could not enter to break them. Here the Parliament horse of that wing received their greatest loss, and a stop for some time to their hoped-for-victory, and that only by the stout resistance of this gallant battalion, which consisted of near four thousand foot, until at length a Scots regiment of dragoons, commanded by Colonel Frizeall [Frazer], with other two, was brought to open them upon some hand, which at length they did; when all their ammunition was spent, having refused quarter, every man fell in the same order and rank wherein he had fought.*

The Duchess of Newcastle agrees with Somerville, stating that the Whitecoats 'showed such an extraordinary valour and courage in that action, that they were killed in rank and file'. Sir Henry Slingsby also writes of the Whitecoats' last stand, although his account has a much more personal feel having lost two relatives in the stand, Colonel John Fenwick, a nephew, and Sir Charles Slingsby, described as a kinsman. Although Fenwick's body could not be identified, Sir Charles' remains were interred in York Minster.

Marston Moor. The pond close to the ditch and Moor Lane. This is a possible site for the Whitecoats' last stand.

Having been brought to a halt by the Whitecoats, who almost certainly numbered much less than the 4,000 reported, the Allied horse awaited the arrival of Frazer's dragoons, supported by two other units according to Somerville, one of which was probably Lilburn's, but the second must remain unidentified. The Royalists had run out of ammunition and were defenceless as Frazer's men pumped musket balls into their packed ranks. Once gaps had appeared the Allied horse closed for the kill and an account of these final moments was written by William Lilly, who although not an eyewitness, heard the story from one Captain Camby, who had been one of Cromwell's troopers and had taken part in the final attack:

A most memorable action happened on that day. There was one entire regiment of foot belonging to Newcastle, called the Lambs, because they were all clothed in white woollen cloth, two or three days before the fight. This sole regiment, after the day was lost, having got into a small parcel of ground ditched in, and not of easy access of horse, would take no quarter, and by mere valour, for one whole hour, kept the troops of horse from entering amongst them at near push of pike; when the horse did enter, they would have no quarter, but fought it out till there was not thirty of them living; those whose hap it was to be beaten down upon the ground as the troopers came near them, though they could not rise for their wounds, yet were so desperate as to get either a pike or sword, or piece of them, and gore the troopers' horses as they came over them, or passed them by. Captain Camby, then a trooper under Cromwell, and an actor, who was the

third or fourth man that entered amongst them, protested, he never in all the fights he
was in, met with such resolute brave fellows, or whom he pitied so much, and said, 'he
saved two or three against their will'.

Although most accounts, modern and contemporary, are in agreement as to the details
of the stand, its location is another matter. As has already been mentioned while
discussing the battlefield, three possible sites have been put forward. The traditional
one is White Syke Close, although artefact evidence seems to have discredited this.
The second, the enclosures on Atterwith Lane, also has little evidence to support it.
Finally, the junction of the ditch and Moor Lane, which has recently been put forward
as a possible location and has a large amount of artefact evidence to support it, is a
strong contender for the site of the Whitecoats' gallant stand. Until the grave pits
where the Whitecoats were buried are discovered it is unlikely that a site for the stand
will be proved beyond doubt.

With the fall of the Whitecoats the Royalist army disintegrated. Most of the
Royalist foot either surrendered or fled back along the lanes towards York and all
that remained for the Allied army to do was pursue the enemy, or so they thought.
Several large bodies of Royalist horse, Goring's returning troopers, were forming on
the ground upon which Sir Thomas Fairfax had originally deployed. Turning from
the destruction of the Royalist foot, Cromwell led his men against the Royalist horse
and in a short, sharp, fight saw them off. Simeon Ashe writes about this closing
action:

Yet their horse there still in full bodies; our left wing was neither wearied by their
former hot service, nor discouraged by the sight of that strength which yet the enemy
had unshaken and entire, but continuing and renewing their valour, they charged every
party remaining in the field, till all were fully routed and put to flight: our men pursued
the enemy's about three miles, till they came near unto York.

The victorious Allied army had cleared the field. Leonard Watson states that the field
was cleared by nine o'clock which, with the battle starting at around seven or half past,
seems a little early, but the pursuit certainly started in daylight, as Captain W.H.
reports nightfall bringing an end to it. Some small bodies of Royalist horse remained
on the fringes of the battlefield and straggled back to York during the night. The weary
Allied soldiers lay down to sleep on the ground on which they had fought and won.
But how great a victory had they achieved? Only the morning would tell.

With the exception of the Earl of Manchester, the Allied commanders were
unaware of the victory their lieutenants had won. Fairfax received news of the victory
while he was at Cawood Castle and immediately wrote a letter to the mayor of Hull:

After a dark cloud, it hath pleased God to show the sunshine of his glory, in victory
over his enemies, who are driven into the walls of York; many of their chief officers
slain, and all their ordnance and ammunition taken, with small loss (I praise God)
on our side. This is all I can now write.

This must have come as a great relief to the mayor, as other fugitives from Fairfax's forces had got as far as Hull and reported an Allied defeat. This news reached London by ship before the true state of affairs and at least one news tract reported Marston Moor as a defeat.

Royalist losses were severe. Out of an army of 17,000 men, 4,000 had been slain – local inhabitants who buried the bodies reported 4,150 – 2,000 taken prisoner, including Sir Charles Lucas and Major-General Porter, and 5,000 wounded, as individuals escaping from the city reported. Twenty-five cannon, the whole of the Royalist artillery train, had been captured, along with a mass of arms and ammunition.

Allied losses were very light in comparison: not many more than 300 were killed. The Earl of Manchester's foot lost only one officer and six men killed and a further twenty wounded. Most of the Allied casualties were among the troops who had routed and the 'carriage-keepers' when Goring's men pillaged the carriages.

The Allied victory had been greater than they could have ever believed as night fell on 2 July. The Royalists had suffered over fifty per cent losses in dead, wounded and prisoners. Much of the Royalist horse had escaped from the field but the foot had suffered horrendous losses, with Newcastle's northern foot almost ceasing to exist. With the return of Fairfax and Leven to the army, the Allies prepared to return to their siege of York and put an end to the business.

The fall of York and the end of the Civil War in Yorkshire

Newcastle, Eythin and Prince Rupert all arrived safely back in York and spent several hours discussing their options. Rupert wanted to withdraw into North Yorkshire where he could begin to rebuild his army. Newcastle would go into Northumberland and Durham to raise troops, while reinforcements were gathered from Lancashire, Westmorland and Cumberland. Once these recruits had been gathered and trained the Royalists would return to the offensive. Newcastle seems to have agreed with this initially but, after further discussions with Eythin, he changed his mind. His fortune was spent and his reputation ruined. Newcastle had no intention of becoming the butt of the Royal court's jokes and decided to take himself into voluntary exile.

On 3 July the Royalist commanders went their separate ways. Rupert, with what troops he could gather, marched into the north of the county. When he realised little support was forthcoming, he crossed the Pennines into Lancashire, where he lingered for several days before marching south to rejoin his uncle in the Midlands. Crossing the Mersey at Hale Ford, the Prince's force had reached Chester by 25 July. Newcastle and his entourage rode directly to Scarborough where, on 5 or 6 July, he took a boat for Hamburg. He would remain in exile until the restoration of King Charles II in 1660. Sir Thomas Glemham and the garrison of York had been left to their own devices.

By 11 July Glemham had realised that no help would be forthcoming and came to terms with the Allied commanders. The garrison of York would march out of the town on 16 July and were free to march to the nearest Royalist garrisons. One of the conditions of the surrender was that York would be occupied only by Yorkshiremen and this indeed was what happened. By the end of July the Allied army had divided into its constituent parts. The Scots had marched north to Newcastle-upon-Tyne, to which they laid siege, while Manchester's Eastern Association army headed south to support Parliament's flagging war effort in the southern counties.

By the end of August Lord Fairfax was once again in sole command in the county. No enemy field army remained to oppose him and the rest of 1644 and 1645 was spent reducing a number of enemy strongholds: Skipton Castle, Knaresborough Castle, Sandal Castle, Pontefract Castle, Helmsley Castle, Scarborough Castle and Bolton Castle. Helmsley Castle fell in early November 1644 and Knaresborough surrendered on 20 December.

Fairfax's troops continued to reduce the enemy strongholds during 1645 and only twice would enemy troops disturb their work. On 1 March 1645 the Northern Horse, now commanded by Sir Marmaduke Langdale, returned from Oxford to the north, in a successful effort to resupply Pontefract Castle. The Northern Horse then returned to the Midlands to rejoin the King's army. On 14 June the King suffered his worst defeat at Naseby, at the hands of the New Model Army, commanded by Sir Thomas Fairfax, with Oliver Cromwell as his lieutenant-general. This would prove to be a war-winning combination.

In the aftermath of Naseby two more Yorkshire fortresses surrendered – Pontefract Castle on 20 July and Scarborough Castle on the 25th. These were followed by Sandal Castle on 1 October.

Only in Scotland was the King's cause flourishing, with the Marquis of Montrose defeating a succession of Scots Covenanter armies. King Charles decide to reinforce Montrose by sending the Northern Horse into Scotland, commanded by Lord George Digby and Sir Marmaduke Langdale. On the morning of 15 October this force surprised the Parliamentarian garrison of Sherburn-in-Elmet. Instead of moving on the Royalist troops halted to eat lunch and loot the prisoners. They in turn were caught and routed by a force of pursuing Parliamentarian horse. The survivors of the Northern Horse continued their march to Skipton and then on into Cumberland. By the time they reached southern Scotland they had received news that Montrose had been defeated by David Leslie at Philiphaugh on 13 September. The Royalist horsemen retraced their steps but were caught at Burgh-on-Sands, near Carlisle, on 20 October and forced to surrender. The last remnants of Newcastle's once-proud army had finally ceased to exist.

In Yorkshire Fairfax continued to besiege the last two remaining Royalist strongholds. On 6 November Bolton Castle capitulated. Six weeks later, on 21 December, Skipton Castle, the last Royalist fortress, surrendered. By the end of 1645, Yorkshire was completely under Parliament's control. In his letter to Prince Rupert, already mentioned, the King had written 'If York be lost I shall esteem my crown little else'. How prophetic his words were.

BATTLEFIELD WALKS

The following section gives five battlefield walks. These battles were selected as they are some of the most interesting and the battlefields are still reasonably open. Three of them – Northallerton, Towton and Marston Moor, are still open fields with few buildings, while the other two are partly built over but still open enough to trace the course of events. The tours do not give a lot of information about the battles and are intended to be used in conjunction with the relevant section of the book.

Yorkshire, and, indeed, the whole British Isles, has a rich military history. Unfortunately, for many years it has been taken for granted. In the United States many of their major battlefields are now national parks, in Britain they are more likely to be industrial parks. Yorkshire battlefields are still under threat. Within the last two or three years a large area of the Adwalton Moor battlefield came under threat from the proposed building of a large factory. This proposal was successfully fought but may reappear in the future.

A large housing estate threatens the probable site of Gate Fulford. This illustrates a problem with battlefield preservation – proving where some battles actually took place. Gate Fulford is a prime example. We know it was fought close to Gate Fulford village and on the banks of the Ouse. This in itself gives a fairly wide area for the battlefield. What also needs to be taken into account is the width of the battlefield. With upwards of 10,000 men on each side, the front lines could have stretched half a mile from the river bank. Because of a lack of firm evidence for the battle's precise location a group of private individuals are having to fight for its preservation.

At Yorkshire's other 1066 battlefield, Stamford Bridge, a large part of the battlefield recently disappeared under a new housing estate. The builder put up an information board, which hardly makes up for the untold damage done to the battlefield.

It is high time that the United Kingdom started looking after its military heritage. If a stately home was demolished to make way for a factory there would be a public outcry. The same would happen if a scheduled ancient monument was built over, even though little, if anything, can be seen above the surface. I see little difference between a stately home and an ancient monument, and a battlefield. Some of the pivotal events in British history took place on these fields and they should be preserved and interpreted.

Fortunately, all is not gloom and doom. Two bodies are now fighting to preserve English battlefields. English Heritage now has the Battlefield Register and will fight to protect any battlefields listed in it. Unfortunately, the register covers a limited number of battlefields. A major criterion for inclusion is solid evidence for the extent of a battlefield. Because of this battlefields such as Gate Fulford are not included and, therefore, not protected. The second body is the Battlefields Trust, a society of like-minded private individuals. Not only does the Trust fight to preserve battlefields but also attempts to interpret them and educate the public. For more details visit their website at <u>www.battlefieldstrust.com</u>.

Battle of Stamford Bridge
25 September 1066

1. It is best to approach the village of Stamford Bridge along the main York to Bridlington road. Approaching the village from the direction of York, you will pass through Gate Helmsley, about one and a quarter miles from Stamford Bridge. This village existed at the time of the battle, and is mentioned in the Domesday Book. The road you have been travelling along follows the route of a Roman road, the very road along which the English army marched to reach the

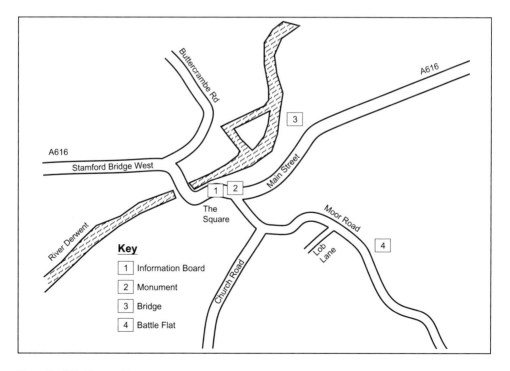

Stamford Bridge walk

A pub sign in Stamford Bridge commemorating one of the most famous incidents from the battle.

battlefield. It was as the English army crossed the ridge at Gate Helmsley that the Norwegians realised that it was an army, and not the expected hostages.

2. The road now descends towards Stamford Bridge. As it approaches the village it bends to the right, to cross the present bridge. The site of the bridge at the time of the battle is open to discussion, and has been covered in the main text. The present bridge was built during the eighteenth century. At the time of the battle, the village did not exist and there was no reason for the road to deviate as it now does. Tracing the line of the Roman road puts the bridge several hundred yards north of the present bridge.

3. Having crossed the bridge, park in the Square or in the car park of the Swordsman public house. The sign of this pub is quite interesting, and illustrates one of the most famous incidents in the battle – the lone Viking warrior holding the bridge. Continue into the Square and examine the information board (1). This originally stood close to the church but has been moved recently.

4. Continue along Main Street until you reach the monument (2). This was raised during the 1950s and gives the following inscription, in both English and Norwegian:

THE BATTLE OF

STAMFORD BRIDGE

WAS FOUGHT IN THIS

NEIGHBOURHOOD ON

SEPTEMBER 25TH 1066

More recently the surround to the monument was raised. On a recent visit to the battlefield, I was informed by a local that this was paid for by an American

The monument to the battle in Stamford Bridge.

Detail from the monument at Stamford Bridge. Calling King Harald of Norway 'King Hardraada' is like calling William I 'King Conqueror' or Richard I 'King Lionheart'. Hardrada, as it is more often spelt, was a nickname meaning ruthless given to him long after his death.

historian. You will also notice a plaque on the rear wall, which mentions 'King Hardraada'. No such king of Norway existed. Hardraada, or Hardradi, is a nickname meaning ruthless, which was attached to King Harald Sigurdsson quite some time after his death. To refer to him by this incorrect name is like using the term King Conqueror or King Lionheart for William I and Richard I, respectively.

5.   If you now go down the left-hand side of the monument, you will be entering the car park of the Mill public house. There is an entrance to a footpath, which runs along the riverbank, at the bottom right corner of the car park. Proceed along this footpath until you reach a wooden landing stage (3). This point gives a clear view along the river. The site of the original bridge lay about 100 yards further north, close to the bend in the river. The original bridge was a narrow wooden one, only wide enough for a single cart to cross. It was this bridge that was held by a Norwegian warrior against the English army. This story is discussed in the main text and has grown over the years.

6.   Turning your back to the river, you will now be looking uphill at the back of the houses along Main Street. The Norwegian army formed at the top of this slope, about 100 yards from the river. The English army formed on the ground immediately to your front. Looking at the buildings and gardens surrounding you, it is very difficult to imagine two shield-walls, half a mile long, stretching either side of you. The initial fighting took place on the slope in front of you, but, once again, little can be seen of the ground.

7.   It is now time to return to the monument. Cross the road at the monument and proceed towards the church. With the church on your right, continue along Dales Walk. This road becomes Moor Lane as it leaves the village. The area to the left of this road is still known as 'Battle Flat' (4). It is traditionally known as the area where the main fighting took place. Over the years remains and relics of the battle have been ploughed up in this area. Unfortunately, much of the area has been built over. The final phase of the battle took place here. Tostig and the surviving Norwegian troops made a stand against the English army. King Harald Sigurdsson had been killed closer to the river in the initial fighting. Ori's reinforcements arrived from the south and almost swung the battle in favour of the Norwegians. The English rallied and routed the Norwegians, pursuing them all the way to their ships, at Riccall.

Battle of the Standard (Northallerton)

1.   To get to the battlefield at Northallerton follow the A167 towards Darlington. Keep your eye open for a small layby on the right-hand side as you go up the hill. When you pull into the layby you should be able to see the monument alongside the road. You are now close to where the English army deployed, in the fields to

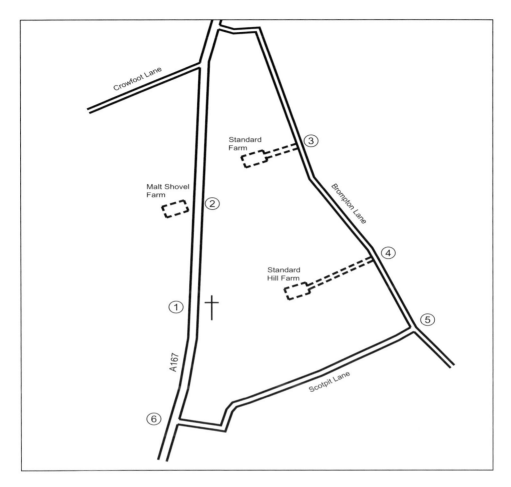

Northallerton walk

the east of the road. To your front is Standard Hill Farm. Looking half left, up the hill, you will see another farm – Standard Farm. This approximately marks the Scots front line. The bulk of the battle was fought on the ground lying between the two farms.

2. Continue up the hill for several hundred yards and you will come to a farm on the left-hand side of the road – Malt Shovel Farm. The Scots mounted troops were deployed close to the area now covered by the farm. The line between Malt Shovel Farm and Standard Farm marks the Scots front line.

3. Continue up the hill for another couple of hundred yards until you reach several houses and a junction on the right-hand side of the road. Turn right into Brompton Lane. Continue along Brompton Lane until you come to the lane leading to Standard Farm. You are now looking at the Scots line from the east.

Detail of the information board at Northallerton.

Memorial to the Battle of the Standard (Northallerton).

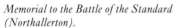

The ground between the two roads was covered by the Galwegians in the Scots front line. It is very likely that the Scots army extended across Brompton Lane into the fields on its eastern side.

4.   Continue down Brompton Lane until you reach the lane leading to Standard Hill Farm. Looking west towards the main road, you are close to the English front line, which comprised levy spearmen and archers, supported by dismounted knights.

5.   A little further down Brompton Lane you will find the entrance to another lane – Scotpit Lane. The lane gets its name from the grave pits that are said to lie close to it, where the Scots dead were buried. Unfortunately, this is a private lane and the current owner does not allow access. The English reserve was positioned just north of the lane.

6. Retrace your steps back up Brompton Lane and down the A167 to the layby. If you feel so inclined you can continue past the layby to the western entrance to Scotpit Lane but, as has already been mentioned, you are not allowed access.

Battle of Towton
29 March 1461

1. Start the walk at Dacre's cross. This position gives an excellent view over the whole battlefield. Stand looking past the cross with the road to your left. You are positioned towards the right of the Lancastrian line, which stretched from the end of the ridge to your right to the A162 about 1,000 yards to your left, running along the ridge line you are standing on. The Yorkist line ran a similar distance along the ridge several hundred yards to your front, from Castle Hill Wood, to your right front, to the A162, past the single hawthorn tree. It is from this tree that a Yorkist archer is supposed to have shot Lord Dacre, standing close to the monument, in the throat as he took his helmet off to take a drink at the height of the battle – an impossible shot of almost half a mile, and certainly local tradition rather than historical fact!

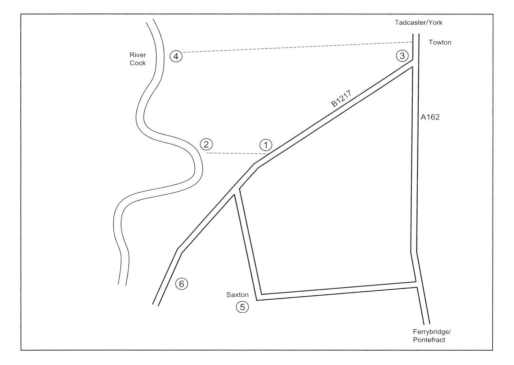

Towton walk

Lord Dacre's Cross stands close to where the Lancastrian army formed its line. It is said to mark the spot where the Lancastrian Lord Dacre was struck in the throat by an arrow after removing his helmet to take a drink.

Look back towards the Yorkist lines. On the day of the battle the Lancastrians had a driving snow storm blowing into their faces, so their view of the Yorkist array must have been intermittent at best. The Yorkists used the wind to their advantage by bringing their archers forward and pouring volleys of arrows into the massed Lancastrians, causing many casualties. The Lancastrians returned their fire but, due to the wind, their arrows fell short. When the Lancastrian commanders realized this they ordered their army to advance – an army under fire that cannot reply has two options, advance or retreat, and in this instance a retreat was not an option.

There then followed a brutal slogging match, which some sources reported as going on for ten hours, although this seems unlikely. Initially, the Lancastrians got the better of the fight pushing the Yorkists back up onto their ridge. One contemporary account talks of some type of disaster befalling the Yorkist left, close to Castle Hill Wood. A number of modern authors have attributed this 'disaster' to a Lancastrian flank attack or ambush from the area of the wood, but there seems to be no real evidence to support this, and it could have been something as simple as a contingent commander falling that caused the Yorkist left to fall back. Things were looking precarious for the Yorkists. Their army had been forced back by the weight of Lancastrian numbers and behind them was the reverse slope dropping towards Saxton village. In the nick of time reinforcements arrived to turn the course of the battle.

The Duke of Norfolk was marching his contingent along the Great North Road from Ferrybridge to Tadcaster road, now the A162. He was not a well man and this could have been the cause of his force being almost a day's march behind the main army. The road brought him on to the field close to the Lancastrian left flank and put new heart into the flagging Yorkist troops. Norfolk's arrival caused the Lancastrian flank to be driven back and turned. This in turn caused the army to begin to dissolve. A trickle of fugitives turned into a torrent and the Lancastrian army broke in rout, fleeing towards Towton village behind you and towards the valley of the Cock Beck to your right. This was the time when most of the casualties on a beaten army were caused, in the pursuit.

2. Walk along the track from the monument to the gate, where there now stands an

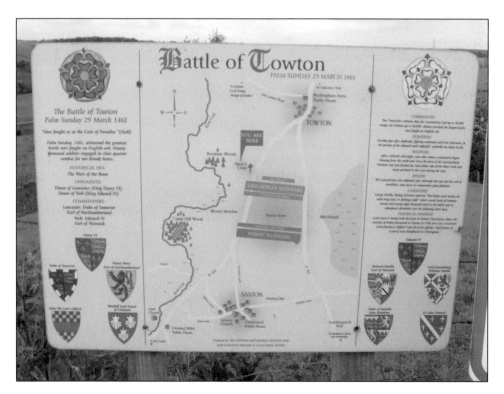

Information board above the Bloody Meadow and the Cock Beck Valley. The board was raised by the Towton Battlefield Society.

Saxton Church.

information board put up by the Towton Battlefield Society. From this point you have a good view down into the valley of the Cock Beck. The area to your front is known locally as the Bloody Meadow. When the Lancastrian army routed many fugitives were pursued and cut down in the valley bottom, while others drowned while attempting to cross the river. Return to the cross.

Lord Dacre's tomb. Dacre was killed during the battle and buried in Saxton churchyard.

3.   Follow the road towards Towton until you reach the junction with the A162. A gate stands close to this junction and this is the entrance to Towton Hall. It was in the grounds of the hall that a grave pit was discovered during building work during the 1990s. The remains were examined by a team at the University of Bradford and clearly show the horrors of medieval warfare. One skull had thirteen wounds in it, most of which would have been fatal. There was also evidence of executions and trophy taking – the cutting off of ears. So much for chivalry.

4.   Continue through the village to the

Front of the monument in Saxton churchyard. The Towton Battlefield Society raised a monument to mark the spot where some of the bodies unearthed at Towton Hall in 1996 were reinterred.

Rear of the monument in Saxton churchyard.

Rockingham Arms – renowned locally for its fish and chips! Just beyond the pub car park is a lane on the left hand side of the road. Follow this lane down the hill towards the Cock Beck. Believe it or not you are walking down what was the Great North Road, which crosses the Cock Beck at the bottom of the hill before turning north towards Tadcaster. The bridge across the Cock Beck is the site of the 'bridge of bodies' where so many Lancastrian troops were killed or drowned that the river could be crossed dry shod. Looking at the river today it seems unlikely that this can be true, but the Cock Beck is said to have been in flood at the time of the battle. Photographs from the 50s show the river in flood and it is a different proposition to the gently running stream we usually see, and the stories from the battle can easily be believed. Close to the modern bridge are the remains – stone footings – of a much older bridge. It is worth considering some of the personalities who have crossed the river here – King Harold Godwinsson on his way to victory at Stamford Bridge and on his return to defeat at Hastings in 1066, Edward IV and Warwick the Kingmaker, Sir Thomas Fairfax and Oliver Cromwell, to name but a few. It is now time to return to the monument and finish the walk.

Two other places close to the battlefield are worth visiting:

5.   Saxton Church. This is the site of two monuments to the battle. The first is Lord Dacre's tomb. Local tradition has it that Lord Dacre, a Lancastrian, was buried sitting on his horse. The tomb was opened in the nineteenth century as part of a restoration of the church. The workers did indeed find the remains of a horse in the tomb, but Dacre was to the side of it not sitting on it. As you stand by Dacre's tomb you will notice an area of the graveyard with no graves in it. This is supposed

Led Church is the only surviving part of a medieval village abandoned during the Black Death.

to be the site of a trench grave where some of the battle casualties were laid to rest. At the side of the tomb stands a new monument. This is dedicated to all the dead of both sides and marks the site where many of the remains found in the grave pit at Towton Hall were reinterred.

6. The Crooked Billet and Led Church. If you follow the road from the monument, in the opposite direction to Towton village, you will come to a pub, the Crooked Billet. Local tradition has it that the Earl of Warwick spent the night before the battle in the inn that stood on the site of the current building. Across the road is a small church standing on its own in a field. This is Led Church, and originally belonged to a village that disappeared after the Black Death, as did many villages throughout the country. A service still takes place there every Palm Sunday to commemorate the battle.

Battle of Adwalton Moor
30 June 1643

1. A good starting point for your walk is Drighlington Library. Here you are standing in the centre of Adwalton Moor, and close to the scene of much of the action in the battle. Walk from the car park to the front door of the library, where an information board is displayed. This board, and four stones placed on the battlefield, were raised in 2000 by Leeds Council, Morley Rotary Club, Groundwork, the English Civil War Society, and the Yorkshire Battlefield

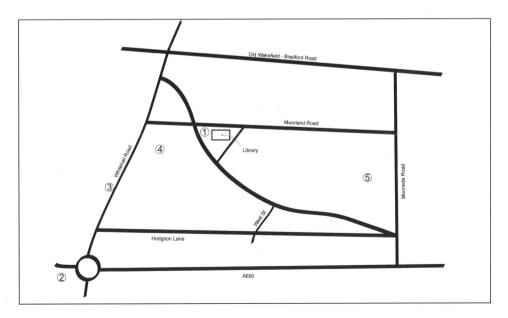

Adwalton Moor walk

Society, and funded by local businesses. Walking back to the car park, the first of the stones can be seen.

2.   At the entrance to the car park turn left and proceed down Moorland Road, continuing past the first junction until you come to its junction with Whitehall Road. Then turn left along Whitehall Road until you arrive at the roundabout. Follow the A650 towards Bradford for a few yards and then cross the road and follow the track up onto the old railway embankment. Find a position from which you can see along the A650 towards Bradford. The hill to your front is known locally as Whiskett, or Westgate Hill, and it is across its slopes that the initial part of the battle was fought. Looking across the A650 you can see a number of houses in the distance, and these mark the line of the old A650. This was the old road from Wakefield to Bradford, and it was along this road that both armies marched on the morning of the battle, the Royalists towards Bradford, and the Parliamentary army towards Howley Hall, in the direction of Wakefield. Half a mile beyond the nearest ridge of Whiskett Hill the advance guards of the two armies collided. The Royalists were driven back to the ridge and, once reinforced, made a stand. In the meantime the remainder of the Royalist army was deploying on to Adwalton Moor, just beyond the Library. The Parliamentary army then

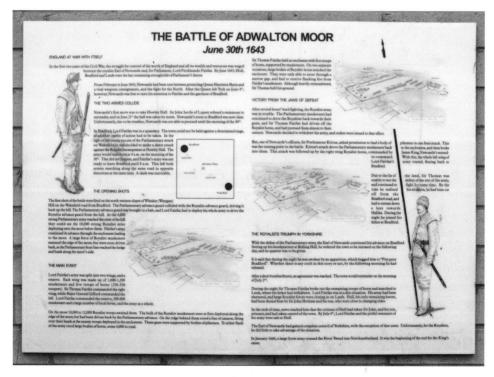

The information board at Drighlington Library.

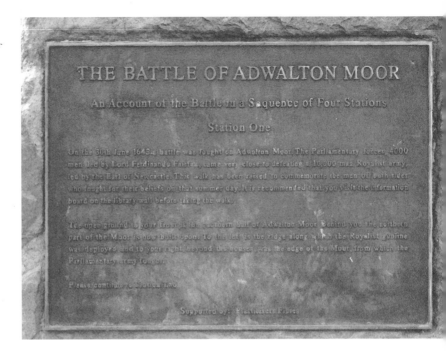

One of a series of four stones raised as part of a battlefield walk.

drove the Royalist musketeers from the ridge, through a number of enclosures to the edge of the moor, marked by a field boundary opposite where you are standing, which joins onto Whitehall Road close to its junction with Moorland Road. While this was happening, the main body of the Parliamentary army deployed along the ridge to your front and prepared to advance.

3. Retrace your steps onto Whitehall Road and proceed for several hundred yards until you come to the Malt Shovel public house. You have a good view of the line of the Parliamentary advance down the hill from the pub's car park. The hedge line across your front marks the original boundary between the enclosures, above the line, and the moor, below the line and to your rear. The Royalist musketeers lined the hedge, and the Parliamentary army marched down the hill to engage them, driving them from their positions back onto the moor.

4. Return to Whitehall Road and turn left, crossing to the other side of the road when you get chance. Follow the buildings around to the right until you are standing looking back towards the library and Hungar Hill beyond. The main Royalist army was deployed on the lower slopes of Hungar Hill, above the library, and stretched from the road to your left, Hodgson Lane, to the old A650 and possibly beyond, with horse on either flank and pike and guns in the centre. The infantry regiments had been split in two, with the musketeers advancing to engage the Parliamentary army among the enclosures, while the pike stood in blocks, waiting to advance. To your right, where the buildings now stand, was an area of

enclosures, which were occupied by Sir Thomas Fairfax's men. These were attacked on two occasions by large bodies of Royalist horse, but held their ground, driving the enemy back towards their guns.

5.   Cross the moor until you are on the hill above the library, close to Moorside Road, and turn back to face the library. You are now standing at approximately the position of the Royalist army. Below you the Royalist musketeers had been driven back onto the moor, and their Parliamentary opponents had begun to advance. Looking half left, towards the building to the left of your last position, you would have seen a large body of Royalist horse being driven back up the hill towards your present location, pursued by a much smaller body of Parliamentary horse, led by Sir Thomas Fairfax. At this stage of the battle the Royalists were on the verge of defeat, and the Earl of Newcastle had issued orders to withdraw. It was at this point that one of his officers, Colonel Posthumous Kirton, led a body of pikemen forward to attack the advancing Parliamentary forces. This was the turning point of the battle, as more Royalist troops joined Kirton's attack the Parliamentary advance was first halted, and then driven back. Within a short time the whole Parliamentary left wing was in flight back towards Bradford, over Whiskett Hill and along the old road. Sir Thomas Fairfax and his men had withdrawn back into the enclosures they had occupied, and held their ground until an order to withdraw reached him, from his father. He successfully disengaged, but was unable to return to Bradford, marching to Halifax instead, before rejoining his father in Bradford that night.

Oakwell Hall. Its owner at the time of the battle, Captain John Batt, served in Newcastle's army, although it is not known if he was present at Adwalton Moor.

There are two other places close to the battlefield that are worth a visit: Oakwell Hall and Bolling Hall:

Oakwell Hall

To get to Oakwell Hall drive back along the modern A650 towards Wakefield. After several hundred yards you will see a sign for Birstall. Turn right and follow the road down into Birstall, where you will see signs for Oakwell Hall. The Hall is a pretty early Jacobean house, owned by the Batt family at the time of the battle. One of the family members was Captain John Batt, one of the Earl of Newcastle's officers, although it is not known whether he served at Adwalton Moor.

Bolling Hall

Follow the A650 towards Bradford. As you approach the city Bolling Hall is clearly sign posted. The Earl of Newcastle used Bolling Hall as his headquarters during the siege of Bradford, which followed the Battle of Adwalton Moor. Local tradition has it that he was visited by a spirit, during the night before the town was taken, imploring him to 'Pity poor Bradford.' The bedroom in which this visitation is supposed to have taken place is still decorated in the style it was during the Earl's stay. The hall also contains a number of artefacts from the battle, including cannonballs, and a helmet.

Bolling Hall. Newcastle spent the night after the battle in Bolling Hall. A spirit is said to have awoken him during the night and implored him to 'Pity poor Bradford'.

Battle of Marston Moor
2 July 1644

1. Start at the obelisk, which lies on the road between Long Marston and Tockwith. Standing between the monument and the information board, with the monument behind you, you are looking towards the Royalist lines, and towards the main area of fighting. To your right is Long Marston, and to your left can be seen the roofs of Tockwith. The two villages marked the east and west extremities of the battlefield. Turning half right, you are looking across the fields towards where George Goring's cavalrymen were deployed in two lines. Turn back to face the information board, and then half left, to where you can see a large house set back in the fields. This is approximately the frontage covered by the Royalist foot, and beyond them was Byron's horse. Now turn to face the monument, and the ridge beyond. It was upon this ridge that the Allied army deployed during the afternoon of the battle. Sir Thomas Fairfax's horsemen were positioned on the western end of the ridge, to your left front. Oliver Cromwell's men were stationed at the eastern end of the ridge, and the Allied foot in between the two wings of horsemen. During the late afternoon the Allied army descended from the ridge and took up a line close to the road. At sometime between 1900 and 1930 hrs the Allies moved forward to attack the Royalists, all along the line.

2. Across the road from the monument a track leads up onto the ridge, ascending the ridge will give you a much better view of the battlefield. To the right of the

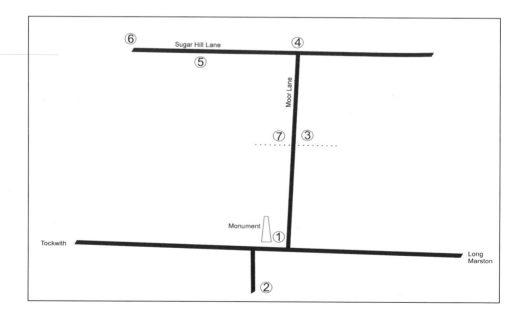

Marston Moor walk

The monument at Marston Moor.

monument is Moor Lane, which leads into the centre of the battlefield. Several hundred yards beyond the road a hedge line can clearly be seen. This was the obstacle described in most contemporary accounts of the battle, which stretched from Long Marston to Tockwith, and covered the whole front of the Royalist army. It varied in composition from a hedge, to a ditch, or a combination of both, and although in some areas it formed a formidable obstacle, in other areas its effects were negligible. Between Sir Thomas Fairfax and George Goring the obstacle was particularly bad, as a six feet high bank had formed between the cultivated land and the moor beyond, down which Fairfax's horsemen had to descend.

3. Walk back to the monument, and then along Moor Lane until you come to the ditch, which was manned by Royalist musketeers as a forlorn hope. Beyond them the main body of the Royalist foot formed, supported by several bodies of horse. Look to your right, towards Long Marston. Across the fields to your front a large cavalry action was fought. The line of the obstacle continued on from where you are standing towards Long Marston, and was formed by a high bank, down which Sir Thomas Fairfax's men had to descend, into the teeth of George Goring's commanded musketeers. A mass of musket balls has been recovered along this line. Disordered by their descent of the bank, and by the heavy musketry poured into them by the Royalist musketeers, Fairfax's horsemen were easy prey to Goring's counterattack, and were driven in confusion back up the ridge. A second line of Royalist horse, commanded by Sir Charles Lucas, then swept towards where you are standing to strike the flank of the Allied foot. Turn around to look along the ditch towards Marston Grange. Close to where you are standing four regiments of Scots foot had fought their way across

the ditch. Beyond them a brigade of Lord Fairfax's had also fought their way over the obstacle, although they were quickly driven back by a fresh body of Royalist foot. Beyond them, close to Marston Grange, two brigades of the Earl of Manchester's foot had advanced quickly, the obstacle in front of them being almost non-existent, and had routed a detached brigade of Royalist foot, positioned to cover the gap in the obstacle.

4. Continue along Moor Lane until you come to the junction at its end. This junction is called Four Lanes Meet. The track running across your front was used by the Marquess of Newcastle's foot, to reach the battlefield as it marched from York. Another track ran north, directly to your front. This has now been ploughed away. The track running to the right is an extension of Moor Lane, and is known locally as Bloody Lane. Local children still dare one another to go up Bloody Lane after dark, such is its reputation!

5. Turn left and walk down the lane that runs across the battlefield; Sugar Hill Lane. After a couple of hundred yards stop and look left towards the ridgeline. You are now behind the centre of the Royalist lines looking towards the ditch. To your front is the area in which Lord Fairfax's foot crossed the ditch, and was then driven back by a body of the Earl of Newcastle's foot. Then a brigade of Royalist horse struck Fairfax's disordered troops and routed them. Several regiments of Scots foot also turned tail and fled, and the ridge in the distance would have been covered with fleeing Allied soldiers and pursuing Royalist horsemen. Looking half left to where the ditch meets Moor Lane (point 3 above), two regiments of Scots soldiers, Crawford-Lindsay and Maitland's stood their ground against the continued charges of the Royalist left wing horse.

6. Continue along Sugar Hill Lane until you come to its end, in a small field. This is White Syke Close, the traditional site of the last stand of Newcastle's Whitecoats. To your front, over towards Tockwith, the Royalist right flank horse were engaged and routed by Cromwell's Eastern Association Horse, supported by David Leslie's three regiments of Scots Horse. The fight was over quickly, and the remnants of the Royalist right wing fled past where you are standing towards Wilstrop Wood, the wooded area to your left. The Earl of Manchester's foot, approaching from the direction of Marston Grange and Cromwell's horse, approaching from your front, then fell upon the flank of the Royalist centre. It is at this point that a body of Newcastle's Whitecoats made a stand and fought virtually to the last man. Tradition has it that the Whitecoats fell, and were buried, in the area now covered by White Syke Close, although the close itself did not exist at the time of the battle. A recently published study of the artefacts found in a long-term survey of the battlefield shows little evidence to support this tradition. The only artefacts found in the area point to this being the route taken by the fleeing Royalist right wing horse. One modern author put forward a theory that the last stand took place in an enclosure on Atterwith Lane much further to the east, but the evidence for this was flimsy. The artefact evidence may point to

another area of the battlefield as the site of the Whitecoats' last stand, and it is to this point that we shall now return.

7. Retrace your steps back along Sugar Hill Lane and Moor Lane until you come to the junction of the ditch and Moor Lane. The area on either side of the lane has revealed a mass of finds, particularly musket ball. The western side of Moor Lane has a massive concentration of finds in a fairly small area, where the ditch crosses the lane, and this area has recently been put forward as the site of the last stand. As well as the artefact evidence another couple of pieces of historical information may support this. The first is a map from the nineteenth century, which shows a wood in this area, called White Syke Whin – could this be how confusion has arisen as to the location of the stand? The second is a newspaper article from 1859. Workmen were building an underground drain and dug into a massive grave pit, about four feet below the surface. They uncovered an area twelve yards long by eight wide and still hadn't got to the edge of the 'vast sepulchre'. Unfortunately, the article does not state exactly where the discovery took place, although an underground drain does pass through the area where you are standing, running east to west. The site of the gallant stand of the Whitecoats is still open to dispute, and will be until their grave pit is found. To the north of the ditch, at its junction with Moor Lane is a pond, in exactly the position of White Syke Whin, and very close to the line of the drain. Could it be that the reason the grave pit has not come to light is that it now lies under water? For the time being, where the Whitecoats met their end must remain one of the mysteries of Marston Moor.

Further Reading

General

Clark, David. *Battlefield Walks in Yorkshire*. Sigma Leisure, 2003.
Rayner, Michael. *English Battlefields*. Tempus, 2004.

Roman period

Barker, Phil. *The Armies and Enemies of Imperial Rome*. Wargames Research Group, 1981.
Cottrell, Leonard. *The Great Invasion*. Pan, 1969.
De la Bédoyère, Guy. *Defying Rome – The Rebels of Roman Britain*. Tempus, 2003.

Dark Ages

Garmonsway, G.N. (Translated and edited by). *The Anglo-Saxon Chronicle*. Everyman, 1994.
Richards, Julian. *Blood of the Vikings*. Hodder & Stoughton, 2001.
Wood, Michael. *In Search of the Dark Ages*. Penguin, 1994.

Medieval

Bell, Graham. *Yorkshire Battlefields – A guide to the great conflicts on Yorkshire soil 937-1461*.
    Wharncliffe Books, 2001.
Burne, Alfred H. *The Battlefields of England*. Greenhill Books, 1996.
Traquair, Peter. *Freedom's Sword – Scotland's Wars of Independence*. Harper Collins, 1998.

Wars of the Roses

Boardman, A. W. *The Battle of Towton – the bloodiest battle of British soil*. Alan Sutton, 1994.
Dockray, Keith and Knowles, Richard. *The Battle of Wakefield*. The Richard III Society, 1992.
Haigh, Philip A. *From Wakefield to Towton – The Wars of the Roses*. Pen and Sword, 2002.
Haigh, Philip A. *The Military Campaigns of the Wars of the Roses*.

The English Civil Wars

Cooke, David. *The Civil War in Yorkshire – Fairfax versus Newcastle*. Pen and Sword, 2004.
Johnson, David. *Adwalton Moor 1643 – The battle that changed a war*. Blackthorn Press, 2003.
Newman, P.R. and Roberts, P.R. *Marston Moor 1644. The battle of the five armies*. Blackthorn
    Press, 2003.
Reid, Stuart. *All the King's Armies – A Military History of the English Civil War 1642-1651*.
    Spellmount, 1998.

INDEX